Survival

GLOBAL POLITICS AND STRATEGY

Volume 66 Number 2 | April–May 2024

'While the salvation of Western Europe, at least, was possible thanks in part to Britain's perseverance, Britain's own survival and then future role as springboard for European liberation was in turn thanks to the awesome industrial power of the United States.'

Benjamin Rhode, Europe Without America, p. 8.

'Neither side is very specific about what a "China model" entails or how it might be followed. Yet each sees a profound benefit in the notion that Western states have no monopoly on the ideas that will drive the Middle East forward.'

Jon B. Alterman, The 'China Model' in the Middle East, p. 76.

'The upheaval in Gaza has mobilised the most radical Iraqi militias, which operate independently of the formal security apparatus. As of spring 2024, it seemed more likely than not that US forces would be asked to leave the country.'

Ellen Laipson and Douglas Ollivant, A Delicate Balance: Iraq's Security Culture Between Iran and the United States, p. 100.

Survival

GLOBAL POLITICS AND STRATEGY

Volume 66 Number 2 | April–May 2024

Contents

On the cover
A painting by Charles Ernest Cundall depicts the evacuation of British and allied forces from Dunkirk, France, in 1940.

On the web
Visit www.iiss.org/publications/survival for brief notices on new books on the United States, Middle East and Asia-Pacific.

***Survival* editors' blog**
For ideas and commentary from *Survival* editors and contributors, visit https://www.iiss.org/online-analysis/survival-online.

Survival
GLOBAL POLITICS AND STRATEGY

The International Institute for Strategic Studies

2121 K Street, NW | Suite 600 | Washington DC 20037 | USA
Tel +1 202 659 1490   Fax +1 202 659 1499   E-mail survival@iiss.org   Web www.iiss.org

Arundel House | 6 Temple Place | London | WC2R 2PG | UK
Tel +44 (0)20 7379 7676   Fax +44 (0)20 7836 3108   E-mail iiss@iiss.org

14th Floor, GFH Tower | Bahrain Financial Harbour | Manama | Kingdom of Bahrain
Tel +973 1718 1155   Fax +973 1710 0155   E-mail iiss-middleeast@iiss.org

9 Raffles Place | #49-01 Republic Plaza | Singapore 048619
Tel +65 6499 0055   Fax +65 6499 0059   E-mail iiss-asia@iiss.org

Pariser Platz 6A | 10117 Berlin | Germany
Tel +49 30 311 99 300   E-mail iiss-europe@iiss.org

Survival Online www.tandfonline.com/survival and www.iiss.org/publications/survival

Aims and Scope *Survival* is one of the world's leading forums for analysis and debate of international and strategic affairs. Shaped by its editors to be both timely and forward thinking, the journal encourages writers to challenge conventional wisdom and bring fresh, often controversial, perspectives to bear on the strategic issues of the moment. With a diverse range of authors, *Survival* aims to be scholarly in depth while vivid, well written and policy-relevant in approach. Through commentary, analytical articles, case studies, forums, review essays, reviews and letters to the editor, the journal promotes lively, critical debate on issues of international politics and strategy.

Editor **Dana Allin**
Managing Editor **Jonathan Stevenson**
Associate Editor **Carolyn West**
Editorial Assistant **Conor Hodges**
Production and Cartography **Alessandra Beluffi, Ravi Gopar, Jade Panganiban, James Parker, Kelly Verity**

Contributing Editors

William Alberque	Franz-Stefan Gady	Nigel Inkster	Benjamin Rhode	Robert Ward
Aaron Connelly	Bastian Giegerich	Jeffrey Mazo	Ben Schreer	Marcus Willett
James Crabtree	Nigel Gould-Davies	Fenella McGerty	Maria Shagina	Lanxin Xiang
Chester A. Crocker	Melissa K. Griffith	Irene Mia	Karen Smith	
Bill Emmott	Emile Hokayem	Meia Nouwens	Angela Stent	

Published for the IISS by
Routledge Journals, an imprint of Taylor & Francis, an Informa business.

ISBN 978-1-032-80658-7 paperback / 978-1-003-49798-1 ebook

About the IISS The IISS, a registered charity with offices in Washington, London, Manama, Singapore and Berlin, is the world's leading authority on political–military conflict. It is the primary independent source of accurate, objective information on international strategic issues. Publications include *The Military Balance*, an annual reference work on each nation's defence capabilities; *Survival*, a bimonthly journal on international affairs; *Strategic Comments*, an online analysis of topical issues in international affairs; and the *Adelphi* series of books on issues of international security.

SUBMISSIONS

To submit an article, authors are advised to follow these guidelines:

- *Survival* articles are around 4,000–10,000 words long including endnotes. A word count should be included with a draft.
- All text, including endnotes, should be double-spaced with wide margins.
- Any tables or artwork should be supplied in separate files, ideally not embedded in the document or linked to text around it.
- All *Survival* articles are expected to include endnote references. These should be complete and include first and last names of authors, titles of articles (even from newspapers), place of publication, publisher, exact publication dates, volume and issue number (if from a journal) and page numbers. Web sources should include complete URLs and DOIs if available.
- A summary of up to 150 words should be included with the article. The summary should state the main argument clearly and concisely, not simply say what the article is about.

- A short author's biography of one or two lines should also be included. This information will appear at the foot of the first page of the article.

Please note that *Survival* has a strict policy of listing multiple authors in alphabetical order.

Submissions should be made by email, in Microsoft Word format, to survival@iiss.org. Alternatively, hard copies may be sent to *Survival*, IISS–US, 2121 K Street NW, Suite 801, Washington, DC 20037, USA.

The editorial review process can take up to three months. *Survival*'s acceptance rate for unsolicited manuscripts is less than 20%. *Survival* does not normally provide referees' comments in the event of rejection. Authors are permitted to submit simultaneously elsewhere so long as this is consistent with the policy of the other publication and the Editors of *Survival* are informed of the dual submission.

Readers are encouraged to comment on articles from the previous issue. Letters should be concise, no longer than 750 words and relate directly to the argument or points made in the original article.

Survival: Global Politics and Strategy (Print ISSN 0039-6338, Online ISSN 1468-2699) is published bimonthly for a total of 6 issues per year by Taylor & Francis Group, 4 Park Square, Milton Park, Abingdon, Oxon, OX14 4RN, UK. Periodicals postage paid (Permit no. 13095) at Brooklyn, NY 11256.

Airfreight and mailing in the USA by agent named World Container Inc., c/o BBT 150-15, 183rd Street, Jamaica, NY 11413, USA.

US Postmaster: Send address changes to Survival, World Container Inc., c/o BBT 150-15, 183rd Street, Jamaica, NY 11413, USA.

Subscription records are maintained at Taylor & Francis Group, 4 Park Square, Milton Park, Abingdon, OX14 4RN, UK.

Subscription information: For more information and subscription rates, please see tandfonline.com/pricing/journal/TSUR. Taylor & Francis journals are available in a range of different packages, designed to suit every library's needs and budget. This journal is available for institutional subscriptions with online-only or print & online options. This journal may also be available as part of our libraries, subject collections or archives. For more information on our sales packages, please visit librarianresources.taylorandfrancis.com.

For support with any institutional subscription, please visit help.tandonline.com or email our dedicated team at subscriptions@tandf.co.uk.

Subscriptions purchased at the personal rate are strictly for personal, non-commercial use only. The reselling of personal subscriptions is prohibited. Personal subscriptions must be purchased with a personal cheque, credit card or BAC/wire transfer. Proof of personal status may be requested.

Back issues: Taylor & Francis Group retains a current and one-year back-issue stock of journals. Older volumes are held by our official stockists to whom all orders and enquiries should be addressed: Periodicals Service Company, 351 Fairview Avenue, Suite 300, Hudson, NY 12534, USA. Tel: +1 518 537 4700; email psc@periodicals.com.

Ordering information: To subscribe to the journal, please contact T&F Customer Services, Informa UK Ltd, Sheepen Place, Colchester, Essex, CO3 3LP, UK. Tel: +44 (0) 20 8052 2030; email subscriptions@tandf.co.uk.

Taylor & Francis journals are priced in USD, GBP and EUR (as well as AUD and CAD for a limited number of journals). All subscriptions are charged depending on where the end customer is based. If you are unsure which rate applies to you, please contact Customer Services. All subscriptions are payable in advance and all rates include postage. We are required to charge applicable VAT/GST on all print and online combination subscriptions, in addition to our online-only journals. Subscriptions are entered on an annual basis, i.e., January to December. Payment may be made by sterling cheque, dollar cheque, euro cheque, international money order, National Giro or credit cards (Amex, Visa and Mastercard).

Disclaimer: The International Institute for Strategic Studies (IISS) and our publisher Informa UK Limited, trading as Taylor & Francis Group ('T&F'), make every effort to ensure the accuracy of all the information (the 'Content') contained in our publications. However, IISS and our publisher T&F, our agents and our licensors make no representations or warranties whatsoever as to the accuracy, completeness or suitability for any purpose of the Content. Any opinions and views expressed in this publication are the opinions and views of the authors, and are not the views of or endorsed by IISS or our publisher T&F. The accuracy of the Content should not be relied upon and should be independently verified with primary sources of information, and any reliance on the Content is at your own risk. IISS and our publisher T&F make no representations, warranties or guarantees, whether express or implied, that the Content is accurate, complete or up to date. IISS and our publisher T&F shall not be liable for any losses, actions, claims, proceedings, demands, costs, expenses, damages and other liabilities whatsoever or howsoever caused arising directly or indirectly in connection with, in relation to or arising out of the use of the Content. Full Terms & Conditions of access and use can be found at http://www.tandfonline.com/page/terms-and-conditions.

Informa UK Limited, trading as Taylor & Francis Group, grants authorisation for individuals to photocopy copyright material for private research use, on the sole basis that requests for such use are referred directly to the requestor's local Reproduction Rights Organization (RRO). The copyright fee is exclusive of any charge or fee levied. In order to contact your local RRO, please contact International Federation of Reproduction Rights Organizations (IFRRO), rue du Prince Royal, 87, B-1050 Brussels, Belgium; email ifrro@skynet.be; Copyright Clearance Center Inc., 222 Rosewood Drive, Danvers, MA 01923, USA; email info@copyright.com; or Copyright Licensing Agency, 90 Tottenham Court Road, London, W1P 0LP, UK; email cla@cla.co.uk. This authorisation does not extend to any other kind of copying, by any means, in any form, for any purpose other than private research use.

Submission information: See https://www.tandfonline.com/journals/tsur20

Advertising: See https://taylorandfrancis.com/contact/advertising/

Permissions: See help.tandfonline.com/Librarian/s/article/Permissions

All Taylor & Francis Group journals are printed on paper from renewable sources by accredited partners.

April–May 2024

 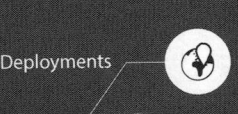
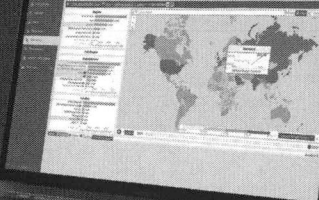

Europe Without America

Benjamin Rhode

The stench of battle and bloodshed wafting over most of Europe's history is common to the human experience across our planet. Europe, however, differs from other strategically significant continents in several important ways. The most recent of these distinctions lies in the nature of the security order established there after the Second World War and expanded after the Cold War, founded on the power and engagement of the United States, which now faces potentially mortal challenges. To appreciate this order's full significance, however, it is worthwhile considering it in the context of other distinctive aspects of Europe's history.

Perhaps one of the most notable of these is that, since the fall of the Roman Empire in the West in 476 CE, no overwhelming hegemon has dominated Western and Central Europe for a sustained period, and certainly has not controlled most of its territory. In 1453, almost 1,000 years after Rome's fall, the Ottoman Empire took Constantinople and the last remnants of what had been the Eastern Roman Empire. In the intervening millennium, while there had been pretenders to the imperial legacy in Western and Central Europe, such as the misnamed Holy Roman Empire, none had truly established itself as the inheritor of Rome's crown. Europe had largely represented a backwater in economic, technological and strategic terms, and its constituent

Benjamin Rhode is Editor of the *Adelphi* book series and IISS Senior Fellow.

Survival | vol. 66 no. 2 | April–May 2024 | pp. 7–18   https://doi.org/10.1080/00396338.2024.2332054

states appeared poor relations to the great empires in East and South Asia and the Middle East.

Some have argued that the very lack of imperial leadership and political unity after Rome's fall itself stimulated the internal competition and dynamism essential to Europe's eventual rise and global dominance.[1] In the five centuries after the Ottomans seized Constantinople, European states succeeded in enslaving, colonising or otherwise controlling much of the rest of the world, or seeded powerful new polities that became world powers in their own right, including the United States of America. At the same time, war remained an almost constant presence in Europe itself.

There were some significant diplomatic efforts to maintain peace. After a quarter of a century of revolutionary and Napoleonic bloodletting ended in 1815, there were several decades of relative quiet under the 'Concert of Europe', in which the more reactionary states combined to suppress incipient unrest. But this system had collapsed by the middle of the nineteenth century, which saw a flurry of significant wars among the European great powers. The so-called 'balance of power' that followed was underpinned by the possibility of a cataclysmic 'European War' which leaders knew could erupt at almost any moment, and eventually did in 1914.

Europe is also unique in the fact that, during the twentieth century, its internal struggles provoked both world wars, with their devastating, global and irreparable consequences for much of humanity. The first of these wars arguably – and the second indisputably – represented an ambition by one of Europe's more powerful states to match its rivals' international imperial exploits by colonising and dominating its own continent. But the Second World War compounded the misery of the First, ending with much of Europe in ruins, millions of its people murdered or maimed, and its treasuries bankrupt, with the continent effectively divided between the influence of two, essentially non-European powers: the US and the Soviet Union.[2]

While the salvation of Western Europe, at least, was possible thanks in part to Britain's perseverance, Britain's own survival and then future role as springboard for European liberation was in turn thanks to the awesome industrial power of the United States. America's internal and isolationist politics prevented its intervention at the beginning of this new European war, but its president had sought reassurance from Winston Churchill that the fight would continue even if Britain itself fell to the Nazis, and provided his own assurance that Washington would then assist that ongoing resistance. Hence Churchill's pledge in June 1940 that even if the homeland were overrun, the British Empire would hold out 'until, in God's good time, the New World, with all its power and might, steps forth to the rescue and the liberation of the old'.[3] While Britain remained free, the New World did indeed liberate its European progenitors, although not before the US was itself attacked in the Pacific. An earlier intervention, while perhaps politically implausible, might have saved much blood, treasure and suffering.

The next 45 years fortunately remained peaceful in terms of conventional military conflict within Europe, although in strategic terms the continent's new role was to serve as a chessboard for the non-European superpowers, and their primary battlefield should the Cold War become a Third World War. If a superpower conflict had gone thermonuclear, Europe would likely have been almost totally destroyed.

The New World liberated its European progenitors

In more positive terms, the post-war period also saw the emergence in Western Europe of a security order founded upon Washington's preponderant military and economic power and the notion of collective security across the North Atlantic. NATO, naturally dominated by the United States, was soon accompanied by nascent economic and political European communities, whose overlapping relationship with the Alliance could be both complementary and conflicting.

While significant elements within Western European states, particularly on the Left, chafed at the enduring post-1945 American presence in their countries, this resentment never extended to the level of hatred towards the USSR felt by most inhabitants of the 'satellite' states in the Warsaw Pact, for whom the Soviet military and intelligence presence represented an active foreign occupation, most obviously in Hungary in 1956 and Czechoslovakia in 1968. Although the US substantially reduced its forces in Western Europe following the collapse of the USSR in 1991, this was due more to Washington's desire to enjoy the 'peace dividend' than to any unsustainable opposition from European populations or leaderships. Indeed, in the post-Cold War era, despite the disappearance of the unifying common adversary of the Soviet Union, the US-led security order in Europe endured and even expanded eastwards.

Europe's trilemma

'Let Europe be whole and free', proclaimed US president George H.W. Bush in 1989, describing Washington's 'larger vision' for a 'Europe that is free and at peace with itself' as the Cold War drew to a close. In an essay published in late 2023, the historian Timothy Garton Ash evaluated Europe's progress in the intervening decades towards the desired 'trinity' of 'whole, free and at peace'.[4] Of course, this 'trinity' – perhaps reformulated as unity, liberty and security – could be applied as an analytic prism to all European history. And on closer inspection, over this longer time frame, it could be understood more accurately as what economists refer to as an 'impossible trinity' or 'trilemma': one in which the three goals are to some extent in tension, and where it is often impossible to achieve all three simultaneously.[5]

For instance, the unity and security brought by the Roman hegemon were accompanied by a lack of liberty or self-determination. The states of Europe in subsequent generations may have enjoyed more liberty, but they were also more politically fragmented and less secure. Later efforts in the nineteenth and early twentieth centuries to create an indigenous European security order of equal and sovereign states, marked by greater cooperation and even forms of collective security, ultimately failed catastrophically.

It was not until the return of the figurative prodigal son, in the shape of the United States, that Europe was able to enjoy all these goals in conjunction. In effect, both during and after the Cold War, the US served as an historically anomalous form of non-territorial hegemon in Europe. This was far from the 'offshore balancing' that certain contemporary 'realists' espouse: Washington maintained hundreds of thousands of troops on the continent, along with nuclear weapons, and remained tightly bound to Europe through NATO's collective-security pact. Yet the US did not occupy or annex European territory, nor did it depose governments within the Alliance which acted against its perceived interests. For example, when, in

1966, Charles de Gaulle withdrew France, one of the major Western powers, from NATO's integrated military command and expelled NATO's military headquarters, American tanks did not roll into Paris. Nevertheless, the European security order was indisputably dependent on America's military (and to an extent its economic) power.

Washington did not perform this role out of self-sacrificing altruism, but enlightened self-interest. It considered the preservation of Western Europe within the free world a key national interest. So was the prevention of further internecine and destabilising European war. The US served not only as a protector against the external Soviet threat but, more implicitly, as a guarantor of peace within Europe. America's engagement in Europe acted as a crucial reassurance to its wartime allies that it would be safe for West Germany to rebuild and act as a bulwark against communism. America's enduring presence after 1989 offered additional comfort to Britain and France, both of whose leaders harboured grave misgivings about German reunification. Europe thus enjoyed many of the security advantages of a hegemonic presence, but without the traditional accompanying disadvantages of tyranny or territorial predation.

This reconciliation of the impossible trinity was assisted by the pooling of national sovereignty through increasing European political and economic union, which saw some movement towards increased unity while largely maintaining national liberty. But this brought with it little meaningful increase in indigenously generated security: Europe's security was still ultimately dependent on the US. A desire for the welcome budgetary relief brought by increasing conventional disarmament after the Cold War, perhaps combined with an overlearning of the lessons of its own destructiveness and self-destructiveness in earlier centuries, saw a succession of disgraceful military hesitancies or impotent performances in Europe itself or its immediate vicinity which required American muscle to resolve – from Bosnia through Kosovo to Libya. Despite these humiliations and countless reasonable demands from multiple US administrations for more equitable 'burden-sharing', most Europeans continued to assume that they would be able to enjoy indefinitely the protection and benefits of a relatively benign and liberal Leviathan.

What happens when the Leviathan leaves? Can Europe continue to enjoy the combination of unity, liberty and security if the US either cannot or will not continue to act as its security guarantor?

Ukrainian crucible

The Biden administration has frequently reaffirmed Washington's commitment to the military support of Ukraine and more generally to the protection of Europe through NATO's Article 5. But both these commitments are dependent on the vagaries of US politics and the larger structural realignment of US security priorities towards East Asia to confront a rising China. The cold realities of Europe's declining global significance – European states accounted for 28.6% of global GDP in 1990, but only 17.9% in 2019 – are hard to ignore.[6] The US has largely abandoned earlier aspirations to be able to fight two wars in different regional theatres simultaneously. If it wishes to prevail in a war against China in East Asia, it may reasonably aim to provide military materiel for its allies in concurrent conflicts elsewhere, but not itself to fight on two fronts.[7] Even the provision of that military equipment, however, is vulnerable to shifting domestic politics.

In the first two years of the Russo-Ukrainian war, Ukraine's defence was heavily dependent on US military aid.[8] In January and February 2024, despite a majority of American voters and their representatives in Congress favouring continued US military support for Ukraine, a small but powerful minority in the Republican Party, under the sway of its likely nominee for the presidential election, Donald Trump, held up the passage of a crucial $60 billion package of military support for Ukraine while Ukrainian forces were forced to ration ammunition.[9] It is possible that, by the time this article appears in print, this squalid episode will have been resolved. But it has underscored that the US and the world face the real prospect of a second Trump presidency in 2025, and that this would prove disastrous for the defence of Ukraine and Europe more broadly.

Trump has demonstrated many times that he does not subscribe to the ideal of collective security. At best, he considers NATO as being akin to an American landlord being bilked by 'delinquent' European tenants, at worst something closer to a Mafia protection racket, and he has boasted that he would 'encourage' Russia to attack any Europeans not paying their dues.[10] It is possible that this is a cynical attempt both to entertain his resentful supporters and to frighten parsimonious and parasitical Europeans into paying for their own defence. But given that in his first term Trump suggested to his advisors that Washington should withdraw from NATO, and one of his former national security advisors, John Bolton, has declared that Trump would certainly follow through on this threat in a second term, any European assumption of indefinite US support for NATO could prove strategically calamitous. As Bolton put it, Trump's 'goal … is not to strengthen NATO, it's to lay the groundwork to get out'.[11] It remains possible that Joe Biden will be re-elected to a second term, especially if Trump is convicted in one or more criminal trials later this year. But the underlying volatility of US politics is likely to continue, as are the structural pressures forcing American strategic attention towards Asia, whichever president is in power.

Europe therefore faces the re-emergence of an old security threat on its borders at the same time that its security guarantor of the past 80 years is threatening either to disappear or at least to diminish. Russia's brutal invasion and attempted annexation of Ukraine has thus far proved less successful than feared two years ago thanks largely, at least in its first crucial few weeks, to a combination of Ukrainian courage and pre-war Anglo-American military training and supplies. But the notion of Russia as a prospective partner in the European security order, nurtured by some until quite recently, appears unthinkable for at least a generation. The judicial murder of Alexei Navalny represented the figurative death of any remaining hope that Russia might evolve into a less confrontational and predatory neighbour. For the foreseeable future, any European security order can only be sustainable if it excludes and defends against Russia. This realisation is epitomised in the statements of French President Emmanuel Macron, previously intent on avoiding Russia's humiliation and retaining a place for it in Europe's security architecture, who in February 2024 declared that European security in fact depended on Russian defeat in Ukraine. Macron and other European leaders have recently underlined the risk of Russia broadening its attacks against Europe, beyond Ukraine, within a matter of years.[12]

It is important not to understate what European states have so far accomplished. Their shared desire to avoid returning to a Europe of territorial conquest and subjugation means that their unity and resolution to resist Russian aggression has been far greater and more sustained than many feared two years ago. Originally (and justifiably) pilloried for its timidity and desultory levels of military assistance to Ukraine, Germany has since sharply increased its military aid and announced a permanent troop presence in the Baltics.[13] The accession of Finland and Sweden, two militarily capable states, has strengthened the Alliance and marks a strategic setback for Russian President Vladimir Putin. European defence spending increased after the initial shock of Russian behaviour in Ukraine in 2014, then increased further as a result of Trump's threats and the full Russian invasion of Ukraine in 2022.[14] Kyiv has signed bilateral security agreements with Berlin, London and Paris.[15] In early 2024, as MAGA Republicans blocked the desperately needed $60bn in aid to Ukraine, the European Union overcame a Hungarian veto to provide a similar amount, although this was financial aid to be distributed over the next three years.[16] Most recently, Macron aired the possibility of NATO ground forces defending Ukraine directly, although the rapid declarations from his counterparts across Europe that they would never do so doubtless undermined the deterrent power of his suggestion, which was soon followed by Putin's threats that NATO forces in Ukraine would produce a direct clash with Russia and the possible use of nuclear weapons.[17]

Europe alone?

A Europe composed of around 30 sovereign states of very different sizes, economic and military capabilities, and strategic perspectives will predictably struggle to achieve unanimity or even consensus on security priorities. This disunity was somewhat sustainable with the American Leviathan acting as a backstop, especially as a federal Europe is in no way a feasible prospect in the foreseeable future. But with the possibility of the Leviathan's withdrawal within a matter of months, rather than years or decades, it is unclear how far the recent encouraging European rhetoric will be matched by meaningful actions. Decades of underinvestment in defence will require significant and sustained expenditure to remedy, at the same time that anaemic economic growth, costly social models and ageing populations put great pressure on those same budgets.

As we approach the 75th anniversary of NATO's founding, much will be heard of its status as the most powerful alliance in history. Probably less will be said, at least in public, of the reality that its members remain overwhelmingly militarily dependent on a single ally, and even less about how Europe would feasibly and sustainably secure itself during a second Trump presidency. Before America's presence on the continent, Europe had never developed a sustainable indigenous security order that allowed it to reconcile the trinity of liberty, unity and security. It is unlikely it would be able to do so now if it found itself once more without America. We are unlikely to see the emergence of a new, indigenous security-providing hegemon that would not be strongly resisted by others. We may observe increased fragmentation of European efforts, and the increasing regionalisation of security cooperation based on geography and alignments of security perceptions. If there were a full and dramatic US retrenchment from Europe, it is conceivable that a number of European states (notably those nearest Russia) could begin the process of acquiring nuclear weapons. In the shorter term, we might see efforts to develop European nuclear-sharing arrangements, although it is unclear whether Eastern European states would have more confidence in the extended deterrence provided by France or Britain than that by Trumpian America. Increased federal unity is also unlikely, although European states will ultimately need to find a way to secure themselves against larger and more cohesive entities such as Russia and China, while at the same time preserving their own liberty. But necessity is not always the mother of invention.

In the first volume of his monumental history of the decline and fall of the Roman Empire, Edward Gibbon remarked that 'if a man were called to fix the period in the history of the world during which the condition of the human race was most happy and prosperous, he would, without hesitation, name that which elapsed from the death of Domitian to the accession of Commodus [96–180 CE]'.[18] It is striking that these 80-odd years in the second century CE, the height of the Pax Romana, might appear to be not only a golden age, but Europe's happiest period thus far as late as 1776, when Gibbon's first volume was published. It would have been impossible, though, for Gibbon to have fully foreseen the long-term consequences for his own continent of the momentous developments taking place that same year across the Atlantic. The birth of the United States of America, and its ultimate role as a security provider, allowed for a period in Europe when relative unity, security and liberty were concurrent and whose happiness and prosperity far outshone that of the second century. It may be that our distant descendants, like Gibbon, will consider the 80-odd years of the Pax Americana in the post-war – and especially the post-Cold War – period as a brief aberration in Europe's long history of bloodshed, and itself a golden age long lost.

Notes

1   See, for example, Walter Scheidel, *Escape from Rome: The Failure of Empire and the Road to Prosperity* (Princeton, NJ: Princeton University Press, 2019).

2   The reader might reasonably argue that Russia is itself a European state. While Russia has made a glorious contribution to what might be called European high culture, and at various points has played a key role in European power dynamics, its political culture has generally been quite distinct. At present, it stands in opposition to all that contemporary Europe represents.

3   Richard Toye, '"We Shall Fight on the Beaches": 3 Things You Never Knew About Churchill's Most Famous Speech', History of Government blog, UK Government, https://history.blog.gov.uk/2013/12/02/we-shall-fight-on-the-beaches-three-things-you-never-knew-about-churchills-most-famous-speech/.

4   Timothy Garton Ash, 'Europe Whole and Free', *New York Review of Books*, 2 November 2023, https://www.nybooks.com/articles/2023/11/02/europe-whole-and-free-timothy-garton-ash/.

5   In economics, the trilemma is between free capital mobility, exchange-rate management and an independent monetary policy. See 'What Is the Impossible Trinity?', *The Economist*, 10 September 2016, https://www.economist.com/the-economist-explains/2016/09/09/what-is-the-impossible-trinity.

6   IISS, 'Changing Alliance Structures', December 2021, p. 7, https://www.iiss.org/globalassets/media-library---content--migration/files/research-papers/2021/alliances-report.pdf.

7   See Raphael S. Cohen, 'Ukraine and the New Two-war Construct', *War on the Rocks*, 5 January 2023, https://warontherocks.com/2023/01/ukraine-and-the-new-two-war-construct/.

8   Christoph Trebesch et al., 'Ukraine Support Tracker – 15th Release (Covering January 24, 2022 to January 15, 2024)', Kiel Working Papers, no.

2218, Kiel Institute for the World Economy, available at https://www.ifw-kiel.de/publications/the-ukraine-support-tracker-which-countries-help-ukraine-and-how-20852/.

9 See Stephen Groves and Lisa Mascaro, 'Ukrainian Troops Are Rationing Ammunition. But House Republicans Plan to Take Weeks to Mull More Aid', AP News, 2 March 2024, https://apnews.com/article/congress-ukraine-resupply-aid-republicans-53db93c5db8ab249503e93b558da5bd8; Stephen Collinson, 'House Speaker Mike Johnson Faces a Defining Dilemma on Ukraine', CNN, 27 February 2024, https://edition.cnn.com/2024/02/27/politics/mike-johnson-urkaine-aid-dilemma/index.html; and Chicago Council on Global Affairs, 'Americans Continue to Support Military and Economic Aid to Ukraine', 28 February 2024, https://globalaffairs.org/research/public-opinion-survey/americans-continue-support-military-and-economic-aid-ukraine.

10 James FitzGerald, 'Trump Says He Would "Encourage" Russia to Attack Nato Allies Who Do Not Pay Their Bills', BBC News, 11 February 2024, https://www.bbc.co.uk/news/world-us-canada-68266447.

11 Kelly Garrity, 'Why John Bolton Is Certain Trump Really Wants to Blow Up NATO', Politico, 13 February 2024, https://www.politico.com/news/magazine/2024/02/13/bolton-trump-2024-nato-00141160.

12 See Roger Cohen, 'Seeking to Unsettle Russia, Macron Provokes Allies', *New York Times*, 28 February 2024, https://www.nytimes.com/2024/02/28/world/europe/macron-nato-russia-putin.html; and Patrick Wintour, 'Russia Could Attack Nato States if West Fails to Support Ukraine, Macron Says', *Guardian*, 26 February 2024, https://www.theguardian.com/world/2024/feb/26/emmanuel-macron-paris-conference-aims-to-show-the-west-has-means-to-defeat-putin.

13 See Trebesch et al., 'The Ukraine Support Tracker'; and 'German Brigade in Lithuania Set to Be Combat Ready in 2027', DW, 18 December 2023, https://www.dw.com/en/german-brigade-in-lithuania-set-to-be-combat-ready-in-2027/a-67754124.

14 For data on European defence spending, see the IISS Military Balance+ database, https://www.iiss.org/the-military-balance-plus/.

15 See Tom Balmforth, 'What Are the Security Deals Ukraine Is Discussing with Allies?', Reuters, 16 February 2024, https://www.reuters.com/world/europe/what-are-security-deals-ukraine-is-discussing-with-allies-2024-02-14/.

16 European Commission, 'EU Leaders Agree on €50 Billion of Reliable Financial Support for Ukraine Until 2027', 2 February 2024, https://ec.europa.eu/commission/presscorner/detail/en/ac_24_621.

17 Pjotr Sauer, 'Sending Troops to Ukraine Would Risk Provoking Nuclear War, Putin Tells Nato', *Guardian*, 29 February 2024, https://www.theguardian.com/world/2024/feb/29/troops-ukraine-risk-provoking-nuclear-war-vladimir-putin-tells-nato.

18 Edward Gibbon, *The Decline and Fall of the Roman Empire*, vol. 1 (London: W.W. Gibbings, 1890 [1776]), p. 73.

A Critical Juncture: Russia, Ukraine and the Global South

Mustafa Kutlay and Ziya Öniş

The first quarter of the twenty-first century will likely be remembered as an era of multiple crises that profoundly shaped the contours of an emerging post-Western order. Firstly, the 2008 financial crisis tilted the balance of the global economy towards China and non-Western powers. Secondly, the failure of the Arab uprisings to produce stable democracies paved the way for a refugee crisis of significant proportions, which in turn fuelled right-wing populism and exposed the fragility of Western democracies. Thirdly, COVID-19 produced a public-health crisis that accelerated geopolitical competition over global supply chains. Yet the biggest shock to the international order came with Russia's invasion of Ukraine in February 2022, which German Chancellor Olaf Scholz credibly stated 'put an end to an era'.[1]

Wars are major drivers of change in global politics. They make and break international orders, reshape state–market relations and restructure political systems.[2] Russian President Vladimir Putin's war against Ukraine undermined one of the central tenets of the current international order by violating the territorial integrity of a sovereign state. It was also the first European war since 1945 that proved to have genuinely global implications, the Bosnian and other Balkan wars, though significant, having had a more limited geopolitical impact. In the initial phase, some suggested that the

Mustafa Kutlay is a senior lecturer in the Department of International Politics at City, University of London. **Ziya Öniş** is a professor of international relations at Koç University in Istanbul.

Survival | vol. 66 no. 2 | April–May 2024 | pp. 19–36   https://doi.org/10.1080/00396338.2024.2332055

war would revive the liberal-international order as it breathed new life into transatlantic relations and energised the NATO alliance. Lucan A. Way, for instance, suggested that 'Putin's attack on international norms could ultimately strengthen the liberal world order'.[3] Kori Schake similarly argued that 'Putin accidentally revitalized the West's liberal order'.[4] US President Joe Biden stated that Russia's invasion was 'nothing less than a direct challenge to the rules-based international order' and claimed that the 'democracies of the world are revitalized with purpose and unity found in months that we'd once taken years to accomplish'.[5]

On balance, however, Russia's full-scale invasion of Ukraine has undermined the post-Cold War liberal-international order in three principal ways. Firstly, it has widened geopolitical rifts between the West and the Global South. Secondly, it has increased pressure on liberal democracy. Thirdly, it has accelerated the weakening of the neo-liberal economic paradigm that has anchored the US-led economic order since the 1980s.[6]

The West versus the Global South

The war has exposed and deepened the geopolitical rift between the West and the non-Western world. The European Union, Australia, Canada, Japan, South Korea and the United States were shocked by Russia's attack, which they considered unprovoked aggression against a sovereign state. Ukraine's independence was established early in the post-Cold War period, in 1991, and there was no ambiguity regarding its sovereign status. Western countries led by the United States displayed strong unity and commitment from the beginning of the war. The NATO alliance was given a new lease on life. The Western powers united in their desire to support Ukraine militarily and economically, extending military aid to Kyiv and imposing unprecedented sanctions on Russia to weaken Putin's regime. A consensus also developed that Ukraine should continue fighting until it recovered all of the territory Russia had seized since February 2022.

For Western actors, Russia was unambiguously the aggressor and Ukraine clearly the victim, and the rules-based order had been trampled. China and the Global South did not see it that way. While they were uncomfortable with the war and expressed a desire that it end as quickly as possible, they did not unequivocally consider Russia fully responsible for starting the war. Global South governments also were unwilling to go along with Western sanctions, and maintained diplomatic and economic ties with Russia. The West greeted this response with astonishment.

Many countries of the Global South perceived the Russia–Ukraine conflict as a 'European war' with no direct impact on their interests. They preferred to keep out of the conflict as much as they could and adopt a neutral position. As Chris Alden has pointed out, 'the same sorts of arguments heard time and again when conflict breaks out in Africa, that the Western public would not support intervention in a country so geographically remote from North America and Europe, were played out in the Global South'.[7] From the perspective of several countries in the non-Western world, the West itself had adopted a similar approach with respect to the Syrian civil war, assuming a relatively detached attitude and becoming genuinely concerned only when their interests, such as containing the refugee crisis or countering terrorism, were directly at stake.

Furthermore, Global South countries harboured the strong, long-term goal of industrialising rapidly and reaching consumption standards enjoyed by Western democracies, and many had forged significant economic, military and diplomatic ties with Russia that they did not want to weaken by bandwagoning with the Western powers. Some also saw opportunities to benefit from Western sanctions, as Russia sought to diversify its economy and expand trade, investment and financial links. While Russia's exports to the US and the EU decreased due to sanctions, its exports to Brazil, China, India and Turkiye increased considerably (see Figure 1).

A view emerged in the Global South that the war distracted attention from serious global challenges such as poverty, debt, climate change and forced migration, as well as creating significant food and energy shortages on a global scale, fuelling a cost-of-living problem. Hence, it was essential to try to end the war as rapidly as possible, without inordinate concern for whether the peace that emerged was a just one. From the West's perspective, however, only a just peace, involving Ukraine's full recovery of lost territory, would do for two reasons: Russia's egregious behaviour could not be rewarded as a matter of principle, and Russia could not

Figure 1: **Russia's exports to selected countries (US$ billions)**

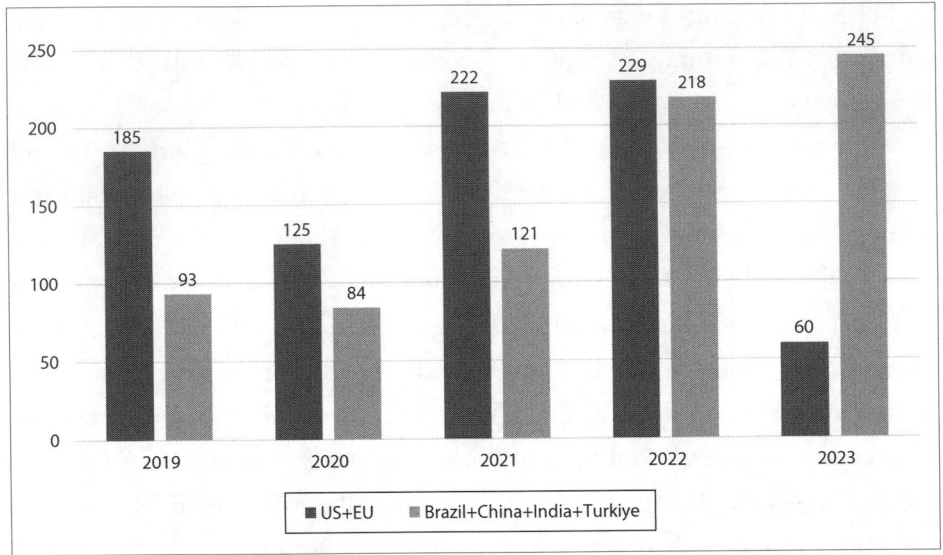

Source: Authors' calculations based on Z. Darvas et al., 'Russian Foreign Trade Tracker', Bruegel Datasets, first published 10 October 2022 (accessed on 4 March 2024), available at https://www.bruegel.org/dataset/russian-foreign-trade-tracker

be encouraged to continue its expansionist behaviour as a matter of geopolitical stability.

From a historical standpoint, many in the Global South were inclined to believe that NATO, through needless enlargement, was primarily responsible for provoking an aggressive Russian response, and that Putin's move was essentially defensive, designed to restore the balance of power. This perspective has gained traction due to strong anti-American and anti-Western sentiments rooted in the legacy of Western colonialism and reinforced by the post-9/11 US invasions of Afghanistan and Iraq. The overarching narrative is that the liberal-international order has been hierarchical, selective and, in certain respects, exclusionary.[8] When Beijing's special representative on European affairs posed the rhetorical question, 'Do we forget the miserable life of the Iraqi people, when they were invaded by a permanent member of the Security Council without the approval of United Nations authority', it resonated strongly in many corners of the globe.[9]

Israel's war in Gaza in response to Hamas's 7 October 2023 terrorist attack deepened the rift between the West and the Global South. Western countries defended Israel's bombardment of Gaza as the 'right to self-defence', while most countries in the Global South supported South Africa's bid to have the International Court of Justice try Israel for war crimes. Although Western support for Ukraine had moral foundations, what they perceived as the United States' and key European powers' unbalanced and unconditional support for Israel, with insufficient sensitivity to the Palestinian cause and the growing humanitarian crisis, undermined the West's claim to the moral high ground. Some divisions did emerge within the Global South: for example, while South Africa and Brazil took a strong stand against Israel, India maintained a pro-Israel position.

China's role

The role that China has played before and during the Russia–Ukraine war is of critical significance in the broader geopolitical contestation. Evan S. Medeiros has described the Chinese position as 'pro-Russia neutrality'.[10] Chinese leaders were not in favour of the war. The China–Russia alignment was bearing fruit and Russia, under peacetime conditions, was in a strong position to help challenge the West, build a multipolar world order and end American hegemony. Nevertheless, Beijing did not condemn the Russian invasion and implicitly supported Moscow by declining to implement Western sanctions. China–Russia trade volume increased markedly during the war, as China purchased massive amounts of Russian energy at discounted prices. Total trade between the two countries increased from $146 billion in 2021 to almost $189bn in 2022.[11] China's tolerance no doubt facilitated Russia's resilience and encouraged other large economies of the Global South to adopt similar approaches. Had China joined the sanctions regime and directly opposed the war, Russia would have found itself far more isolated, with less capacity to conduct the war. Chinese President Xi Jinping and Putin have expressed their commitment to continue working together. In his visit to Russia in March 2023, Xi told Putin that 'change is coming that hasn't happened in 100 years. And we're driving this change together.'[12]

The Russia–Ukraine war has militarily weakened Russia and exposed the limits of Russian military capabilities. The Russian economy has also suffered under Western sanctions. But China has emerged geopolitically stronger, burnishing its credentials as a global peacemaker and increasing its external influence and reach. In particular, it brokered the limited rapprochement between Saudi Arabia and Iran, which appear more comfortable dealing with an outside power that is relatively unconcerned with human-rights violations in their respective domestic spheres. China has sought to broker 'authoritarian peace' in an effort to consolidate non-democratic political regimes, and its comparatively pro-Palestine position has set it apart from Western powers. The Chinese government has also put forward a 12-point plan aiming to end the Russia–Ukraine war.[13] While China's peace plan has not been acceptable to Ukraine or the Western powers since it does not press Russia to return all occupied territory, it could get more purchase as the war drags on, the possibility of Ukraine reclaiming lost land by military means becomes more remote, and Western support for Ukraine diminishes.

The Global South's 'active neutrality'

One of the war's most striking impacts is its elevation of the concept of 'strategic autonomy' among several countries of the Global South in the context of intensifying geopolitical rivalry.[14] These countries have taken to balancing their relations, economically, diplomatically and militarily engaging with both the West and the Russia–China axis. The most important of these are Brazil, India, Saudi Arabia and Turkiye.

In October 2022, former Brazilian president Luiz Inácio 'Lula' da Silva defeated the incumbent president, Jair Bolsonaro. It was a rare case of an authoritarian, right-wing, populist leader losing an election, the other key example being Donald Trump's defeat in the 2020 US presidential election. In other elections – including those in Hungary, Turkiye and India – authoritarian, populist leaders maintained and consolidated their power in successive electoral victories. Pro-democracy figures and key leaders of the Western alliance, especially Biden, welcomed Lula's return, which coincided with Biden's launch of the 'Presidential Initiative for Democratic Renewal'.[15]

During his presidential visit to the United States in February 2023, however, Lula made it clear that his stance on Ukraine differed markedly from the common position of the Western alliance. Although he was critical of Putin's actions, he voiced the opinion that the West also had responsibility for provoking the war. His position was that the war was costly and must end as quickly as possible, without further damage to both sides and the rest of the world. Brazil has maintained strong trade and diplomatic ties with Russia, and has shown no inclination to join democratic Western states in implementing sanctions against Russia, which could be extremely costly to a country struggling to achieve rapid economic development. Lula has thus promoted democracy at home while practising 'active neutrality' in world affairs by striking a balanced position between the West and the China–Russia axis with an eye to advancing a multipolar international order.

India under Prime Minister Narendra Modi has much in common with Lula's Brazil. The two countries have a long history of cooperation, and constitute the more democratic side of the BRICS framework, though Indian democracy under Modi has seen serious illiberal backsliding. Over the past decade, the Indian economy has enjoyed strong growth, which has been key to Modi's efforts to elevate India's status as a global actor. On the one hand, India has maintained good relations with the US and the Western alliance to balance the rise of Chinese power. On the other hand, it has cooperated with China and Russia within BRICS, the Shanghai Cooperation Organisation and the G20, sharing the view that a multipolar international order should be encouraged to offset Western hegemony. This is hardly surprising in light of India's historical position as leader of the Non-Aligned Movement.

India was critical of the war but did not actively take sides.[16] Modi's approach to Putin has been much more reserved than Xi's, but Russia was already a key trading partner for India, especially in energy and military equipment. New Delhi also perceived a calibrated partnership with Moscow as an important means of balancing Chinese power. Consequently, India had no intention of joining the Western-led sanctions against Russia, and indeed, its buoyant market afforded Russia an escape from Western sanctions. Russia's exports to India increased from $6.25bn in 2019 to $40bn at the end of 2022 and stood at $61bn in 2023.[17] Energised by India's assumption of the G20 presidency in December 2022, Modi, much like Lula, is looking to play a diplomatic mediating role in the Russia–Ukraine war to showcase

India's global engagement and influence, and to underline other critical challenges like development, poverty, debt, security and climate change.

Saudi Arabia is also seeking a more autonomous role in foreign affairs. Under Crown Prince Muhammad bin Salman, it has been trying to diversify its national economy and gradually modernise Saudi society. Despite its strong ties to the United States, Saudi Arabia has been acting more 'BRICS-like' in recent years, manifesting ambitions to play a more prominent regional and global role, and in fact was accepted as a new member of the grouping following the BRICS Summit in August 2023. Saudi Arabia is another fence-sitter when it comes to the Russia–Ukraine war. On the one hand, Riyadh wants to maintain economic, diplomatic and military ties with the United States. On the other hand, it seeks to diversify politically based external alignments to distance itself from the West, in part to avail itself of partners – in particular, China – less critical of its human-rights record. The war has provided additional impetus for this tilt, as Saudi Arabia has emerged as one of its winners by virtue of rising oil prices. The war in Gaza has accentuated Saudi Arabia's status as a pivotal regional actor. Riyadh will likely play a key role as a mediator, especially when the military phase of Israel's response gives way to post-conflict negotiations and recovery. This function, and the potential normalisation of relations between Saudi Arabia and Israel, appear important to Western actors' calculations, particularly those of the United States.

Saudi Arabia has tried to position itself as a mediator in the Russia–Ukraine war too. Its efforts have included a summit of national-security advisers in summer 2023, to which more than 30 countries were invited.[18] Interestingly, they did not include Russia, which suggests a more cautious Saudi attitude towards Moscow than Brazil's or India's. But the initiative does reflect an inclination to move towards a post-Western international order.

Finally, Turkiye's position on the war deserves special emphasis owing to the country's position in the Western alliance. As a NATO member since 1952, it has been an integral part of the Western security architecture. It has also had close institutional relations with the EU and its predecessors throughout the post-war period. It joined the Customs Union in 1996 and has been a candidate country for EU membership since December 1999. It developed strong economic and security linkages with the transatlantic alliance through a multilayered institutional framework shaping the country's position in the international system. But Ankara has been deeply disappointed by the stagnation of its EU-membership process and, over the past decade, has increasingly positioned itself as a BRICS-like country embedded in Western institutions. President Recep Tayyip Erdoğan, long the dominant figure in Turkish politics, sees himself as a pre-eminent leader of the Global South, and supports the idea of a multipolar international order and an end to American dominance.[19] Accordingly, Turkish policymakers have stepped up efforts to expand economic, diplomatic and military ties with Russia and China. Of particular note, Turkiye purchased the S-400 anti-aircraft missile system from Russia, generating considerable resentment among Turkiye's NATO partners.

Turkiye has been one of most proactive players in the Russia–Ukraine negotiating process, with Erdoğan committing significant political capital. Turkiye's broader activity has differed from that of other NATO partners and could well be described as one of 'active neutrality', leveraging strong economic and diplomatic ties with both sides. For example, while drones manufactured in Turkiye have proved instrumental in Ukraine's defence, especially during the initial phases of the conflict, Ankara has refrained from implementing Western sanctions, Erdoğan and Putin have maintained close relations, and Turkiye has increased trade and investment with Russia. One notably concrete achievement was the Black Sea Grain Initiative struck in Istanbul (under the auspices of the UN) in July 2022, which helped to remove the Russian blockade of Ukrainian grain shipments in the Black Sea. Russia withdrew from the deal in July 2023, but for a year Ukrainian grain exports could reach the world market and help alleviate food shortages, especially in African countries. Turkiye has taken a strongly pro-Palestine approach with respect to the Gaza war, sharply deviating from the Western powers' position. But its economic relations with Israel have continued without any significant interruption, and its political and security role in the conflict is not as central as the one it has assumed in the Russia–Ukraine war.

Democracy versus authoritarianism: a shifting balance

The second major impact of the war on the liberal-international order is normative. In the first stages of the conflict, the unified response of the Western alliance and massive support – military and economic – for the defence of a Western-leaning, relatively democratic country suggested that the liberal order on a global scale might end up stronger from this conflict. Optimistic expectations were based on two interrelated propositions. Firstly, Ukraine, with Western assistance, would be able to defeat Russia and emerge victorious from the war by recovering all the territory lost during the war. As the war progressed, however, it became clear that this proposition was not viable. Ukraine, with Western assistance, displayed extraordinary resilience on the battlefield against the Russian army, whose capabilities, though far superior on paper, were exposed as weak. The Russian economy also suffered under the sanctions regime. The significant indirect support provided by the United States and its NATO allies, however, has not decisively tilted the balance in Ukraine's favour, and it now seems less likely that Ukraine will be able to recover all of its territory. Nevertheless, Ukraine and the Western partners remain prepared to engage in a prolonged effort to deny legitimacy to Russian aggression.

Secondly, some believed severe economic sanctions would isolate Putin's regime and trigger intra-elite conflict in Russia, leading to regime change. But both the economy and Putin's regime have turned out to be more resilient than expected. Although Russia's real GDP shrank by 2.1% in 2022, China and the rest of the Global South helped keep its economy afloat. According to IMF projections, the Russian economy is expected to grow more than Germany's, Japan's and the United Kingdom's over the next two years (see Figure 2). Furthermore, Putin was able to take advantage of the war to tighten his grip on the Russian state and Russian society. Any remaining opposition was effectively dismantled, and the regime became more repressive. The possibility of a regime breakdown, which many Western analysts had predicted or hoped for, now appears far-fetched.

Western countries, for their part, have become more defensive in promoting and protecting democratic values in global politics. Biden's initiative to build a new alliance of democracies has lost its initial momentum. American

Figure 2: **Percentage-growth projections of selected countries, 2023–24**

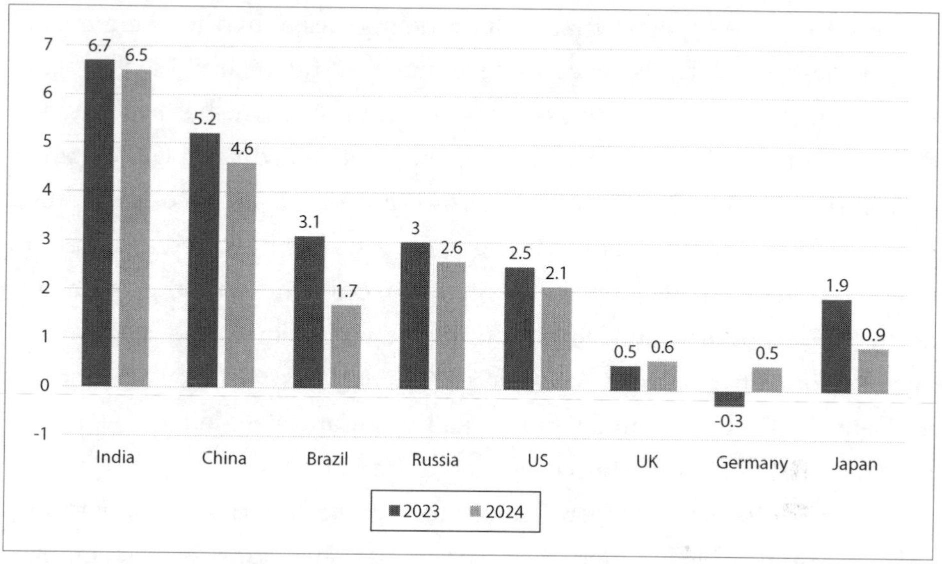

Source: Authors' calculations based on IMF, 'World Economic Outlook', January 2024 projections, available at https://www.imf.org/en/Publications/WEO

policy towards many countries has become more pragmatic and less idealistic, marred by normative inconsistencies. For instance, the White House's criticism of human-rights violations in countries such as Saudi Arabia and India has become more muted owing to Washington's economic concerns and its desire not to lose these countries altogether. European countries, concerned about their own security and domestic stability, have also become much less energetic in promoting democratic values. Enthusiasm for a new wave of EU enlargement has appeared limited, given that certain member states themselves have significantly diverged from democratic norms. Even in the case of Ukraine, EU membership is now considered a long-term outcome that would materialise only after arduous membership negotiations.

In contrast, the China–Russia axis has proactively supported authoritarian regimes. The current wave of BRICS enlargement can be interpreted in part as an attempt to enlarge the autocracy coalition under Chinese influence. In addition, China and Russia have effectively crushed protest movements – in Hong Kong and in Belarus and Kazakhstan, respectively – that could have paved the way for democratic openings in their immediate neighbourhood.

The Global South is, of course, politically heterogeneous, comprising a variety of governments that include democracies, hybrid regimes and autocracies with different levels of development. Still, their unified stance in rejecting the Western narrative on Russia's war in Ukraine has been a major disappointment to key Western actors, and explains why the United States and Europe have become more defensive and pragmatic in downgrading pro-democracy rhetoric in their foreign policies. They have had to adapt to a new international context in which many governments and large segments of the world population reject the normative viewpoint of the Western alliance; historically based anti-Western sentiments constrain the West's ability to engage effectively; and China's authoritarian, state-led development model is challenging Western economic dominance.

Closer South–South cooperation certainly presents a salutary opportunity to build a more inclusive international order that better addresses the concerns of the developing world. But BRICS enlargement is also likely to weaken democratic governance. China's dominance in the BRICS grouping was evident before the Russia–Ukraine war. The BRICS countries' response to the war differed sharply from the West's, which increased the interest of many countries in joining the bloc despite differences on other matters. At the 15th Annual BRICS Summit, held in Johannesburg in August 2023, BRICS membership was extended to six new countries, effective from January 2024. These were Argentina, Egypt, Ethiopia, Iran, Saudi Arabia and the United Arab Emirates, though Argentina declined to join. This expansion reflects China's growing weight and influence, which the war has facilitated by diverting the resources and attention of the United States and the Western alliance to supporting Ukraine and containing Russia. Any new members are likely to maintain their ties to the United States and other Western actors, but they will probably be inclined to use BRICS membership and closer ties to China to establish greater strategic autonomy and increase their bargaining power with Western actors.[20]

Towards post-neo-liberalism

In the post-Cold War era, with the stagnation of the Keynesian paradigm in the West and the collapse of the Soviet economic model, neo-liberalism gained currency because most American policymakers believed it would increase economic interdependence and drive convergence towards improved living conditions, political liberalisation and strategic stability. Although globalisation has helped decrease global poverty since the 1990s, it has also contributed to growing income inequality and fuelled right-wing populism.[21] Moreover, the rise of China and Russia's invasion of Ukraine have deflated the hope that economic interdependence would advance political liberalisation and contain conflict.[22] Although the hope for neo-liberalism was not entirely wrong or naive, it prompted many to question the logic of globalisation and reorder their economic priorities.

The neo-liberal economic paradigm has emphasised efficiency, and in particular the idea that free trade and the free flow of capital would boost economic growth and productivity on a global scale. Such a dynamic is sustainable, however, only if it is underpinned by a stable international political system free of major geopolitical conflict. Growing great-power competition between the US and China, and military escalation between Russia and the West, have broken this condition, compelling states to shift their priorities away from efficiency and towards resilience to reduce their exposure to external economic shocks, ruptures in global supply chains and the adverse effects of sanctions, financial restrictions, and trade and technology wars. The Biden administration, for example, introduced the Inflation Reduction Act and the CHIPS and Science Act to reduce US dependence on overseas high-technology sectors. China, for its part, has adopted the 'dual-circulation' framework to encourage domestic demand and reduce China's dependence on exports.[23]

This trend has increased the risk of geo-economic fragmentation.[24] Economic security and protectionism are becoming integral to national policy. Heavy state-driven investment in domestic production capacities has prompted *The Economist* to anxiously announce 'the rise of homeland economics'.[25] The US is leading the current Western surge in domestic re-industrialisation, partly due to its growing geopolitical rivalry with China. Biden's ambitious industrial policies entail massive government subsidies to encourage domestic production in high-value-added industries, such as semiconductors, and in green technologies. This policy shift aims not only to address justifiably growing concerns about unacceptable levels of income and wealth inequality, but also to reduce America's economic and technological dependence on China. European policymakers have similar concerns. French President Emmanuel Macron has suggested that 'Europe needs more factories and fewer dependencies' to secure 'European sovereignty'.[26] The EU has acted to accelerate green industrial transformation and increase its resilience in key strategic sectors such as semiconductors, artificial intelligence, clean energy and defence.

Post-neo-liberalism, such as it is, has taken on a different character in the Global South. Unprecedentedly severe Western sanctions imposed on Russia exposed many developing countries to the negative effects of 'weaponised interdependence'.[27] Owing to the United States' willingness to exploit the reserve-currency status of the American dollar and its control over the global financial infrastructure for geopolitical purposes, many non-Western countries are searching for alternative forms of economic statecraft to reduce their vulnerability to US-led sanctions and financial constraints. Although replacing the US dollar as the reserve currency seems very remote, one of the drivers of BRICS enlargement is a desire to reduce the dominance of the American dollar in the international financial system by promoting local currencies for some international payments. Lula said in his visit to China in April 2023: 'Every night I ask myself why all countries have to base their trade on the dollar.'[28]

The erosion of neo-liberal globalisation is likely to transform the liberal-international order in two significant ways, one salutary and the other dubious. On the plus side, it will open more space for development-oriented policies to reduce income and wealth inequality, promote more inclusive growth and hasten the much-needed return of the welfare state. Less auspiciously, since the primary driver appears to be geopolitics, 'beggar-thy-neighbour' policies and self-destructive economic protectionism may intensify, fragmenting and militarising the global economy.

* * *

Russia's invasion of Ukraine has helped undermine the post-Cold War liberal-international order by widening and deepening the geopolitical rift between the West and the Global South. China's disingenuous behaviour has been critical. Beijing adopted a purportedly neutral position on the war that was in fact heavily tilted in Moscow's favour. Despite portraying itself as a mediator, Beijing's peacemaking efforts have been structured to Russia's advantage. Key countries of the Global South, such as Brazil and India, have displayed more genuine neutrality than China but have essentially followed its lead. If the war ends without Ukraine's full recovery of its territory – which looks increasingly likely – the Western-centred rules-based international order would appear at least partially incapable of protecting the security of democratic regimes.

Even if the war is settled on terms relatively favourable to Ukraine, China and the Global South may claim the moral high ground through diplomatic facilitation and economic assistance for Ukraine's post-war reconstruction. Some damage to the liberal-international order as a result of the war now appears inescapable. Attempts to revive it encountered a significant setback with the Gaza war, which raised serious concerns about the moral standing of the United States and major European powers, widening the West's legitimacy gap in the Global South.

Notes

[1] Scholz also said that the 'world is facing a *Zeitenwende*: an epochal tectonic shift'. See Olaf Scholz, 'The Global Zeitenwende', *Foreign Affairs*, vol. 102, no. 1, January/February 2023, pp. 22–38.

[2] See, for example, Robert Gilpin, *War and Change in World Politics* (Cambridge: Cambridge University Press, 1981).

[3] Lucan A. Way, 'The Rebirth of the Liberal World Order?', *Journal of Democracy*, vol. 33, no. 2, April 2022, pp. 5–17.

[4] Kori Schake, 'Putin Accidentally Revitalized the West's Liberal Order', *Atlantic*, 28 February 2022, https://www.theatlantic.com/international/archive/2022/02/vladimir-putin-ukraine-invasion-liberal-order/622950/.

[5] White House, 'Remarks by President Biden on the United Efforts of the Free World to Support the People of Ukraine', 26 March 2022, https://www.whitehouse.gov/briefing-room/speeches-remarks/2022/03/26/remarks-by-president-biden-on-the-united-efforts-of-the-free-world-to-support-the-people-of-ukraine/.

[6] We focus on the post-Cold War liberal-international order in this article because that order 'is a dynamic order exhibiting different

features across time and space'. David A. Lake, Lisa L. Martin and Thomas Risse, 'Challenges to the Liberal Order: Reflections on *International Organization*', *International Organization*, vol. 75, no. 2, Spring 2021, pp. 225–57. In the economic realm, for example, 'embedded liberalism' with limited capital mobility and more extensive welfare-state policies was the predominant economic paradigm in the post-1945 Western order, but in the 1980s gave way to neo-liberalism, which expanded globally with the collapse of the Soviet Union. See John Gerard Ruggie, 'International Regimes, Transactions, and Change: Embedded Liberalism in the Postwar Economic Order', *International Organization*, vol. 36, no. 2, Spring 1982, pp. 379–415.

7   Chris Alden, 'The Global South and Russia's Invasion of Ukraine', *LSE Public Policy Review*, vol. 3, no. 1, September 2023, pp. 1–8.

8   On conceptual debates concerning the key features of the liberal-international order, see Alexander Cooley and Daniel Nexon, *Exit from Hegemony: The Unraveling of the American Global Order* (Oxford: Oxford University Press, 2020), pp. 18–53; and Lake, Martin and Risse, 'Challenges to the Liberal Order'.

9   Quoted in Andy Bounds and Joe Leahy, 'EU Trade Commissioner to Seek Relief from Export Barriers During China Visit', *Financial Times*, 23 September 2023, https://www.ft.com/content/20e60f3a-53eb-46aa-bd92-f1dff61ebd7b.

10 Quoted in Kathrin Hille, 'Xi Pursues Policy of "Pro-Russia Neutrality"

Despite Ukraine War', *Financial Times*, 27 February 2022, https://www.ft.com/content/bf930a62-6952-426b-b249-41097094318a.

11 Z. Darvas et al., 'Russian Foreign Trade Tracker', Bruegel Datasets, first published 10 October 2022 (accessed 14 October 2023), available at https://www.bruegel.org/dataset/russian-foreign-trade-tracker.

12 Quoted in James Kynge, 'China Is Tightening Its Embrace with Russia as It Builds Bulwarks Against the West', *Financial Times*, 24 March 2023, https://www.ft.com/content/bbaa4006-318e-4dbe-b7d4-3c21aa5e8887.

13 See Ministry of Foreign Affairs of the People's Republic of China, 'China's Position on the Political Settlement of the Ukraine Crisis', 24 February 2023, https://www.mfa.gov.cn/eng/zxxx_662805/202302/t20230224_11030713.html.

14 See Alden, 'The Global South and Russia's Invasion of Ukraine', pp. 5–6.

15 See White House, 'Remarks by President Biden at the Summit for Democracy Opening Session', 9 December 2021, https://www.whitehouse.gov/briefing-room/speeches-remarks/2021/12/09/remarks-by-president-biden-at-the-summit-for-democracy-opening-session/.

16 By trying to maintain good relations with the US and Russia simultane-ously, 'India has hoped to run with the hare and hunt with the hound', as the editors of the *Financial Times* put it. 'India's Disappointing Silence over Ukraine', *Financial Times*, 13 March 2022, https://www.ft.com/content/9e8af1a9-da07-4fb4-ae0e-6f6986ea5b75.

17 Darvas et al., 'Russian Foreign Trade Tracker'.

18 See Henry Foy, Samer Al-Atrush and Felicia Schwartz, 'Saudi Seeks to Woo Developing Nations for Ukraine Peace Talks', *Financial Times*, 29 July 2023, https://www.ft.com/content/5d69508a-e8c3-46b7-82cf-8c033499b445.

19 See Mustafa Kutlay and Ziya Öniş, 'Turkish Foreign Policy in a Post-Western Order: Strategic Autonomy or New Forms of Dependence?', *International Affairs*, vol. 97, no. 4, July 2021, pp. 1,085–104.

20 See Ziya Öniş and Mustafa Kutlay, 'The New Age of Hybridity and Clash of Norms: China, BRICS, and Challenges of Global Governance in a Post-liberal International Order', *Alternatives: Global, Local, Political*, vol. 45, no. 3, May 2020, pp. 123–42.

21 See Dani Rodrik, 'Why Does Globalization Fuel Populism? Economics, Culture, and the Rise of Right-wing Populism', *Annual Review of Economics*, vol. 13, August 2021, pp. 133–70.

22 America's 'liberal interventionism' also weakened the legitimacy of the rules-based order.

23 See Jude Blanchette and Evan S. Medeiros, 'Xi Jinping's Third Term', *Survival*, vol. 64, no. 5, October–November 2022, pp. 61–90.

24 See IMF, 'World Economic Outlook: Navigating Global Divergences', October 2023, https://www.imf.org/-/media/Files/Publications/WEO/2023/October/English/text.ashx.

25 'Are Free Markets History?', *The Economist*, 5 October 2023, https://www.economist.com/leaders/2023/10/05/are-free-markets-history.

26 Emmanuel Macron, 'Europe Needs More Factories and Fewer Dependencies', *Financial Times*, 12 May 2023, https://www.ft.com/content/7ff1123d-51b1-482c-ba86-b3a95a347df9. The EU's attempt to boost its industrial capabilities (especially in defence) is related to its quest to become a more autonomous actor in global politics vis-à-vis other great powers. This has long been on the EU's agenda, but progress has been limited. As Pierre Buhler points out, 'many tools, procedures and institutions have been set up and concept papers written to allow the EU to become a more potent and capable actor in the international area ... Yet little of substance has been achieved.' Pierre Buhler, 'About European Sovereignty', *Survival*, vol. 65, no. 2, April–May 2023, p. 62.

27 See Henry Farrell and Abraham Newman, *Underground Empire: How America Weaponized the World Economy* (London: Allen Lane, 2023); and Henry Farrell and Abraham Newman, 'Weaponized Interdependence: How Global Economic Networks Shape State Coercion', *International Security*, vol. 44, no. 1, Summer 2019, pp. 42–79.

28 Quoted in Bryan Harris and Joe Leahy, 'Lula Vows Partnership with China to "Balance World Geopolitics"', *Financial Times*, 15 April 2023, https://www.ft.com/content/766ed3aa-3f51-4035-8573-43254c9756d5.

The Return of Geopolitical Blocs

Zeno Leoni and Sarah Tzinieris

In his first major speech as British secretary of state for defence, Grant Shapps warned in January 2024 that the West had 'come full circle' from the Cold War and was now moving from a 'post-war' to a 'pre-war world'. Shapps, a long-standing senior minister of the ruling Conservative Party, painted a bleak picture in which the 'foundations of the world order are being shaken to their core' and the West is engaged in an existential crisis triggered by old and new adversaries. He went so far as to warn that 'in five years' time we could be looking at multiple theatres including Russia, China, Iran and North Korea'.[1] While Shapps's intervention lacked nuance – and notably came ahead of a general election, when incumbents often play up external threats – his warning about a bifurcation in global politics is in line with a growing consensus that the world is moving away from the US-led liberal-international order to something new.[2]

It is clear that strategic competition will turn on the tension between globalisation and protectionism, the financial primacy of the US dollar and the struggle for control over global trade, particularly in strategic technologies and critical minerals. Much of this activity will be centred in the vast Indo-Pacific maritime space, though it will also emerge in new frontiers like the Arctic and outer space. Yet it is not just about capabilities and resources,

Zeno Leoni is a lecturer in defence studies in the Defence Studies Department of King's College London. **Sarah Tzinieris** is a research fellow in the Department of War Studies of King's College London.

Survival | vol. 66 no. 2 | April–May 2024 | pp. 37–54   https://doi.org/10.1080/00396338.2024.2332056

but also involves a more fundamental tension between the pursuit of narrow national interests focused on economic and military resources, and the promotion of values, ideas and norms, manifested in the re-emergence of bloc politics. Less tangible than the Eastern and Western blocs of the Cold War and less ideologically driven, new geopolitical poles are emerging, with associated spheres of influence. They include a renewed, albeit diminished, Western bloc, a large but fragmented and leaderless Eurasian bloc, and a confluence of swing states not bound to any particular hegemon but potentially wielding substantial influence. The two key global trends that will shape the world order in 2024 and beyond are resurgent conflict between the West and Russia and, perhaps more significantly, intensifying rivalry between the United States and China.[3] The predominant view is that America's might will fade as economies like China and India come to the fore. Discussions of strategic scenarios tend to cleave to an intense struggle for global primacy or a manageable way to 'share' the twenty-first century. Yet a closer examination of the three emerging blocs suggests that the West will continue to hold sway, provided – and this is a big if – the authoritarian influences now threatening America's liberal traditions and achievements do not prevail.

A new Iron Curtain?

In the 1990s, Daniel Deudney and G. John Ikenberry warned that the Cold War settlement was 'unravelling'.[4] While Russia's annexation of Crimea in 2014 came as a shock to the West, it sealed Ukraine's fate as a 'grey zone' between the competing spheres of influence of a complacent West and a resurgent Russia.[5] With hindsight from the full-scale invasion in 2022, these events suggest that the end of the Cold War was not as conclusive as most had hoped. As Stephen Kotkin notes, 'to argue that the Cold War ended … is to reduce that conflict to the existence of the Soviet state'.[6] The fabled post-Cold War era lasted just over two decades, when the doctrine of liberal internationalism was at its zenith. Pushed by Western leaders like Tony Blair and Barack Obama, it rested on the assumption that a strategic pause was under way.[7] In retrospect, this was overly optimistic. The same competitive dynamics that characterised the Cold War had been simmering under the surface of what Richard Sakwa calls a 'cold peace' and were rekindled in 2014.[8] While differences abound over the semantics of the present moment, its dynamics look similar to those of the Cold War.

.How did it come to this? There are multiple reasons, but two stand out. Firstly, during Washington's roughly 75-year leadership of the international order, US grand strategy has focused on maintaining the primacy of global capitalism and, where possible, protecting and cultivating democratic regimes. These efforts did not end with the Soviet Union's dissolution, but continued with vigour into the 1990s and beyond.[9] As China emerged as an economic heavyweight, the US also became preoccupied with curbing its rising influence.[10] The American objective, however, was always to maintain the status quo – that is, US primacy – rather than to effectuate a genuine balance of power. Secondly, Russia's invasion of Ukraine constitutes a convergence of the two traditional Cold War vectors of competition.[11] China's refusal to condemn Russia's belligerency confirmed Beijing as an adversary of the West, and thus the emergence of America's tripolar nuclear problem.[12] China and Russia have aligned in an anti-Western bloc, formalised by their 'no limits' friendship with 'no "forbidden" areas of cooperation' announced just 20 days before the invasion, in February 2022.[13] Meanwhile, the neutral stance of other influential states – including India, an important emerging economy[14] – further dampened expectations that Russia would be diplomatically isolated. In turn, it seemed less likely that Russia's experience with Ukraine would discourage China from moving on Taiwan.[15]

A firm West

On account of the newly drawn East–West fault lines, a reinvigorated Western bloc is emerging. US grand strategy under President Joe Biden has focused on cultivating minilateral frameworks – discrete groups of like-minded allies and partners that have common strategic objectives. Although the liberal internationalism of the earlier decades facilitated an order in which differences between East and West gradually eroded as states became more capitalistic and democratic, and better governed, the new Western geopolitical bloc is becoming more exclusive. This is primarily due to a stricter set of rules relating to global trade, but there is a strong China dimension. The US is attempting to reassert American primacy through order-engineering, an essentially conservative strategy that eschews any effort to accommodate China or Russia through a genuine balance of power.

Notwithstanding the tensions and disappointments involving Ukraine, the reconfigured East–West fault line has in fact provided a more favourable diplomatic environment for the Biden administration to shape America's alliances than is commonly appreciated.[16] With Beijing taking Moscow's side, Western states have reunited against common enemies. The most obvious consequence has been NATO's renaissance, including strengthened consensus, increased defence spending and expansion to include Finland and Sweden. The G7 had also been struggling to forge a consensus, but as US National Security Advisor Jake Sullivan has observed, now 'it is the steering committee of the free world'.[17] Kotkin points out that retaining this unity vis-à-vis China and Russia is vital, not least to restore the momentum that Washington lost over its mistakes in withdrawing from Afghanistan and early fumbles over the security pact between Australia, the United Kingdom and the US, known as AUKUS.[18]

The ideological glue for this unity is the Western conviction that relations between countries should be determined by their respective political frameworks, and that democracies should be preferred and promoted.[19] This 'democratic internationalism' yields a stark division of the world into autocracies and democracies, in that it ultimately 'reproduces the cold war logic' – that is, the logic of blocs.[20] The US under Biden is seeking to create a new liberal-international order by excluding those states that threaten US leadership, primarily China, and pursuing deeper integration among like-minded allies and partners.[21] On a practical level, two vehicles appear instrumental in US order-engineering. Firstly, AUKUS has revealed itself to be not merely the strategic-technology accelerator that it first appeared, but also a framework for a much broader set of objectives aimed at curbing China's influence, as well as a tentative signal of a strengthened Anglospheric core to safeguard US primacy.[22] Secondly, traditional vectors of Western military power are consolidating the trend towards bloc politics. In its new 'Strategic Concept' document, NATO explicitly identifies China as a 'systemic challenge' that is seeking to 'subvert the rules-based international order'.[23] There have even been suggestions that the Alliance might extend its reach – albeit informally – as far as East Asia.[24] Meanwhile, the US has pursued security integration with partners in Asia through a series of minilateral initiatives, reviving the Quadrilateral Security Dialogue, which importantly includes India and Japan, renewing a defence agreement with the Philippines, and increasing freedom-of-navigation exercises with various Indo-Pacific partners.

Nevertheless, the West is a smaller political construct than it was even a decade ago. It is compelled to moderate its Manichaean world view and engage across the wider international community, including with autocracies and adversaries; constructive trade talks between Washington and Beijing in autumn 2023 are a case in point. Washington itself has shifted towards a more inclusive, rules-based world order, underscored by its improved ties with India.[25] While this notional order has broad potential geographic scope, however, its normative scope remains contested.[26] The line between capitalism and communism was clear during the Cold War, but that between contemporary democracies and autocracies is far murkier, further complicated by the economic interdependence between the West and most of Asia.

Despite such challenges, the overall weakness of current political leadership plays to the West's advantage. The West is unlikely to endure as a 'geopolitical and ideological colossus', as Ikenberry put it.[27] But it will remain highly competitive through its relative political cohesion, vast reservoirs of capital, goods, technological know-how, and military capacity and capability.[28] Democracies are also better able to collaborate with one another, while open societies enable them to be more resilient and adaptable.[29]

Autocratic Eurasia

The new geopolitical bloc taking shaping in Eurasia rests, above all, on the constellation of shared strategic interests between China and Russia. Well before Russia's invasion of Ukraine, the US was concerned about Beijing and Moscow forming an anti-Western alliance.[30] Since their 'no limits' proclamation in February 2022, that prospect has become an existential issue for the West. They have also opposed further enlargement of NATO and criticised 'the formation of closed bloc structures and opposing camps in the Asia-Pacific region'.[31] Sakwa casts China and Russia as the 'political East', shaped by the dynamics of a second cold war and, even more importantly, the establishment of a multipolar system whereby alternative political and financial institutions seek to blunt Western sanctions and the weaponisation of the dollar.[32]

The Shanghai Cooperation Organisation is the bloc's main diplomatic forum, even if New Delhi and other members might chafe at this characterisation. China has been promoting initiatives that, while nascent, provide competing visions to America's minilateral designs.[33] A Eurasian bloc is also nested in the China-led '16+1' initiative, whose members mostly include states that are east of the former Iron Curtain. While some are also now members of the European Union, it appears that China wants to instrumentalise this framework to reinforce oligarchic elements of Central and Eastern European states, and make them more susceptible to its state-led-capitalism model.[34]

The bloc could also extend to BRICS, the intergovernmental organisation of leading emerging economies founded by Brazil, Russia, India, China and South Africa. Not only are Beijing and Moscow prominent in this forum, but several important economies, such as South Africa, have moved closer to them in recent years.[35] With more than 40 states having expressed interest in joining BRICS, it could become the key intergovernmental framework of the Eurasian bloc while also tapping into the Global South.[36] An expanded BRICS could conceivably represent around 30% of global GDP and 43% of global oil production, profoundly impacting the balance of power.

A new Eurasian bloc, however, faces significant constraints that will take time to overcome and may never be surmountable. Firstly, although China and Russia are united in a desire for a more multipolar world, they have not yet arrived at, much less elaborated, a shared long-term vision for it.[37] Their relationship is still informal, and it remains unclear what China's intentions are towards Russia.[38] Chinese equivocation vis-à-vis Russia may be a deliberate strategy for maintaining the upper hand. Aside from supporting each other in the United Nations Security Council, they have demonstrated little capacity for combining diplomatic efforts to address global challenges.[39] Secondly, contradictions in Chinese grand strategy call into question whether any Eurasian bloc could achieve the degree of political cohesion required to function effectively. China remains ambiguous about how politically entrepreneurial it wants to be on a global scale, maintaining traditional Panchsheel principles of respect for territorial sovereignty and non-interference.[40] Beijing's leadership on international controversies has been quite weak, its facilitation of reconciliation between Iran and Saudi Arabia being the exception rather than the rule.[41] Compared to the US, China still appears too inward-looking to lead a bloc. Thirdly, the BRICS framework is primarily orientated towards economic growth rather than geopolitics, and many potential new members would blanch at intense politicisation. Finally, as a normative organising principle, sovereign internationalism remains a poor fit for most states in Eurasia.[42] They may be united in opposing US unipolarity and on other particular issues, but alignment will only be achievable on specific issues, where interests happen to coincide.[43]

On balance, the Eurasian bloc appears to be a soft, opportunistic grouping rather than a hard alliance, with consensus relying narrowly on mutual Chinese and Russian opposition to a US-led order. The new Eurasian bloc is highly fragmented, which hinders the delineation of a clear set of members, although they can be expected to include China, Iran, North Korea, Russia and Syria. Pakistan could also be a member given its long-established 'special relationship' with China based on economic and military cooperation – a scenario that would pose stiff and possibly existential strategic challenges for India and perforce complicate geopolitics for the new bloc.

Non-binary swing states

The recent revival of BRICS correlates with the potential emergence of another geopolitical bloc: that of 'global swing states', led by Brazil, India and other rising economic powers. Often associated with the Global South, and roughly synonymous with middle powers, swing states have been defined as countries 'with significant leverage in international politics but varying preferences for international cooperation'.[44] They generally favour multipolarity.[45] India is a case in point, with its principle of 'strategic autonomy'. It has become a member of the Quad and BRICS, and established the Russia–India–China trilateral. It has also cultivated relations with Brazil and the Gulf states, and secured technology and defence deals with France while maintaining robust arms-trade relationships with both Russia and the United States. While America is prone to characterising India as Western-facing due to its purportedly secular democratic system, shared political values alone are unlikely to prove sufficient to sustain a strong partnership given Prime Minister Narendra Modi's promotion of Hindu nationalism with an authoritarian edge.[46]

Though important, swing states don't easily add up to a distinct geopolitical entity. They do not even perceive themselves as parts of a bloc, let alone seek to consolidate one. Still, the flexibility of alliances amid the diminishing influence of great powers on lesser powers has become increasingly salient since the Ukraine invasion. During UN General Assembly votes on the crisis, a much larger number of states than expected remained neutral rather than siding with the West. Many non-Western states believe that too often, the West has hypocritically violated its own values and rules, especially in neglecting global humanitarian issues.[47] Yet there is no evidence that swing states see themselves as bound to a hegemonic China, which to many does not appear any more benevolent than the West. Beijing has not, for example, offered to share technical know-how to help developing countries build their own national industries.[48] As great-power rivalry sharpens, swing states may be willing to cooperate with China or Russia, but probably not to the point of shoring up an anti-Western Sino-Russian bloc.[49] Furthermore, in their quest for autonomy, they tend to focus on their near abroad, which suggests that smaller powers may be hard to influence geopolitically owing to local security and political priorities.[50] Their aim may be to retain agency and selectivity in helping to shape the rules of the world order, with non-interference in other states being an abiding principle.[51] These factors cut against Ikenberry's thesis that the West and China could engage in a 'creative' struggle for the approval and backing of the Global South.[52]

The political autonomy of swing states, assuming it can be sustained in the long term, will limit the manoeuvrability of both the West and the Eurasian bloc. There is no uniformity among swing states and no monolithic Global South.[53] It is also unlikely that Washington, Beijing or Moscow will be able to cultivate genuine alliances with these states, which would require flexible diplomatic outreach and an appreciation of deeply nuanced regional contexts and national interests, both elusive. Compared with the Non-Aligned Movement, a product of the Cold War whose ideological solidarity was based on anti-colonialism and anti-imperialism, today's swing states are both more powerful and more transactional. Their main concern is to protect themselves from great-power competition.[54] For them, 'unaligned' or even 'multi-aligned' may be a better adjective than 'non-aligned'.[55] Many swing states may ultimately aim to reap benefits from both the Western and Eurasian blocs, which would allow for partnerships of convenience but contraindicate alliances.

A clash of blocs?

The preponderance of evidence points towards three porous blocs, each seeking avenues of self-interested cooperation with the others. Rather than the East–West Iron Curtain – which could be somewhat porous itself – the US–China relationship will probably continue as grudging coexistence characterised by both competition and cooperation. A kind of co-hegemony may persist for a considerable period, with China becoming the world's largest economy and the United States remaining its largest military power. Washington and Beijing will have equal 'attractive power', as Jean Kachiga puts it, such that states orbiting in the sphere of influence of one may still be able to gravitate towards the other.[56] While the previous level of cooperation that Washington and Beijing enjoyed – a fleeting marriage of convenience – is unlikely to be restored, both sides are exploring ways to move forward.[57] A new bilateral framework may yet be on the cards, as suggested by the autumn 2023 bilateral trade talks. A deep freeze of cooperation and dialogue across the board, like that arising between the United States and the Soviet Union during the Cold War, thus seems unlikely.[58] As Richard Higgot and Simon Reich have said, the 'bifurcation' will be 'fuzzy'.[59]

The present order is different than the Cold War in several clear ways. It features more influences on state behaviour and a wider range of actors, including prominent non-state ones. Alliances are no longer hermetically sealed as they were during the Cold War.[60] And great powers have decreased ability to influence the strategic choices of weaker states. These factors, especially the last one, inhibit great powers' capacity to engineer the world order.

How geopolitically determinative these three blocs will become, then, is highly debatable. At present, there is no single issue that could draw any particular bloc into direct conflict with another, nor any issue that could compel any of the blocs to act in unison. But dangerous crises – the Russia–Ukraine war being the most obvious – have arisen that could, in the long term, impose harder political barriers between blocs. Changes in government in swing states could also have significant impacts on international affairs. On account of Javier Milei's victory in Argentina's 2023 presidential election, for instance, Buenos Aires turned down the invitation to join BRICS.[61] Regional, national and local conflicts might at any given point undermine efforts towards geopolitical cohesion. The most significant challenge to American or Chinese primacy may well come from swing states or Global South states looking to modulate strategic competition. A putative hegemon can no longer claim automatic entitlement to a customary sphere of influence, which suggests that great powers would be unwise to back lesser states into a corner.[62] Despite retaining substantial global leadership on account of its relative political cohesion, the West will need to compromise on particular issues over which other blocs or their leaders – especially China and Russia – enjoy greater clout.[63]

An inside challenge to Western primacy

The greatest apparent threat to Western primacy is not any rival bloc but rather the percolating domestic right-wing challenge to American democracy. Another Trump presidency would produce global turbulence rather than order, and the prospect of an enduring liberal-internationalist America committed to democracy might well not survive it. America's assumption of substantial responsibility for the West was crucial not only for Allied victory in the Second World War but also for instilling trust in its vision and guidance in American allies and partners during the critical Cold War decades that followed. Even if policy differences emerged from time to time, the United States, as a like-minded superpower, reciprocated by providing its allies with reliable protection. The AUKUS episode provides a modest recent example of the post-war settlement's staying power. When Australia scrapped the diesel-submarine deal with France in favour of procuring nuclear-powered subs from the US and the UK as part of a broader security arrangement in 2021, Paris was furious, recalling its ambassadors. Yet France's close relationships with the three AUKUS partners were never in real danger. Diplomatic ties and normal relations were quickly restored, France having subordinated its indignation to the West's larger strategic interests.

Under the spectre of Donald Trump, putative American values cannot be taken for granted. Should he win in November, Western allies may get an 'illiberal America that is increasingly anti-democratic at home and crudely transactional, protectionist and undiplomatic abroad'.[64] In February 2024, for instance, he publicly suggested that he would acquiesce to Russian President Vladimir Putin invading financially feckless NATO members.[65] Such conduct as president would increase the likelihood of conflict between the West and other blocs. The impending US presidential election in November therefore will be strategically pivotal. Yet Trump is not the only factor in the potential crystallisation of an illiberal, quasi-isolationist America. Broader right-wing tribalism and crude partisanship have widened the chasm in American politics.[66] Bullish US allies are betting that a liberal America will endure, when recent evidence also supports a contrary outcome.[67]

There do remain some structural constraints that could stave off the American Right's abject destruction of the liberal-international order. In December 2023, a solid bipartisan majority in Congress approved the Fiscal 2024 Defense Spending Bill, which includes a provision barring the president from withdrawing from NATO without the advice and consent of the Senate.[68] Likewise, minilateral security arrangements such as the Quad and AUKUS are unlikely to completely implode under Trump, as they enjoy wide bipartisan support. In addition, European governments are apt to accede to Trump's ultimatums – such as hitting the 2%-of-GDP target for NATO-member defence spending – as long as they aren't too jarring.[69] And the extraordinary strength of post-war transatlantic relations, extending to the wider Western geopolitical bloc, could still help moderate Trump's most radical impulses, if not to the degree that they did in his first presidency. At the very least, however, another four years of Trump would compromise the West's power at a time when it was already at a historically low ebb and facing energised competition.

* * *

The loosening of the US-led liberal-international order amid the erosion of globalisation and multilateralism has made the re-establishment of distinct geopolitical blocs more palpable. But it is far too early for the extant groupings to constitute true blocs. Geopolitical polarity is further complicated by other dynamics, including the West's economic interdependencies with fast-rising Asian economies, fragile leadership and weak integration within the Eurasian bloc, and the lack of coherence among swing states. Accordingly, any blocs that do emerge are unlikely to be consolidated and demarcated as readily as they were during the Cold War. Pronouncements of a Chinese century seem excessive.[70]

Asia may someday lead the world order owing to its demographic mass, fast-growing industries, abundance of natural resources and centres of technical excellence. Yet Eurasia has little political cohesion, and most governments do not envision Beijing as a global leader in the American mould. Chinese leaders still have to determine to what extent they want their country to supervise the Indo-Pacific, multilateral institutions and, indeed, the world order. Washington, however fitfully, has managed to re-energise the West in the face of threats to Ukraine, Taiwan and Israel, and the West retains a vast reservoir of financial and military resources. Provided the United States can escape Trumpism and the cynical insularity it would bring to world affairs, the West should still be able to take the lead in resolving critical strategic issues, and thus steer the orderly conduct of world affairs.[71]

Notes

1   Grant Shapps, 'Defending Britain from a More Dangerous World', UK Ministry of Defence, 15 January 2024, https://www.gov.uk/government/ speeches/defending-britain-from-a-more-dangerous-world.

2   See, for instance, Fareed Zakaria, *The Post-American World and the Rise of the*

Rest (London: Penguin, 2008), pp. 1–2. US Secretary of State Antony Blinken likewise told the US Senate Committee on Foreign Relations in March 2023 that the 'post-Cold War world is over, and there is an intense competition underway to determine what comes next', which he said would be characterised by strong rivalry between the US and its adversaries, China and Russia. Antony Blinken, 'American Diplomacy and Global Leadership: Review of the FY24 State Department Budget Request', Senate Foreign Relations Committee, 22 March 2023, https://www.foreign.senate.gov/imo/media/doc/2d392f68-f342-6511-8716-757358078495/032223_Blinken_Testimony.pdf. While it is true that several dangerous touchpoints are now coalescing – Russia's unprovoked war in Ukraine, the eruption of war between the Israelis and Palestinians, and ongoing skirmishes in the South China Sea – the inflection point arguably occurred in the late 2000s, in the aftermath of the global financial crisis.

3   See Yuen Foong Khong, 'The US, China, and the Cold War Analogy', *China International Strategy Review*, vol. 1, no. 2, February 2019, pp. 223–37.

4   Daniel Deudney and G. John Ikenberry, 'The Unravelling of the Cold War Settlement', *Survival*, vol. 51, no. 6, December 2009–January 2010, pp. 39–62.

5   Iain Ferguson, 'Between New Spheres of Influence: Ukraine's Geopolitical Misfortune', *Geopolitics*, vol. 23, no. 2, April 2018, pp. 285–306.

6   Stephen Kotkin, 'The Cold War Never Ended', *Foreign Affairs*, vol. 101, no. 3, May/June 2022, p. 67.

7   See Lawrence Freedman, *The Revolution in Strategic Affairs*, Adelphi Paper 318 (London: Routledge for the IISS, 1998), pp. 5–10; and Edward Luttwak, 'From Geopolitics to Geo-economics', in G.Ó. Tuathail, S. Dalby and P. Routledge (eds), *The Geopolitics Reader* (London: Routledge, 1990), pp. 125–30.

8   Richard Sakwa, 'The Cold Peace: Russo-Western Relations as a Mimetic Cold War', *Cambridge Review of International Affairs*, vol. 26, no. 1, February 2013, pp. 203–24. See also Walter Russell Mead, 'The Return of Geopolitics', *Foreign Affairs*, vol. 93, no. 3, May/June 2014, pp. 69–74.

9   See Leo Panitch and Sam Gindin, 'Global Capitalism and American Empire', in L. Panitch and C. Leys (eds), *The New Imperial Challenge: Socialist Register 2004* (London: Merlin Press, 2004), pp. 1–42.

10   See Zeno Leoni, 'The Economy–Security Conundrum in American Grand Strategy: Foreign Economic Policy Toward China from Obama to Biden', *China International Strategy Review*, vol. 4, November 2022, pp. 320–34.

11   See Jude Blanchette and Bonny Lin, 'China's Ukraine Crisis', *Foreign Affairs*, 21 February 2022, https://www.foreignaffairs.com/articles/china/2022-02-21/chinas-ukraine-crisis?

12   See Charles L. Glaser, James M. Actor and Steve Fetter, 'The U.S. Nuclear Arsenal Can Deter Both China and Russia', *Foreign Affairs*, 5 October 2023, https://www.foreignaffairs.com/united-states/us-nuclear-arsenal-can-deter-both-china-and-russia.

13   President of Russia, 'Joint Statement of the Russian Federation and the

People's Republic of China on the International Relations Entering a New Era and the Global Sustainable Development', 4 February 2022, http://www.en.kremlin.ru/supplement/5770.

14 India is projected to be the world's third-largest economy by the late 2020s. See International Monetary Fund, 'India', April 2023 update, https://www.imf.org/en/Countries/IND.

15 See Bonny Lin and John Culver, 'China's Taiwan Invasion Plans May Get Faster and Deadlier', *Foreign Policy*, 19 April 2022, https://foreignpolicy.com/2022/04/19/china-invasion-ukraine-taiwan.

16 See White House, 'Remarks by President Biden, Prime Minister Morrison of Australia, and Prime Minister Johnson of the United Kingdom Announcing the Creation of AUKUS', 15 September 2021, https://www.whitehouse.gov/briefing-room/speeches-remarks/2021/09/15/remarks-by-president-biden-prime-minister-morrison-of-australia-and-prime-minister-johnson-of-the-united-kingdom-announcing-the-creation-of-aukus/.

17 White House, 'Remarks by National Security Advisor Jake Sullivan on the Biden–Harris Administration's National Security Strategy', 12 October 2022, https://www.whitehouse.gov/briefing-room/speeches-remarks/2022/10/13/remarks-by-national-security-advisor-jake-sullivan-on-the-biden-harris-administrations-national-security-strategy/.

18 See Kotkin, 'The Cold War Never Ended', p. 67.

19 See Daniel Deudney and G. John Ikenberry, 'Democratic Internationalism: An American Grand Strategy for a Post-exceptionalist Era', Working Paper, Council on Foreign Relations, November 2012, https://cdn.cfr.org/sites/default/files/pdf/2012/11/IIGG_WorkingPaper11_Deudney_Ikenberry.pdf.

20 Richard Sakwa, 'What Role for Russia in a Multipolar World?', in Aldo Ferrari and Eleonora Tafuro Ambrosetti (eds), *Multipolarity After Ukraine: Old Wine in New Bottles?* (Milan: Ledizioni LediPublishing, 2023), pp. 33–6.

21 See Kyle M. Lascurettes, *Orders of Exclusion: Great Powers and the Strategic Sources of Foundational Rules in International Relations* (Oxford: Oxford University Press, 2020), pp. 36, 237; and James Crabtree, 'Indo-Pacific Dilemmas: The Like-minded and the Non-aligned', *Survival*, vol. 64, no. 6, December 2022–January 2023, pp. 23–30.

22 See Selim Kurt, Göktürk Tüysüzoğlu and Cenk Özgen, 'The Weakening Hegemon's Quest for an Alliance in the Indo-Pacific: AUKUS', *Journal of the Indian Ocean Region*, vol. 18, no. 3, February 2023, p. 232.

23 NATO, 'NATO 2022 Strategic Concept', 29 June 2022, p. 5, https://www.nato.int/nato_static_fl2014/assets/pdf/2022/6/pdf/290622-strategic-concept.pdf.

24 See Gorana Grgić, 'Why Is NATO Expanding Its Reach to the Asia-Pacific Region?', *Conversation*, 10 July 2023, https://theconversation.com/why-is-nato-expanding-its-reach-to-the-asia-pacific-region-209140.

25 See Zachary Paikin, 'After the Ukraine War: Liberal Order Revisited',

in Ferrari and Ambrosetti (eds), *Multipolarity After Ukraine*, p. 17.

26 See *ibid*.

27 G. John Ikenberry, 'Three Worlds: The West, East and South and the Competition to Shape Global Order', *International Affairs*, vol. 100, no. 1, January 2024, p. 123.

28 See Matthew Kroenig, *The Return of Great Power Rivalry: Democracy Versus Autocracy from the Ancient World to the U.S. and China* (Oxford: Oxford University Press, 2020).

29 See Ikenberry, 'Three Worlds', p. 123.

30 See Brian Carlson, 'China–Russia Relations and the Inertia of History', *Survival*, vol. 58, no. 3, June–July 2016, pp. 213–22.

31 President of Russia, 'Joint Statement of the Russian Federation and the People's Republic of China on the International Relations Entering a New Era and the Global Sustainable Development'.

32 See Sakwa, 'What Role for Russia in a Multipolar World?', p. 34.

33 See Ministry of Foreign Affairs of the People's Republic of China, 'The Global Security Initiative Concept Paper', 21 February 2023, https://www.fmprc.gov.cn/mfa_eng/wjbxw/202302/t20230221_11028348.html; and State Council Information Office of the People's Republic of China, 'A Global Community of Shared Future: China's Proposals and Actions', September 2023, http://english.scio.gov.cn/node_9004328.html.

34 See Martin Hala, 'China in Xi's "New Era": Forging a New "Eastern Bloc"', *Journal of Democracy*, vol. 29, no. 2, April 2018, pp. 83–9.

35 See 'Why South Africa Is Drifting into the Sino-Russian Orbit', *The Economist*, 19 February 2023, https://www.economist.com/middle-east-and-africa/2023/02/19/why-south-africa-is-drifting-into-the-sino-russian-orbit.

36 See Heather Ashby et al., 'What BRICS Expansion Means for the Bloc's Founding Members', United States Institute of Peace, 30 August 2023, https://www.usip.org/publications/2023/08/what-brics-expansion-means-blocs-founding-members.

37 See Paul J. Bolt, 'Sino-Russian Relations in a Changing World Order', *Strategic Studies Quarterly*, vol. 8, no. 4, Winter 2014, pp. 47–69.

38 See Nien-Chung Chang-Liao, 'The Limits of Strategic Partnerships: Implications for China's Role in the Russia–Ukraine War', *Contemporary Security Policy*, vol. 44, no. 2, February 2023, pp. 226–47.

39 See Bonnie S. Glaser and Andrew Small, 'China: On the Russian Axis', in Heather A. Conley et al., *Alliances in a Shifting Global Order: Rethinking Transatlantic Engagement with Global Swing States* (Washington DC: German Marshall Fund, 2023), p. 15, https://www.gmfus.org/sites/default/files/2023-04/Global%20Swing%20States_27%20apr_FINAL_embargoed%20until%202%20May%202023.pdf.

40 See Chen Zheng, 'China Debates the Non-interference Principle', *Chinese Journal of International Politics*, vol. 9, no. 3, Autumn 2016, pp. 349–74.

41 See Liu Ruonan and Liu Feng, 'Contending Ideas on China's Non-alliance Strategy', *Chinese Journal of International Politics*, vol. 10, no. 2, Summer 2017, pp. 151–71.

42 See Sakwa, 'What Role for Russia in a Multipolar World?', pp. 34–5.

43 See Stephen Aris, 'A New Model of Asian Regionalism: Does the Shanghai Cooperation Organisation Have More Potential than ASEAN?', *Cambridge Review of International Affairs*, vol. 22, no. 3, September 2009, pp. 451–67.

44 Gesine Weber, 'Methodology: Conceptualizing Global Swing States', in Conley et al., *Alliances in a Shifting Global Order*, p. 7.

45 See Michal Baranowski and Thomas Kleine-Brockhoff, 'Why Aren't Swing States Swinging Toward Us?', in Conley et al., *Alliances in a Shifting Global Order*; Len Ishmael, 'A World Divided: A Multi-layered, Multipolar World', in Len Ishmael (ed.), *Aftermath of War in Europe: The West vs. the Global South?* (Rabat: Policy Center for the New South, 2022), pp. 23–4; and Alexandra De Hoop Scheffer, 'Fluid Alliances in a Multipolarizing World: Rethinking US and European Strategies Toward Global Swing States', in Conley et al., *Alliances in a Shifting Global Order*.

46 See Daniel Markey, 'India as It Is', *Foreign Affairs*, vol. 102, no. 4, July/ August 2023, pp. 128–41.

47 See David Miliband, 'The World Beyond Ukraine', *Foreign Affairs*, vol. 102, no. 3, May/June 2023, pp. 36–43.

48 See Barbara Stallings, *Dependency in the Twenty-first Century? The Political Economy of China–Latin America Relations* (Cambridge: Cambridge University Press, 2020).

49 See Glaser and Small, 'China', p. 15.

50 See Arta Moeini et al., 'Middle Powers in the Multipolar World', White Paper, Institute for Peace and Diplomacy, March 2022, pp. 1–2, https:// peacediplomacy.org/wp-content/ uploads/2022/03/Middle-Powers-in-the-Multipolar-World-2.pdf.

51 See Ishmael, 'A World Divided', p. 14. See also James Adams, David C. Gompert and Thomas Knudson, 'From Quad to Quint? Vietnam's Strategic Potential', *Survival*, vol. 66, no. 1, February–March 2024, pp. 57–65.

52 See Ikenberry, 'Three Worlds'.

53 See Ian O. Lesser, 'The Myth of the Monolithic "Global South"', in Conley et al., *Alliances in a Shifting Global Order*, pp. 17, 19.

54 See Crabtree, 'Indo-Pacific Dilemmas'; and Matias Spektor, 'In Defense of the Fence Sitters', *Foreign Affairs*, vol. 102, no. 3, May/June 2023, pp. 8–16.

55 Shivshankar Menon, 'Out of Alignment', *Foreign Affairs*, 9 February 2023, https:// www.foreignaffairs.com/world/ out-alignment-war-in-ukraine-non-western-powers-shivshankar-menon.

56 Jean Kachiga, *The Pulse of China's Grand Strategy* (Abingdon: Routledge, 2022), p. 207.

57 See Jishe Fan, 'Managing China–U.S. "Strategic Competition": Potential Risks and Possible Approaches', *China International Strategy Review*, vol. 3, December 2021, pp. 234–47.

58 See Robert S. Ross, 'It's Not a Cold War: Competition and Cooperation in US–China Relations', *China International Strategy Review*, vol. 2, June 2020, pp. 63–72.

59 Richard Higgott and Simon Reich, 'The Age of Fuzzy Bifurcation: Lessons from the Pandemic and the Ukraine War', *Global Policy*, vol. 13, no. 5, September 2022, pp. 627–39.

60 See *ibid*.

61 See Irene Mia, 'Argentina's Foreign Policy Under Milei: Limited Disruption?', *Survival*, vol. 66, no. 1, February–March 2024, pp. 49–56.

62 See Da Wei, 'Security Concerns Are Reasonable, Spheres of Influence Are Not', *Washington Quarterly*, vol. 45, no. 2, Spring 2022, pp. 93–104.

63 See Stephen Wertheim, 'The Price of Primacy', *Foreign Affairs*, vol. 99, no. 2, March/April 2020, pp. 19–29.

64 Brendon O'Connor, Lloyd Cox and Danny Cooper, 'Australia's AUKUS "Bet" on the United States: Nuclear-powered Submarines and the Future of American Democracy', *Australian Journal of International Affairs*, vol. 77, no. 1, January 2023, p. 47.

65 See 'Trump Says He Would "Encourage" Russia to Attack Nato Allies Who Do Not Pay Their Bills', BBC, 11 February 2024, https://www.bbc.co.uk/news/world-us-canada-68266447.

66 See Nathan P. Kalmoe and Lilliana Mason, *Radical American Partisanship: Mapping Violent Hostility, Its Causes, and the Consequences for Democracy* (Chicago, IL: University of Chicago Press, 2022).

67 See O'Connor, Cox and Cooper, 'Australia's AUKUS "Bet" on the United States'.

68 See US Congress, 'National Defense Authorization Act for Fiscal Year 2024', 118th Congress, H.R.2670, https://www.congress.gov/bill/118th-congress/house-bill/2670/.

69 Hugo Meijer and Stephen G. Brooks, 'Illusions of Autonomy: Why Europe Cannot Provide for Its Security If the United States Pulls Back', *International Security*, vol. 45, no. 4, Spring 2021, pp. 7–43.

70 See Hal Brands, 'The Chinese Century?', *National Interest*, no. 154, March/April 2018, pp. 35–45; and 'The Chinese Century Is Well Under Way', *The Economist*, 27 October 2018, https://www.economist.com/graphic-detail/2018/10/27/the-chinese-century-is-well-under-way.

71 See Wertheim, 'The Price of Primacy'.

Ukraine: The Balance of Resources and the Balance of Resolve

Nigel Gould-Davies

The third year of Russia's war in Ukraine has begun. What are the results of the first two years, and what lessons follow for the future?

2022 was a year of Russian aggression and failure. Not only was Russia unable to seize Kyiv and install its own regime in the first week of the war, but in the autumn it lost huge swathes of occupied territory around Kharkiv and Kherson. By the end of the year, it held just 17.5% of the country – equivalent to 0.6% of its own legally recognised territory.

2023 began with a new Russian offensive that petered out. Ukraine then spent months preparing for a counter-offensive. Despite a heavy burden of expectation, Ukrainian forces barely shifted the front line, though Kyiv's ingenious Black Sea campaign continues to inflict losses on Russia's navy.

It might thus be tempting to say that 2022 and 2023 showed the limits of Russian and Ukrainian power, respectively, and that 2024 should be a year of compromise and peacemaking supported by the West. This would be a grave error for three reasons.

Firstly, neither side is ready to compromise. Ukraine is not politically or morally prepared to accept an outcome that would sacrifice land and people to aggression and leave it permanently weaker. Some would say this is beside the point. However justified Ukraine's moral and legal claims to the full restoration of its sovereignty, its policy and that of the supporting West should be governed by the realities of power. Compromise and equilibrium,

Nigel Gould-Davies is IISS Senior Fellow for Russia and Eurasia. This essay is adapted from a shorter version published by IISS Online Analysis in February 2024.

Survival | vol. 66 no. 2 | April–May 2024 | pp. 55–62   https://doi.org/10.1080/00396338.2024.2332057

not moral outrage and victory over evil, must define the end of this war. Wisdom lies in the recognition of necessity.

Some voices quietly press this view in larger Western capitals. It is now heard, less quietly, from the smallest. Pope Francis is the first head of state to call publicly for Ukraine to show the 'courage of the white flag' – that is, to surrender its aspirations and negotiate – rather than for Russia to end its invasion.[1] It is surprising that the leader who asserts the grandest claim to spiritual authority should speak in such openly temporal terms. Josef Stalin famously asked: how many battalions has the Pope? The Pope now asks in turn: how many battalions has Ukraine? John Paul II might have answered differently.

Realism and reality

The realist argument, more subtly expressed, has a respectable, indeed venerable, pedigree. The domain of choice is defined by power, not right. Where these do not align – and this side of eternity, they almost never do – the familiar agony of compromise intrudes. To ignore this, to insist *fiat iustitia et pereat mundus* – 'let justice be done though the world perish' – is to risk perishing. There thus might conceivably be a case, however unpalatable, for pressing Ukraine to agree to an unjust peace if this would end the war, stem its human losses and secure the future of the remainder of the country. Grown-up diplomacy does morally hard but necessary things, not easy and virtuous ones.

This case for realism founders on misunderstood realities. An end to war requires that the aggressor, not the victim, wishes it or is compelled to accept it. Yet few proponents of a negotiated peace argue that Russia should be pressured. Fewer still understand Russia. As the stronger side, Russia does not feel it faces the necessity of compromise. There is no evidence that Russian President Vladimir Putin has abandoned his initial goal of subordinating Kyiv. Having failed to win a short war, he has formed a theory of victory for a long one: wear down Ukraine militarily and outlast the West politically. As he told senior officers last December, Russia's military production is increasing while the Ukrainians 'are running out … They don't have their own foundation. When you have no foundation of your own … then there is no future. But we do have one.'[2]

Putin seeks victory, not negotiation, because he sees events moving in his favour. Domestic constraints have proved looser than he expected. More than 300,000 Russian troops have been killed or wounded in Moscow's war of aggression without sparking major protest. Despite huge losses, Russia now has more forces in Ukraine than it did at the start of the war. The capture of Avdiivka, civil–military friction in Kyiv and a more anxious mood in Ukraine embolden Russia to push further. Europe's under-delivery of weapons, the United States' failure to pass a new Ukraine-aid bill and the prospect of Donald Trump's return to the White House all cast doubt on the future of Western support. In these realities Putin sees vindication for his strategy of slow, relentless attrition. As he has put it, 'a hen pecks grain by grain'.[3]

The second reason peacemaking does not lie ahead is that the war has not reached a stalemate, but remains dynamic and unpredictable. Several narratives have framed its course so far, each persuasive until confounded by events – not least when Ukraine broke the mid-2022 deadlock with dramatic advances. There is no guarantee that the present lack of mobility will endure. Putin's growing confidence may not be misplaced. The war may turn against a weary Ukraine.

Thirdly, while last year saw little change on the battlefield, the wider geopolitics of the war were transformed. NATO is enlarging and reforming. Several European states have signed bilateral security agreements with Ukraine, with which the European Union has begun accession negotiations. Russia has few allies, but its dependence on drones and ballistic missiles from Iran and ammunition from North Korea has drawn it closer to both. Since Russia and Ukraine each depend on external support, the capacities and choices of the states that supply them will probably determine the outcome of the war.

In long wars involving vital interests, the richer side wins. The sinews of power are fed by plenty and wealth is turned into weapons.[4] The West's margin of superiority is vastly greater now. It is 12 times richer than Russia (when calculated by purchasing-power parity, the method of comparison most favourable to Russia).[5] During the Cold War it was only around three times richer than the Soviet bloc. The balance of resources decisively favours the West.

The balance of resolve, however, favours Russia. Moscow now spends around 7.5% of its GDP on defence and security, while only 11 NATO members spent more than 2% last year.[6] By devoting a larger slice of a smaller pie, Russia's repressive regime may prevail against a prosperous coalition of democracies. It commands fewer resources but possesses a stronger will to use them. As a result, Ukraine is now heavily outgunned and faces growing pressure on the battlefield.

Winning Ukraine

The West urgently needs a geo-economic strategy for the war to harness its superiority in resources to its security imperatives. This should have three elements.

Firstly, the West should mobilise military-industrial production for Ukraine and for itself, thereby matching economic means to security ends. It can easily afford to spend the relatively modest sums this would require.[7] The decision to do so should have been made in 2022. It should now be done without delay.

Implementation is not straightforward: while the Russian state can direct resources to military production at will, Western states must incentivise the private sector. Defence companies have been willing and waiting but have not received the political signal they need – and in at least one country have been actively discouraged from planning to raise production. Civil society as well as public policy can play a role. Having pressured companies to withdraw from Russia early in the war, they can now go further and call for investment ethics to align with security realities. Environment, social and governance criteria brand shares in defence companies as 'sin stocks', thereby depriving them of capital. This makes little sense when the products are used to resist a violently and unjustly aggressive invader.[8] In these circumstances, the moral case for investing in defence production is impeccable.

Secondly, the West should move towards a general prohibition on trade with Russia. Successive rounds of sanctions have constrained Russia more effectively than many realise, precipitating a 40% fall in the value of global exports of high-priority military items to Russia.[9] But these measures are reactive and incremental, and still permit plenty of trade.

Since every transaction makes Russia better off, the goal should be to eliminate as many transactions as possible. As with other sanctions regimes, exceptions may be carved out. In a few cases, the West may have an overriding interest in maintaining some economic relationship. But the presumption should be that no Western company should enrich a regime that poses the primary threat to Western security.

Thirdly, the West should use the $300 billion in Russian central-bank assets, immobilised in its financial systems since February 2022, to provide urgent support for Ukraine and ease the pressure on taxpayers. There is now a clear legal path to doing so.[10] The underlying concerns are economic and financial. The biggest is that confiscation could undermine Western reserve currencies and fuel financial instability. There is no realistic danger of this. Freezing the assets was a far more decisive step than confiscating them and caused no market turbulence. If the countries that issue the major currencies – dollar, euro, sterling and yen – move together, there is nowhere else for large funds of money to be safely held. The rule of law, often a hindrance to rapid and effective action by democracies, in this case confers a decisive advantage.

An exaggerated fear of adverse consequences is the latest form of chronic self-deterrence in economic affairs. Before 2022, it prevented the United States from imposing significant sanctions on Russian sovereign debt, and Europe from weaning itself off Russian pipeline gas. Since the full-scale invasion of Ukraine, both measures have been taken without creating the problems that had been predicted. Economics is the West's greatest area of natural strength, one against which Russia cannot effectively retaliate. The wisdom of restraint in military matters may be debated. There is little case for it in economic and financial ones.

* * *

The realist argument for compromise is that constraints impose choices. The geo-economic rejoinder is that constraints are choices, too, and can be changed. The West can mobilise far more of its superior resources to hinder Russia and to sustain and arm Ukraine. Doing so would properly harness financial and industrial power to moral and security imperatives.

No one should doubt the stakes. A rapid defeat for Ukraine in the first days of the war would have been a disastrous failure of Western foresight and planning. A slow defeat – despite endless declarations of support and countless visits to Kyiv – would be a fundamental failure of credibility. If Russia succeeds despite the mantra that it must fail, the unambiguous lesson, amplifying that of Afghanistan, will be that a weaker but more determined adversary can always outlast the West. This would demoralise its allies and embolden its adversaries around the world.

Notes

1   Kathryn Armstrong, 'Ukraine War: Vatican Envoy Called In over Pope "White Flag" Remarks', BBC, 12 March 2024, https://www.bbc.co.uk/news/world-europe-68538267.

2   '"Ukraine Has No Future, We Do": Putin', Al Arabiya English, 11 December 2023, available at https://www.youtube.com/watch?app=desktop&v=jpaAWmjcdxQ.

3   'Putin ob''iasnaet taktiku Rossii na Ukraine: "kurochka po ziornyshky kliuet"' [Putin explains Russia's tactics in Ukraine: 'A hen pecks grain by grain'], Tsargrad TV, 22 December 2022, https://tsargrad.tv/news/putin-objasnil-taktiku-rossii-na-ukraine-kurochka-po-zjornyshku-kljuet_690906.

4   As Paul Kennedy put it, the success or failure of a great power has historically been 'the consequence of lengthy fighting by its armed forces; but it has also been the consequences of the more or less efficient utilization of the state's productive economic resources in wartime'. Paul M. Kennedy, *The Rise and Fall of the Great Powers: Economic Change and Military Conflict from 1500 to 2000* (New York: Vintage, 1987), p. xv.

5   See World Bank, 'GDP, PPP (Constant 2017 International $) – Russian Federation, European Union, United States, United Kingdom, Canada', 2023, https://data.worldbank.org/indicator/NY.GDP.MKTP.PP.KD?locations=RU-EU-US-GB-CA.

6   IISS, 'Dr Bastian Giegerich's Launch-event Remarks', 13 February 2024, https://www.iiss.org/publications/the-military-balance/2024/bastian-giegerich-launch-event-remarks/; and NATO, 'Defence Expenditure of NATO Countries (2014–2023)', Press Release, 7 July 2023, https://www.nato.int/nato_static_fl2014/assets/pdf/2023/7/pdf/230707-def-exp-2023-en.pdf.

7   One estimate suggests this could be as low as 0.25% of GDP per year specifically for military aid to Ukraine. See 'Estonia's 0.25 Percent GDP Aid to Ukraine Proposal Needs Support of Western States', ERR.ee, 15 January 2024, https://news.err.ee/1609222386/estonia-s-0-25-percent-gdp-aid-to-ukraine-proposal-needs-support-of-western-states.

8   There is now growing recognition of the need for such a realignment. See,

for example, James Cartlidge and Andrew Griffith, 'Joint Opinion Piece on ESG', Gov.uk, 12 September 2023, https://www.gov.uk/government/news/joint-opinion-piece-on-esg-july-2023; and Peggy Hollinger, 'Ukraine War Prompts Investor Rethink of ESG and the Defence Sector', *Financial Times*, 9 March 2022, https://www.ft.com/content/c4dafe6a-2c95-4352-ab88-c4e3cdb6obba.

9   Heli Simola, 'Latest Developments in Russian Imports of Sanctioned Technology Products', BOFIT Policy Brief no. 15, Bank of Finland Institute for Emerging Economies, 29 November 2023, https://publications.bof.fi/bitstream/handle/10024/53179/bpb1523.pdf.

10   See, for example, Viktoria Dendrinou and Alberto Nardelli, 'Seizing Frozen Russian Assets over Ukraine War Wins Endorsement of Legal Experts', Bloomberg, 21 February 2024, https://www.bloomberg.com/news/articles/2024-02-21/seizing-frozen-russian-assets-over-ukraine-war-wins-endorsement-of-legal-experts?sref=fCrVhgAM.

India's Fraying Restraint

Antoine Levesques

Early in the Gaza war, *New York Times* columnist Thomas Friedman offered a hypothetical comparison. What if, instead of Israel's brutal response to Hamas's 7 October 2023 massacre, Israel had chosen to emulate India's choice in November 2008, when ten jihadists from Pakistan-linked Lashkar-e-Taiba came by sea to infiltrate India and terrorised Mumbai for three days, killing more than 160 people? The response from Manmohan Singh, then Indian prime minister, was rather surprising and in its own way resounding. As Friedman put it, 'he did nothing'.[1]

The choice had the effect of keeping opprobrium focused on the terrorists and on Pakistan, where, in Friedman's view, it belonged. Friedman conceded that such restraint was never likely from Israel, which has a different strategic culture and very different strategic circumstances. Nevertheless, the comparison for Friedman highlighted Israel's moral and strategic failures in terms of the scale of death and suffering inflicted on Gazan Palestinians in the effort to root out Hamas. The comparison raises another question: would India act with comparable restraint in similar circumstances today? The answer: probably not.

Reinforcing their decision not to retaliate against Pakistan, Indian officials subsequently assessed that, should they have decided to do so, it would have been difficult for New Delhi to avoid an escalatory spiral. In particular, they lacked confidence in India's ability to use airpower surgically, so

Antoine Levesques is IISS Research Fellow for South and Central Asian Defence, Strategy and Diplomacy.

Survival | vol. 66 no. 2 | April–May 2024 | pp. 63–71   https://doi.org/10.1080/00396338.2024.2332059

as to minimise collateral damage. They were also keen to maintain India's focus on economic growth in the wake of the global financial crisis, and concerned about potential American reactions given the United States' fraught dependence on Pakistan in its prosecution of the war in Afghanistan, which the US was about to intensify.

India's leadership also had more value-based arguments: it wanted to be seen as doing the 'right' thing in exercising restraint. Singh merely warned terrorists and their supporters not to let 'our commitment to civilized norms be misconstrued as a sign of weakness'.[2] The country's national security advisor later called the decision to not respond massively to the Mumbai attacks India's 'finest hour'.[3]

Shifting political positions

The Hindu-nationalist Bharatiya Janata Party (BJP), then in opposition, was quick to criticise the government. Two days after the attack, it took out a full-page newspaper advertisement reading 'brutal terror strikes at will. Weak government. Unwilling and incapable. Fight terror – Vote BJP.'[4] The BJP backed its accusation that the Congress Party was 'soft' on security with a call for reinstating stronger counter-terrorism legislation, which the Congress Party had repealed.[5] This shrill opportunism jarred against the government's more sober tone and may help explain why the Congress Party prevailed in the May 2009 election. In the longer term, however, India's security community gradually moved to the right. The prevailing view was that India's failure to respond forcefully to the Mumbai attack had diminished India's national security and, in particular, effectively neutered the military's 'Cold Start' doctrine, which prescribed conventional armoured thrusts into Pakistani territory under the nuclear threshold to bolster strategic deterrence.[6]

China, India's other strategic rival, exploited India's reaction to the terrorist attack in several ways. In view of its own heightened terrorist-threat perceptions in connection with its Uyghur population, China expressed solidarity with India. At the same time, however, Beijing continued to support Pakistan, which procrastinated in responding to India's demand for evidence and a judicial inquiry. China also blocked or delayed the United

Nations Security Council from imposing sanctions on those Pakistani political figures accused of involvement in the Mumbai attack. Narendra Modi of the BJP, then the chief minister of Gujarat – an industrial-powerhouse state bordering Pakistan – raised his profile as a national politician in part by publicly accusing both Pakistan and China of hostile and destabilising intent, and the Congress Party of weakness against terrorism.[7]

The Modi era

Modi became prime minister in June 2014, riding a wave of dissatisfaction with the Congress Party, and was re-elected in 2019. He has been a divisive but visible leader with an assertive personal style. He has faced two particular challenges. The first was to burnish his credentials as a strong and decisive leader without courting excessive risk vis-à-vis Pakistan and China. The second was to minimise disruptions to domestic Indian politics, albeit while steadily tightening his own brand of hardline Hindu nationalism. There was tension between these two objectives, as a 2016 Pew poll found that 62% of Indians believed that overwhelming military force was the best way to defeat terrorism, including in Pakistan.[8]

Modi's solution was to showcase and emphasise his personal ties to leaders of major powers, including Donald Trump, Xi Jinping and Vladimir Putin, as well as British and French leaders and those of middle powers, such as Australian prime minister Malcolm Turnbull and even Nawaz Sharif of Pakistan. Modi also made selective diplomatic interventions designed to valorise India's non-aligned approach. For instance, he chastised Russia when it appeared to be contemplating the use of low-yield nuclear weapons in Ukraine.[9] He also repeatedly employed tough nationalist messaging, clearly referring to Pakistan and China as adversaries, though usually not by name. He refrained from disavowing a 2014 manifesto pledge to 'revise and update' India's nuclear doctrine.[10] And he abjured any appearance of restraint or loss of face with respect to India's regional security interests.

Trumpeting assertiveness and underplaying restraint have strengthened Modi's electoral position, conditioned most of India's foreign and security establishment, and energised India's foreign brand. But space has shrunk for public advocacy and discussion of restraint.

India's statecraft and the use of force

Modi's resort to military force – including a 2016 cross-border special-forces raid into Kashmir in response to a terrorist attack – remained quite calibrated until February 2019, when a vehicle-borne suicide bomber from the Kashmiri militant group Jaish-e-Mohammed attacked a convoy carrying Indian security personnel in the Pulwama district of Jammu and Kashmir, killing 40. With elections coming, India responded with deep airstrikes targeting a Jaish-e-Mohammed facility in Balakot, Pakistan.[11] The number of casualties and overall efficacy of the strikes were disputed. Pakistan took defensive action but elected not to retaliate in kind. India had not carried out air attacks across the Line of Control since the Indo-Pakistani War in 1971. Modi highlighted the decisive character of India's use of force and its now proven ability to respond to terrorist provocations forcefully with conventional military power while precluding escalation. Modi also personally warned Pakistan that if a downed Indian pilot were not returned safely, Pakistan would suffer further Indian punishment.[12] India reportedly threatened missile strikes.[13] Modi plainly underplayed restraint in favour of aggression.[14]

Against China, Modi has likewise taken calculated risks of escalation. In May 2020, after weeks of non-lethal skirmishing between Indian and Chinese forces, the latter objected to Indian road construction in the disputed Galwan River Valley. The Indians stood their ground, and in subsequent fighting several soldiers from each side were killed. The government clearly intended India's ensuing military mobilisation on the border – characterised by one BJP official as 'proactive diplomacy' together with 'strong ground posturing' – to signal its martial resolve as opposed to restraint.[15] Even minor Indian territorial concessions to the Chinese seemed to end, and demilitarised zones dwindled.[16] In August 2020, at the height of summer tensions, Indian special forces deployed in an area that both sides had previously agreed not to occupy. The Indian Ministry of Defence released an unusual statement claiming India had 'pre-empted' Chinese action.[17] Nearby, both sides mobilised tanks, and they exchanged small-arms fire for the first time since 1975.[18] Although India later vacated the position as part of mutual 'de-escalation' efforts, China labelled India's initial actions 'provocations'.[19]

More broadly, in 2021 India fiercely supported the right to self-defence at the UN.[20] It controversially made good on that theoretical position in lodging support for Israel's maximal response to the 7 October Hamas attack[21] and for Iranian airstrikes in Pakistan this year to counter cross-border terrorism.[22] In 2023, the US and Canada alleged that India had sought to assassinate individuals it regarded as terrorists hostile to the BJP government on American and Canadian soil. Modi himself neither confirmed nor denied the allegations.[23] If they are true, India was breaching basic rules of diplomacy and spycraft between friends, thus undertaking a major political gamble. Some diplomatic damage may have been done in any case, as US President Joe Biden declined Modi's invitation to India's 2024 Republic Day celebrations.[24]

India has taken pains to minimise statecraft that is not in line with Modi's narrative of assertiveness. In 2022, India waited almost two days to acknowledge its firing of an unarmed supersonic *BrahMos* cruise missile into Pakistan, even then merely calling the incident 'deeply regrettable' and attributing it initially to a technical malfunction, later to human error.[25] There is no evidence that New Delhi tried to use any of the hotlines in place with Islamabad to discuss the matter or to make informal contact. Later, India left unchallenged a Pakistani narrative that India may have intentionally launched the missile to test Pakistan's defences.[26] Given the nuclear risk inherent in a military confrontation between India and Pakistan, and the mistaken but widespread belief in Pakistan that India's *BrahMos* missile can be nuclear-enabled, India appeared diplomatically careless and Pakistan strategically irresponsible.

At the same time, Modi refrains from specifically criticising his counterparts in Pakistan and China, and India may seek to establish secret backchannels with Pakistan and China to insure against miscalculation. Such a backchannel may have contributed to India and Pakistan's reaffirmation of the ceasefire agreement on the Line of Control in 2021.[27] With respect to China, India has taken an uncompromising public stance, refusing to talk at any meaningful diplomatic or political level until there is 'disengagement', 'de-escalation' and 'de-induction' of Chinese troops at the border.[28] Yet, in 2023, a recently retired senior Indian national-security official participated in a security conference in Beijing.

* * *

As Modi seeks a third term in India's 2024 general election, his decade in office has displaced much of the explicitly principled foreign and security policy of the Congress Party. Much of this shift is attributable to India's growing international profile, and probably would have occurred under any Indian leader. Furthermore, many Indians see the fraying of their country's restraint as a natural consequence of Pakistan's repeated attempts to provoke India into a crisis since the early 1980s. Accordingly, the domestic opposition has challenged Modi's claims that he has been indispensable in pioneering India's new assertiveness.[29] Whatever its exact genesis, what many have called his 'ruthlessly pragmatic' approach, or the 'Doval doctrine' in reference to his powerful National Security Advisor Ajit Doval, amounts to a distinct embrace of risk as a strategic asset.[30] As India's economy continues to grow, Modi's assertive statecraft will pose a dilemma. While India's means of implementing it will become more potent, it will have more to lose from the instability it can cause.

Notes

1   Thomas L. Friedman, 'The Israeli Officials I Speak With Tell Me They Know Two Things for Sure', *New York Times*, 29 October 2023, https://www.nytimes.com/2023/10/29/opinion/israel-hamas-ceasefire.html.

2   Government of India, 'Excerpts of PM's Intervention in Lok Sabha During Discussion on the Recent Terrorist Attacks in Mumbai', 11 December 2008, https://archivepmo.nic.in/drmanmohansingh/speech-details.php?nodeid=739.

3   Quoted in Suhasini Haidar, 'India, Pakistan Will Inevitably Return to Talks, Says Kasuri', *Hindu*, 6 October 2015, https://www.thehindu.com/news/national/india-pakistan-will-inevitably-return-to-talks-says-kasuri/article7727584.ece.

4   Raju Gopalakrishnan, 'India Directs Anger at Politicians After Mumbai Attacks', Reuters, 30 November 2008, https://www.reuters.com/article/idUSCOL205967/.

5   See, for example, Antara Desai, 'India: Counterterrorism Under the New Government', *Counter Terrorist Trends and Analyses*, vol. 6, no. 5, June 2014, pp. 16–20.

6   See 'What Is India's "Cold Start" Military Doctrine?', *The Economist*, 31 January 2017, https://www.economist.com/the-economist-explains/2017/01/31/what-is-indias-cold-start-military-doctrine.

7   See Narendra Modi, 'Full Text of Shri Narendra Modi's Speech at Ex-servicemen's Rally, Rewari', 15 September 2013, https://www.narendramodi.in/full-text-of-shri-narendra-modis-speech-at-ex-servicemens-rally-rewari-2798.

8   Bruce Stokes, 'How Indians See Their Place in the World', Pew Research Center, 19 September 2016, https://www.pewresearch.org/global/2016/09/19/3-how-indians-see-their-place-in-the-world/.

9   See 'India's Defence Minister Warns Against Nuclear Weapons in Call with Russian Counterpart', Reuters, 26 October 2022, https://www.reuters.com/world/indias-defence-minister-warns-against-nuclear-weapons-call-with-russian-2022-10-26/.

10 See Antoine Levesques, Desmond Bowen and John H. Gill, 'Nuclear Deterrence and Stability in South Asia: Perceptions and Realities', IISS, May 2021, p. 17, https://www.iiss.org/globalassets/media-library---content--migration/files/research-papers/nuclear-deterrence-and-stability-in-south-asia---perceptions-and-realities.pdf.

11 See 'The India–Pakistan Security Crisis', IISS *Strategic Comments*, vol. 25, no. 10, April 2019, https://www.iiss.org/publications/strategic-comments/2019/india-and-pakistan/.

12 See 'Had Pakistan Not Returned Abhinandan It Would Have Been "Qatal ki Raat": PM Modi', *Indian Express*, 21 April 2019, https://indianexpress.com/article/india/had-warned-pakistan-of-consequences-if-iaf-pilot-abhinandan-varthaman-not-returned-pm-modi-5687029/.

13 See Sanjeev Miglani and Drazen Jorgic, 'India, Pakistan Threatened to Unleash Missiles at Each Other: Sources', Reuters, 18 March 2019, https://www.reuters.com/article/idUSKCN1QZ0F0/. India's position may have been influenced by Trump's unsolicited offer to mediate. See White House, 'Remarks by President Trump in Press Conference', Hanoi, Vietnam, 28 February 2019, https://trumpwhitehouse.archives.gov/briefings-statements/remarks-president-trump-press-conference-hanoi-vietnam/.

14 At the same time, Modi's jingoism, expressed on social media, may have created space for quiet de-escalation by overstating India's assertive response. See Lawrence Freedman and Heather Williams, *Changing the Narrative: Information Campaigns, Strategy and Crisis Escalation in the Digital Age*, Adelphi 493–495 (Abingdon: Routledge for the IISS, 2023).

15 'India–China Standoff: Confident Present Conflict Will Be Resolved Through Diplomacy, Says BJP's Ram Madhav', *India Today*, 25 May 2020, https://www.indiatoday.in/india/story/india-china-stand-off-tension-bjp-ram-madhav-resolved-diplomacy-1681575-2020-05-25.

16 See Sanjeev Miglani, 'Insight – With Canal and Hut, India Stands Up to China on Disputed Frontier', Reuters, 24 September 2014, https://www.reuters.com/article/idUSKCN0HJ2FT/; and Shams Irfan and Gerry Shih, 'Age-old Cashmere Trade Ensnared in Military Tensions High in the Himalayas', *Washington Post*, 2 January 2023, https://www.washingtonpost.

com/world/2023/01/02/
india-china-himalaya-cashmere-wool/.

17 Government of India, Press
Information Bureau, 'Situation
Update: Eastern Ladakh',
31 August 2020, https://pib.
gov.in/PressReleseDetailm.
aspx?PRID=1649940.

18 See 'India–China Border Tension:
Both Sides Position Tanks Within
Firing Distance at Pangong Tso',
Business Today, 8 September 2020,
https://www.businesstoday.in/latest/
economy-politics/story/india-china-
border-clash-indian-chinese-army-
tanks-within-firing-distance-pangong-
lake-lac-271808-2020-09-01; and
'India and China Exchange the First
Gunshots in 45 Years', *The Economist*,
8 September 2020, https://www.
economist.com/asia/2020/09/08/
india-and-china-exchange-the-first-
gunshots-in-45-years.

19 Embassy of the People's Republic
of China in the Republic of India,
'Ambassador Sun Weidong's Remarks
Regarding Recent Media Queries
on the Bilateral Meeting Between
Foreign Ministers of China and
India', 14 September 2020, http://
in.china-embassy.gov.cn/eng/embassy_
news/202009/t20200914_2146831.htm.

20 See Ambassador K. Nagaraj Naidu,
'Upholding the Collective Security
System of the UN Charter: The
Use of Force in International Law,
Non-state Actors and Legitimate
Self-defense', Permanent Mission of
India to the UN, 24 February 2021,
https://www.pminewyork.gov.in/
IndiaatUNSC?id=NDE3Nw.

21 'I thank Prime Minister @netanyahu
for his phone call and providing an
update on the ongoing situation.
People of India stand firmly with
Israel in this difficult hour. India
strongly and unequivocally con-
demns terrorism in all its forms
and manifestations.' Narendra
Modi (@narendramodi), post
to X, 10 October 2023, https://
twitter.com/narendramodi/
status/1711669988116050142.

22 See Indian Ministry of External
Affairs, 'Official Spokesperson's
Response to Media Queries Regarding
Iran's Air Strikes in Pakistan', 17
January 2024, https://www.mea.gov.
in/response-to-queries.htm?dtl/37515/
Official_Spokespersons_response_to_
media_queries_regarding_Irans_air_
strikes_in_Pakistan.

23 See Roula Khalaf, Benjamin Parkin
and John Reed, 'Narendra Modi
Responds to Assassination Claims',
Financial Times, 20 December 2023,
https://www.ft.com/content/160235af-
1584-4ec7-8aad-a3de70753f30.

24 See Shishir Gupta, 'Why Joe Biden
Is Skipping [*sic*] Republic Day
Celebrations on January 26? This Is
the Real Reason', *Hindustan Times*,
15 December 2023, https://www.
hindustantimes.com/india-news/
why-joe-biden-is-skipping-republic-
day-celebrations-on-january-26-this-is-
the-real-reason-101702644721372.html.

25 See Christopher Clary, 'The Curious
Case of the Accidental Indian
Missile Launch', *War on the Rocks*, 17
March 2022, https://warontherocks.
com/2022/03/the-curious-case-of-the-
accidental-indian-missile-launch/; and
Debak Das, 'Not Much Happened After
India's Accidental Cruise Missile Launch
into Pakistan – This Time', *Bulletin of the*

Atomic Scientists, 25 March 2022, https://thebulletin.org/2022/03/not-much-happened-after-indias-accidental-cruise-missile-launch-into-pakistan-this-time/.

26 See, for example, Aarish U. Khan, 'Reassessing the BrahMos Missile that Landed in Pakistan', *Diplomat*, 29 September 2022, https://thediplomat.com/2022/09/reassessing-the-brahmos-missile-that-landed-in-pakistan/.

27 See Suhasini Haidar and Kallol Bhattacherjee, 'Backchannel Diplomacy Played Its Part in India, Pakistan Decision to Cease Fire Along LoC', *Hindu*, 25 February 2021, https://www.thehindu.com/news/national/analysis-indications-that-india-and-pakistan-have-been-in-back-channel-talks/article61747025.ece.

28 Rajat Pandit, 'India Wants First Disengagement at Depsang-Demchok', *Times of India*, 25 August 2023, https://timesofindia.indiatimes.com/india/india-wants-first-disengagement-at-depsang-demchok/articleshow/103038383.cms.

29 Claims of restraint and punishment alike feature in India's publicly released military doctrines between 2006 and 2018. The 2022 Indian Air Force doctrine does not refer to restraint, but does refer to punishment. See Indian Air Force, 'Doctrine of the Indian Air Force', 2022, https://indianairforce.nic.in/wp-content/uploads/2023/01/2MB.pdf.

30 See Mahima A. Jain, '"A New, Emerging Indian Security Doctrine in the Indian Ocean Is Set to Challenge the Narrative and Impact of China's Influence" – Rahul Roy-Chaudhury', LSE Blogs, 27 October 2017, https://blogs.lse.ac.uk/southasia/2017/10/27/a-new-indian-security-doctrine-is-emerging-in-the-indian-ocean-which-is-set-to-challenge-the-narrative-and-impact-of-chinas-influence-rahul-roy-chaudhury/. The expression tends to be used pejoratively. For an in-depth, first-hand account of Doval's conception of national-security statecraft, see Ajit Doval, 'State Security, Statecraft and Conflict of Values', Speech to the Lalit Doshi Memorial Foundation, 4 August 2015, https://ldmf.org.in/pdfs/State_Security_Statecraft_and_Conflict_of_Values.pdf.

Noteworthy

Alexei Navalny, 1976–2024

'If they decide to kill me, it means that we are incredibly strong. We need to utilise this power to not give up, to remember we are a huge power that is being oppressed by these bad dudes.'

> *Russian opposition activitist Alexei Navalny gives an interview for a documentary released in 2022 investigating his poisoning during a trip from Tomsk to Moscow in 2020.*[1]

'Loathing. People ask me a lot about it, and I started receiving letters again: do you hate the judge? Do you hate [Russian President Vladimir] Putin even more? I have said many times before that hate is the main thing that must be overcome in prison. There are so many reasons for it, and your powerlessness is a strong catalyst for the process. So if you let it go, it will eat and end you up.

[…]

I get furious after the sessions of the local district court. There are simple cases, there is no space for legal tricks, and the judges simply and frankly say about the black: "Oh this is white, look, the reference says white" and make demonstratively illegal decisions.

[…]

I am sitting in my SHIZO [solitary-confinement cell] and reading a book by Natan Sharansky, "Fear No Evil" (I recommend it).

[…]

In the introduction (I remind you, the year is 1991), Sharansky writes that it is in prisons that the virus of free-thinking persists, and he hopes that the KGB will not find "an antidote to this virus." Sharansky was wrong. The antidote was found. The antidote that now, in 2023, seems to have more political prisoners in Russia than in the Brezhnev–Andropov times. What has the KGB got to do with it? There was no creeping or overt coup in our country led by people from the special services. They did not come to power by pushing the democrat reformers out of power. They did it themselves. They called them themselves. They invited them themselves. They taught them how to fake elections. How to steal property from entire industries. How to lie to the media. How to change laws to suit themselves. How to suppress opposition by force. Even how to organize idiotic, stupid, talentless wars.

That is why I can't help it and I fiercely hate those who sold, drank, and wasted the historical chance that our country had in the early 90s. I hate [Boris] Yeltsin and "Tanya and Valya", [Anatoly] Chubais, and the rest of the corrupt family who put Putin in power. I hate the swindlers, whom we used to call reformers for some reason. Now it is very clear that they did nothing but intrigue and take care of their own wealth. Is there any other country where so many Ministers of the "Government of Reforms" became millionaires and billionaires? I hate the authors of the most stupid authoritarian constitution, which they sold to us idiots as democratic, even then giving the president the power of a full-fledged monarch.

I especially hate everyone for the fact that there was not even a serious attempt to remove the basis of lawlessness – to carry out judicial reform, without which all other reforms are doomed to failure.

Survival | vol. 66 no. 2 | April–May 2024 | pp. 72–74   https://doi.org/10.1080/00396338.2024.2332060

[…]

We let the goat in the cabbage warehouse, and then we wonder why it ate all the cabbage. It is a goat, its mission and goal is to eat cabbage, it can't think of anything else. It is useless to agitate him. Similarly, Putin's FSB [Federal Security Service] official can't think of anything else but to build a huge house and imprison those they don't like. I can't stand the goat, but I hate those who let it in the cabbage warehouse.

Though, of course, I realize that it's better to not hate anyone at all, but to think about how not to do it again. Here comes my greatest fear. I don't just believe, I know that Russia will still have a chance. This is a historical process. We will again be at a crossroads.

[…]

Real life is complicated, hard and full of compromises with unpleasant people. However, at least we ourselves should not become unpleasant people and welcome corruption and cynical fraud even before circumstances require compromise.

[…]

Only when the vast majority of the Russian opposition consists of those who under no circumstances accept fake elections, improper judicial proceedings, and corruption, then we will be able to make the right use of the chance that will surely come again. So that no one in 2055 will be reading Sharansky's book in the SHIZO, thinking: Wow, it's just like me.'

Navalny, who was imprisoned by Russian authorities in 2021, posts on his website on 11 August 2023 after his jail term was extended by 19 years.[2]

'Your honour, I will send you my personal account number so that you can use your huge federal judge's salary to fuel my personal account, because I am running out of money, and thanks to your decisions, it will run out even faster. So send it over.'

Navalny jokes with a judge during a video-link court hearing on 15 February 2024, the day before his death.[3]

'A statement from FSIN [Federal Penitentiary Service] which came shortly before our bulletin: Alexei Navalny has died.'

Russian state TV announces Navalny's death on 16 February.[4]

'You've probably all seen the terrible news coming in today. I thought for a long time whether I should come out here or fly straight to my children. But then I thought about what Alexei would do in my place. And I'm sure he'd be here, he'd be on this stage.

I don't know whether or not to believe the news, the terrible news that we only get from government sources in Russia, because for years – and you all know this – we can't believe Putin and Putin's government. They're always lying. But if this is true, I want Putin and all of his entourage, Putin's friends and his government to know that they will be held accountable for what they have done to our country, to my family and to my husband. And that day will come very soon – and I want to call on the entire world community, everyone in this room and people around the world, that we come together to unite and defeat this evil, defeat the horrific regime that is now in Russia. And this regime and Vladimir Putin must be held personally responsible for all the terrible things that they have been doing to my country, to our country Russia, in recent years.'

Yulia Navalnaya, Navalny's widow, delivers a speech at the Munich Security Conference on 16 February.[5]

'He was our hero who united the opposition. Navalny gave us a Russian dream, that maybe in a decade we'd live in a free Russia.

There is still opposition. Although it's very difficult, there are still people who support Ukraine and want peace negotiations. We love our country and want the best for it.'

Nikolai, a student in Moscow, speaks to the Guardian *newspaper about Navalny's death.*[6]

Sources

1 Tucker Reals, 'Alexei Navalny's Message to the World "If They Decide to Kill Me," and What His Wife Wants People to Know', CBS News, 17 February 2024, https://www.cbsnews.com/news/alexey-navalny-message-if-they-decide-to-kill-me-wife-yulia-message-today/.

2 Alexei Navalny, 'My Fear and Loathing', blog post, 11 August 2023, https://navalny.com/p/6652/.

3 'Alexei Navalny Appears Healthy in Video-link Court Hearing on Day Before His Death', Guardian News, Youtube.com, 16 February 2024, https://www.youtube.com/watch?v=cFGIH9WS5yI.

4 'Russian State TV Announces Death of Alexei Navalny – Video', *Guardian*, 16 February 2024, https://www.theguardian.com/world/video/2024/feb/16/russian-state-tv-announces-death-of-alexei-navalny-video.

5 'Alexei Navalny: Wife Yulia Emotional in Address to Munich Security Conference', *Telegraph*, Youtube.com, 16 February 2024, https://www.youtube.com/watch?v=8Kc4ZuyRAbc.

6 Clea Skopeliti, '"He Was Our Hero": Six Russians on the Death of Alexei Navalny', *Guardian*, 17 February 2024, https://www.theguardian.com/world/2024/feb/17/he-was-our-hero-six-russians-on-the-death-of-alexei-navalny.

The 'China Model' in the Middle East

Jon B. Alterman

In spring 2023, China seemed to be on a roll in the Middle East. The previous December, President Xi Jinping had conducted a successful two days of meetings with Arab leaders in Riyadh. The kings, princes and presidents in attendance had warmly embraced Xi, with none of the scratchiness – or the awkward fist bump – that had marked US President Joe Biden's seemingly reluctant Saudi visit the prior July. A Chinese Foreign Ministry spokesman characterised the visit as an 'epoch-making milestone in the history of China–Arab relations', and that didn't seem especially hyperbolic.[1] On 10 March, Saudi and Iranian representatives in Beijing stunned the world when they announced that, thanks to Chinese mediation, their countries had agreed to normalise ties.

Coinciding with his December 2022 visit to Riyadh, Xi published an opinion piece in a local newspaper that articulated his rationale for his trip and the appeal of closer Arab ties with China. He argued that the 'Arab people value independence, oppose external interference, stand up to power politics and high-handedness, and always seek to make progress'.[2] China was a partner in that. It was not hard to figure out who he was implicitly criticising, nor why many Arabs considered the meetings such a success. Afterwards, the Saudis touted more than 30 agreements with China involving about $50 billion of investment.[3]

Jon B. Alterman is senior vice president, Zbigniew Brzezinski Chair in Global Security and Geostrategy, and director of the Middle East Program at the Center for Strategic and International Studies (CSIS). This article is drawn from a longer CSIS study that will be published at www.csis.org.

Survival | vol. 66 no. 2 | April–May 2024 | pp. 75–98   https://doi.org/10.1080/00396338.2024.2332062

In stark contrast, when Biden had visited five months earlier, he claimed that he had raised the 2018 murder of Saudi journalist Jamal Khashoggi at the beginning of his meeting with Saudi Crown Prince Muhammad bin Salman, 'making it clear what I thought of it at the time and what I think of it now'. According to Biden, the prince 'basically said that he was not personally responsible for it. I indicated that I thought he was.'[4] While agreements were made during the visit, the tensions were palpable.

Over the last six months, however, China has no longer seemed ascendant in the Middle East. As the United States has assumed a leading role in both regional and global diplomacy over the conflict in Gaza, China has drifted increasingly to the margins. It is becoming clear not only that China does not aspire to replace the United States in the Middle East, but also that China and most Arab states alike want the United States to remain committed to Middle East security.

At the same time, both China and the Arab states appear driven to loosen what they see as an undesirable US grip on the region. While the motivations are different – China fears the United States will seek to block its access to the Middle East's resources, and the Arab states seek to escape what they see as onerous conditions that Western states impose, bolster their bargaining power and gain access to what Western powers will not deliver – they are united in seeking a more multipolar future for the region. In pursuit of it, they find common purpose in a single, simple idea: China presents a new model for domestic and international governance, and there are large parts of China's model that are worth emulating.

What is so striking about this pursuit is its vagueness. Neither side is very specific about what a 'China model' entails or how it might be followed. Yet each sees a profound benefit in the notion that Western states have no monopoly on the ideas that will drive the Middle East forward. Whether the Chinese have a coherent set of ideas for so doing, or those ideas are applicable in the Middle East in the long term, often seems beside the point. What each side is urgently seeking is a tool for pushing back on the West. A vague 'China model' that all sides can embrace serves that need, and in some ways, the vaguer the better.

Trouble for the *liberal* model

The idea that states can forge long-term success without evolving towards liberal democracy sits uneasily in many Western capitals. Western states' self-confidence in the potential universality of their success has both missionary and colonial roots. While missionaries professed to be less self-interested than the colonisers, baked into each viewpoint is a strong sense of Western superiority. Many believe that emulating the West promotes progress, and the greater the emulation, the greater the progress. That it serves Western political and economic interests is beside the point. Rather, Western missionaries, colonial administrators, diplomats and others have argued for five centuries that they were merely advancing common interests when they pushed others to be more like them.

The Middle East had been at the receiving end of those Western efforts for many of those 500 years. What some in the Middle East saw as growing Western encroachment, many in the West saw as virtuous efforts to invigorate immiserated biblical lands and to fill the vacuum left by a slowly crumbling Ottoman Empire. Over time, what had originated as a battle for souls turned into one for hearts and minds. The Cold War, combined with the world's transition from coal to oil, raised the regional stakes and turned what had been merely economic and political struggles into civilisational ones. Fear of communism helped provoke Anglo-American intervention in Iranian politics in the early 1950s. Later, the strong anti-communist tilt of the oil-rich Persian Gulf monarchies reassured Western states, and Egypt's pivot towards the US camp in the 1970s further indicated Western ascendancy.

With Deng Xiaoping's embrace of 'socialism with Chinese characteristics' and the fall of the Soviet Union, the world seemed to enter a new phase. As Francis Fukuyama famously argued in 1989, 'the triumph of the West, of the Western *idea*, is evident in the total exhaustion of viable systematic alternatives to Western liberalism'.[5] Middle Eastern states seemed to accept that analysis. By the late 1990s, every country in the Middle East had close relations with the United States or was seeking to improve them.[6]

That moment did not last. In the early 2000s, as the United States reeled from the 11 September attacks, the mood changed. China had only become a net energy importer in about 1993, but as it entered a period of breakneck economic growth in the early 2000s, it consistently imported about half of its oil from the Middle East. China was soon the driving force behind growing global energy demand, and in the process, it became the largest trading partner of successive Middle Eastern countries.

The United States was simultaneously expanding its Middle Eastern footprint, but in a different way. The US strategic response to the 9/11 attacks had three principal elements: a war in Afghanistan, another in Iraq and a focused effort to democratise the Middle East. The first was not a major concern of most Arab states, but the latter two hit close to home. Arab states resented Iraq because of its 1990 invasion of Kuwait, but they respected it as a bulwark against Iran. In waging war there, the United States had seemingly empowered two groups that they feared: Iran's Iraqi allies and a jihadi movement that fought the Iranians, fought the Americans and threatened to fight others in the region too. To Arab states – and other US partners around the world – watching the US flounder in Iraq was unsettling. Indian Minister of External Affairs S. Jaishankar captured the attitude perfectly when he observed that 'for two decades, China has been winning without fighting, while the US was fighting without winning'.[7]

Part of China's strategy of winning was persuading global audiences to appreciate China's modern accomplishments. Joseph Fewsmith has observed that Peking University's Pan Wei sought to popularise the idea of a 'China model' in the early 2000s. There were early signs of success in the Middle East. Nobel Prize-winning author Naguib Mahfouz argued in 2002 that Arab societies should diversify what they borrow from abroad, including lessons from China, as the Middle East's historical and social traditions more closely resemble China's than the West's.[8] An Emirati scholar of China wrote in 2008 that the China model proves 'there is another pathway for governments of the world to follow in order to successfully pursue economic growth'.[9] The idea of a China model took off at this moment. An internet search for articles with the phrase 'China model' in the title yielded 500 articles in 2007, 750 in 2008, and fully 3,000 in 2009.[10]

What is the China model?

The world's growing embrace of the China model happened despite the rise of a lively debate within and outside of China about exactly what constitutes a China model for development, or if one even exists. Western analysts have tended to treat it as an argument for authoritarian-led economic development that is exemplary in its ability to 'make large, complex decisions quickly, and to make them relatively well, at least in economic policy'.[11] Yet one can also argue that when the Chinese economy was growing most strongly, some of the country's greatest successes occurred in cities that took very divergent approaches to economic development. Chongqing's charismatic Chinese Communist Party (CCP) secretary pushed an approach that some scholars described as populist and 'Maoist-revivalist', Guandong pursued a policy that seemed largely neo-liberal and capitalist, and the Shanghai government appeared technocratic and technologically focused. Yuen Yuen Ang argues persuasively that the Chinese have pursued varying strategies at different times and places, and she argues that Chinese government policy is best characterised as 'directed improvisation'. Whereas Mao Zedong pursued ruinous top-down strategies, his successors set dynamic parameters that established boundaries, defined criteria for success and encouraged the flow of industry and capital to less-developed regions, but ultimately relied on local officials rather than central planners.[12]

While Chinese leaders speak openly and persistently about a 'China solution' (alternately translated as 'China proposal'), Chinese leaders take pains not to use the word 'model' themselves. Xi told a group of leaders of political parties in 2017: 'We do not want to "import" models from other countries, nor do we want to "export" the Chinese model, still less will we ask other countries to copy the Chinese practice.' Noting that China itself adopted communism from overseas, he continued:

> As a Chinese saying goes, a stone taken from another mountain may serve as a tool to polish the local jade … The [CCP] will embrace and approach the achievements of other cultures with an open mind and a broad perspective. We stay committed to engaging in dialogue, exchanges and cooperation with the people and political parties of other countries.

Implicit in Xi's assertion that China was 'eager to draw on the achievements of other cultures and apply them in the Chinese context' is an invitation to them to draw on Chinese achievements and apply them in diverse local contexts.[13]

Also in 2017, at a Belt and Road Initiative conference, Xi put great emphasis on China's fundamental belief in mutual benefit. Suggesting that the
ancient Silk Road was all about reciprocity, he noted that

> Chinese silk, porcelain, lacquerwork and ironware were shipped to the West,
> while pepper, flax, spices, grape and pomegranate entered China. Through
> these routes, Buddhism, Islam and Arab astronomy, calendar and medicine
> found their way to China, while China's four great inventions [papermaking,
> printing, gunpowder and the compass] and silkworm breeding spread to
> other parts of the world. More importantly, the exchange of goods and
> know-how spurred new ideas. For example, Buddhism originated in India,
> blossomed in China and was enriched in Southeast Asia.[14]

For good measure, he added: 'We are ready to share practices of development with other countries, but we have no intention to interfere in other
countries' internal affairs, export our own social system and model of development, or impose our own will on others.'[15]

The Chinese leadership's soft-sell rhetorical approach is strikingly different than the Western push for adherence to Western standards. Chinese
officials argue that they merely seek to inculcate respect for difference.
For example, Xi noted in his September 2020 speech to the United Nations
General Assembly: 'We should respect a country's independent choice
of development path and model. The world is diverse in nature, and we
should turn this diversity into a constant source of inspiration driving
human advancement.'[16]

Elizabeth Economy suggests that appeals to tolerate diversity serve to
obscure a more pointed strategy. Since 2017, she argues, 'both in rhetoric and
reality, China has become increasingly comfortable in its efforts to export its
state-centered political and economic model globally' and has done so by
'supporting the creation of laws and regulations that enhance state control,
limit individual freedoms, and favor state-led economic development'.[17]
Such a strategy has two potential and ultimately compatible goals: 'acting
offensively to forge a more illiberal world or defensively to make the world
safe for China's brand of autocracy'.[18]

The ideological challenge

From the perspective of authoritarian regimes in the Middle East, China's objectives are not immediately relevant here. What they value in the Chinese approach is that it legitimises their resistance to Western calls for liberalisation, democratisation and human rights, has no problems with a commanding public sector and provides living proof that there are multiple paths to combining economic growth with social peace.

For many in the US foreign-policy community, however, the US insistence on pushing for better governance is a key instrument of national power. As Hal Brands wrote in *Survival*,

> the chief defender of the existing international order is a liberal democracy that has traditionally sought to shape the global environment in accordance with its ideological values as well as its strategic interests. The leading revisionists are autocracies that practice a distinctly authoritarian version of capitalism and see the advance of liberal ideals as an existential threat to their legitimacy and power.[19]

This situation is different from the US–Soviet Cold War, in which each side competed to spread its ideology.

In the current ideological contest, China is not seeking to promote its own ideology, but rather to undermine an opposing one. It is not hard to understand why. Authoritarianism broadly challenges a liberal world order, but liberalism poses a much more acute threat to authoritarian rule. Liberal states were born amid authoritarian peers, and it is relatively rare that liberal states slide into authoritarianism, which does not have wide appeal in most democracies. Yet a democratic wave would pose a profound challenge to governance models in authoritarian states. Not only did authoritarians fear both the 'colour revolutions' in the post-Soviet space and the Arab Spring, but some academics in China claimed to this author that the United States 'caused' the Arab Spring in order to weaken China. If liberal democracies are attractive to their own populations, they represent an existential threat to authoritarian leaders.

One of China's leading strategic thinkers, Wang Jisi, argues that Chinese officials take this challenge seriously. 'In Chinese eyes, the most significant threat to China's sovereignty and national security has long been US interference in its internal affairs aimed at changing the country's political system and undermining the CCP.'[20] He adds that

> Beijing believes that Washington was the driving force behind the 'color revolutions' that took place in the first decade of this century in former Soviet states and that the US government has ginned up protest movements against authoritarian regimes around the world, including the Arab revolts of 2010–11. The CCP believes that those alleged US interventions will supply a blueprint for Washington to undermine and eventually topple the party.[21]

China's response has been a broader campaign to portray the United States as both hegemonic and homogenising, imposing not only its own political model but also social and cultural mores premised on the American experience and American beliefs. For authoritarian regimes in the Middle East, this is an attractive proposition.

The particular lessons that China might offer to Middle Eastern governments are less important than the general idea that it has lessons. It can certainly point to dramatic successes. Although China's decade of double-digit GDP growth in the late 1990s and early 2000s will not return, bringing 800 million people out of poverty remains an enduring accomplishment.[22] Similarly, China has managed tremendous economic and social change with relatively little political disruption. China shifted from a country where fewer than one in five citizens were urban in 1979 to two in three today, accompanied by the creation of a massive, literate and consumption-oriented middle class that drives the country's economy. Throughout, the CCP has maintained control over public life and sustained its coherence and solidarity. To have done so in the face of such extraordinary material, social and demographic change is not an obvious outcome, and no mean achievement.

Still, Gulf understandings of the Chinese political economy are almost entirely impressionistic. There is no literature in Arabic on China's economic and political development aside from a few newspaper columns. Academic articles about China's role in the region rely almost entirely on secondary

English-language sources rather than Arabic or Chinese material or primary documents.[23] There is no community of elite Gulf businesspeople who have lived in China and could act as a bridge. Similarly, there is no community of Chinese living in the Gulf who mix easily with their Arab counterparts. On the popular level, Chinese goods are widely thought to be of inferior quality, and Chinese construction is below the standard of Western or Northeast Asian firms.[24]

Egypt's stake

For Middle Eastern states with deep insecurities about the enormity of the economic and social tasks ahead of them, China's success is an inspiration. In many ways, the country that feels most in need of a Chinese embrace is Egypt, whose challenges and opportunities seem closest to China's experience. Both feature vibrant countrysides that have been pouring into rapidly growing cities for decades. The World Bank estimates that in 2019, 21% of Egyptians worked in agriculture, versus 25% of Chinese. Identical percentages in the two countries' populations – 27% – were engaged in industrial employment.[25] As with China, state-owned enterprises constitute an important part of the industrial base. Also like China, Egypt has a sprawling military–industrial complex, although in the Egyptian case the military's economic interests dip deeply into normally civilian matters such as bottled water, gas-station convenience stores and cement manufacture.

After first going to China in 2014, Egyptian President Abdel Fattah al-Sisi visited six times in six years and signed at least 25 bilateral agreements.[26] A former Egyptian ambassador to China, now the vice-chairman of the Egypt–China Friendship Association, gushed to the Chinese-published *Global Times*:

> Egypt and China enjoy a lot of similarities, that has been so obvious since their two leaders took over as president. They have both almost identical and profound appreciation of world politics. Their mutual understanding got deeper and deeper over the past few years. They met many times and developed mutual understanding, in particular with regard to the priority that should be given to sustainable development in their nations, to the

building up of their economies, to striving to aim at raising the standards
of living of their people and to the preservation of our two nations' national
security, peace and stability, because any country, if it's stable and strong
from within, no other country could threaten its peace and stability.[27]

One businessperson who has dealt extensively with China raved about
implicit comparisons between China and the United States that favour the
former. 'There is no conditionality on financing, and they finance on comfortable terms', she said. 'They provide financing and know-how … and
they provide long installments with a grace period. It is a less arrogant
model, and they are not interfering in politics.'[28] Another businessperson
with extensive investments in Egypt's New Administrative Capital also
highlighted the financing issue: 'The Germans, French and Chinese are
investing with financing on easy terms.'[29]

In fact, China's engagement with Egypt has been measured, and China
has pulled back when it has judged Egypt to be overreaching. For example,
Chinese firms originally were slated to play a major role in constructing the
government administrative district in Egypt's New Administrative Capital,
but, as one senior Egyptian official said, 'it didn't work for economic and
political reasons'.[30] A Chinese colleague commented privately that the
dispute was over commercial terms, and 'the Egyptians thought they were
the only ones who were supposed to make money'. The Chinese focus shifted
to building towers only in the central business district, a smaller area for
which they have specific technical expertise that the Egyptians hope will be
transferred during the construction process. The commonly accepted figure
for Chinese investment in the central business district is $3bn, although its
terms are hard to discern.[31]

There often seems to be a gap between the perception and the reality
of Chinese investment in Egypt. Agreements are struck and heralded, but
sometimes projects are quietly shelved without clear explanations of when or
why. For example, the Egyptian press widely reported in January 2016 that
the Ministry of Transportation had signed a memorandum of understanding
with China Railway Construction Corporation for a $3.5bn project to design,
plan and build Cairo's sixth metro line, noting that financing was still being

negotiated.[32] Eighteen months later, the press reported that Egypt's National Authority for Tunnels had signed a non-binding agreement with Quebec-based Bombardier to develop a plan for the sixth metro line and made no reference at all to the prior Chinese agreement.[33] There is no public record of what went wrong with the earlier project or when it foundered.

By contrast, sustained attention has been paid to the Chinese role in constructing the electrified light rail connecting Cairo, 10th of Ramadan City and the New Administrative Capital. The $1.25bn project, whose first phase is a 66-kilometre line with 11 stations, opened in July 2022, approximately five years after being agreed. The railway is an example of China's ability to build infrastructure more quickly and affordably than Western firms, drawing on its extensive domestic experience building railways and helping to drive Egypt's economic development. Because Egyptians see China as a fellow developing country, the Egyptian press portrays the railway as part of a partnership of equals, with an implicit hope that some of China's economic magic rubs off on Egypt.

A line of argument has arisen in Egypt that the turn towards a Chinese option is a practical one that has been forced on them. One businessperson commented that 'the US–Egypt relationship is in the DNA of Egypt. Egyptian officials hate dealing with the Chinese.'[34] Another said, 'we have no hostility to China, but it is not like the American dream'.[35] But however much they might prefer dealing with the United States, Egyptians assess that China is interested in Egypt, and the United States is not. 'The US is letting go and blaming Egypt', one businessperson said.[36]

The Gulf Arab states' position

Oil-rich countries in the Persian Gulf are far less concerned than Egypt with attracting investment, but they are much more concerned with how to guide their countries' economic, social and political development. In the 1980s, many Western observers doubted that Saudi Arabia could modernise its economy without also encouraging social and political liberalisation. The Egyptian-American Harvard scholar Wilson Bishai openly wondered, 'how can a population whose majority is conservative and still living in a Medieval time frame accommodate and absorb the technology of the Western world, which is mainly based on a liberal and material background?'[37] In the four decades since, Saudi Arabia has provided an answer to that question. For several decades, it aggressively co-opted most potential domestic opposition and paid particular attention to pursuing a symbiotic relationship with the clerical establishment, which legitimated the ruling family's patrimony. More recently, under the Vision 2030 plan, the country has pursued an aggressive policy, perhaps most accurately described as a strategy to coerce tolerance, that promotes many forms of social and economic liberalisation while becoming even more sensitive than it had been to expressions of political liberalisation.

The United Arab Emirates (UAE) faced much the same challenge, but the country had a different institutional history. Because it was founded as a relatively loose union of seven emirates, diversity – and sometimes, inefficiency – was an inherent part of its structure. From the beginning, individual emirates were each pursuing development independently, often replicating one another's efforts. For example, each emirate built its own cement plant, and four different emirates raced to build their own international airports. The Ministry of Planning conceived of a five-year plan to begin in 1981, but it lacked the authority to enforce its will nationwide and proved ineffective even in communicating with local development planners, let alone coordinating with them.[38]

Despite the lack of central control, or perhaps because of it, the UAE developed robustly. Arguably, divergent approaches and shared hunger for results resembled the multiple strategies China pursued in the 1990s. Dubai in particular developed a reputation for urgency and ambition, which Abu Dhabi has sought to match.[39] The state – in this case, both the federal government and the governments of individual emirates – remains the key driver of economic decision-making, which it maintains through state-owned conglomerates such as Dubai World, Dubai Holding and a government-controlled property-development firm named Emaar. Dubai has an 'Executive Office' that allows rulers to mesh their governmental and economic roles, which in recent decades Abu Dhabi has sought to match with its 'Executive Affairs Authority'.

As a consequence of the oil boom, the whole notion of economic development in the Gulf took on a different cast than it did in a country like

Egypt. The region was not ideologically attracted to socialism – indeed, the Gulf monarchies had a strong aversion to Gamal Abdel Nasser and his Arab-socialism project – but still set up what were essentially socialist systems funded by oil revenues. Almost all citizens were quickly brought out of poverty, often on the backs of non-national workers who laboured in poverty. Guaranteed government jobs, free education and healthcare, and subsidised utilities were all part of the ruling bargain for citizens, and there was still plenty of money to spare.

The resultant economic systems blended capitalism and socialism in ways that had few antecedents in either the United States or China. Politically and socially, the tribal, clan and family systems of the Gulf increasingly had to cope with the cosmopolitan demands of fast-growing cities, mobility and generational change. Here too, there was no obvious direction in which they might adapt.

Gulf systems blended capitalism and socialism

For some, economic development called for more democratic, or at least more liberal, systems. The dynamism of the modern world was synonymous with greater individualism, which in turn would encourage excellence and intellectual independence. Talal bin Abdulaziz, the so-called 'Red Prince' of Saudi Arabia, went into exile for several years in the early 1960s for his embrace of such reforms, and he was just one example of the region's liberalising current. Kuwait first established a legislature in 1938, as a way for merchants to ensure that the ruler was sharing oil revenues with the population.[40] Although it was soon dissolved, it has proven mostly durable since its re-establishment in 1963. But democratic systems have not always correlated with liberalisation. The advent of democratic politics in Kuwait, for example, had the paradoxical effect of nurturing tribal politics. Tribes organise to ensure their representation in parliament, and then use that representation to maximise their share of state benefits. Rather than push individualism, Kuwaiti elections have spurred collective consciousness.

From the Gulf rulers' perspective, collective consciousness is not a bad thing as long as the leaders of the collectivities respect the leadership's rule.

Indeed, it can be easier to manage individuals by delegating authority to a small number of subnational bodies that can both reward compliance and punish deviation. Unlike Egypt, Iraq and Syria, Gulf governments have not embraced systems of large domestic-security forces with widely placed informants. Rather, networks of primordial affiliation that pervade Gulf societies serve to reinforce loyalty and obedience.

Governments in the region rule through what they characterise as benign authoritarianism, arguing that liberalism would open the door to the social ills of the West as well as a conservative reaction by extremists that would undermine necessary progress. That is, they insist that governments play a central role in managing contestation in society, and that more open politics would only drive polarisation and hostility.

It is on this score that the Chinese model of government management centred on the confluence of economic, social and political change becomes especially attractive. As one UAE-based think-tank scholar put it, 'the UAE is asked to be apologetic for lots of stuff, especially its political system … The China model achieved success. They are doing more than any Third World democratic country. They created a parallel model. We don't need to apologise anymore.' This scholar continued: 'We have an Islamic background, so family is first. But in civilisation we are closer to the West because Islam is an Abrahamic religion. Even so, the radical individualism of the West is sometimes offensive. For example, the right to decide gender doesn't resonate with our sense of the boundaries of individualism.' Another UAE-based scholar asked, 'Who comes first, the individual or society?' He suggested that democracy was one way of improving governance, but that improved governance without democracy also represents an appealing path forward. 'China is making people think we have another choice.'[41]

A senior Arab League official similarly argued that there is a sense of revelation that comes from Chinese success. 'They did a miracle. The West said it wasn't possible. If you want economic progress, there is one way forward, and that requires liberalisation and democratisation.' China refutes that premise. And from an economic point of view, China can represent a more conservative bet. 'The China model has continuity', said the Arab League official. 'The democratic model has disruptions all the time.'[42]

For Middle Eastern authoritarians, China is not only an example of a country that has grown despite defying Western rules, it also one whose path has defied Western expectations. Twenty years ago, senior Western officials thought that the economic attractions of Western societies would prompt Chinese liberalisation. For example, then-deputy secretary of state Robert Zoellick said in 2005 that 'China does not believe that its future depends on overturning the fundamental order of the international system. In fact, quite the reverse: Chinese leaders have decided that their success depends on being networked with the modern world.' As a more integrated China became more prosperous, Zoellick suggested, China would open up internally, because 'closed politics cannot be a permanent feature of Chinese society. It is simply not sustainable – as economic growth continues, better-off Chinese will want a greater say in their future, and pressure builds for political reform.'[43]

China has begged to differ, and has gained significantly by emboldening others to refrain from imitating the United States without inspiring a simultaneous imitation of China. The China model, from this perspective, can be seen as promoting global resistance to the adoption of Western liberalism. It isn't much of a stretch to suggest that it also signals governments around the world that they can follow the Chinese path in maintaining flourishing economies and political stability while picking and choosing those aspects of modernity that their populations will embrace and rejecting aspects they see as destabilising or immoral.

Western responses

Western governments do not have an easy response at hand, but, a US military veteran with long experience in the Middle East explained, 'we have to find an alternative to condescendingly screaming at people not to follow the China model. I think that liberal democracy, capitalist democracy, scares the shit out of them. It's not entirely consistent with their culture and their history … and it was brought there by the colonisers.'[44]

For the United States and its allies, an accurate assessment of the situation is the first step to addressing it. China is not trying to supplant the United States, it is trying to supplement it. US partners and allies in the

Middle East – the region contains eight major non-NATO allies of the United States – are seeking to supplement their US relationship. They want military equipment the United States is reluctant to sell, and they want investment and financing for capital-development projects. Even more, though, they want to be courted rather than taken for granted, and to be able to pursue benefits from every corner. All four of Donald Trump's addresses to the UN General Assembly called for the United States to pursue an 'America first' strategy and for every other country to do the same. In turn, virtually all Middle Eastern states believe they would benefit from more aggressively advancing their own individual interests and adopting stronger positions of non-alignment.

Middle Eastern governments see improved governance as a tool with both costs and benefits, and they see it as obtainable irrespective of whether they follow an authoritarian or liberal path. Indeed, there are aspects in which China's governance outperforms the United States. These countries view themselves not as choosing one option to the exclusion of another but rather as selecting aspects of all options, experimenting with contradictory initiatives in hopes of making gradual but steady improvements in an increasingly crowded and noisy policy environment.

To many in the Middle East, pure imitation of the Western path is both unwise and unrealistic. It relies on citizens who are entirely different from their own, rooted in a robust legal and policy environment and a vibrant economy. For years, Arab officials visiting Washington have noted that US democracy took 200 years to reach its current state, and they need a century and a half to catch up. The Arab uprisings of 2011 continue to reverberate in the region. In countries such as Iraq, Libya, Syria and Yemen, governments still struggle to assert control over their entire territory; in others, governments see potential revolutionaries lurking. The United States should be more understanding of the charge that it is both sanctimonious and reckless, and that it is prone to lecturing partners while leading them into anarchy. Under current conditions, many regional governments consider mainstream Western advice to constrain government authority, liberalise political activity, dispense with patronage, expand free speech and empower political opponents to be disruptive madness.

While China will continue to make inroads into the Middle East, it is increasingly clear that the terms on offer are highly circumscribed. China does not provide or enhance security, nor does it invest in the sorts of human capital that are essential to the Middle East's success amid the energy transition. China has been reluctant to push the Iranians to constrain their clients, the Houthis, who have attacked global shipping in recent months. Chinese inaction, despite the costs of Houthi attacks to both Chinese manufacturers and their European customers, suggests both limited interest and limited capacity on China's part. Despite talk of 'win–win', China is revealing itself to be a deeply self-interested power, and its Middle East strategy is rooted in both its need for energy security and its efforts to undermine the United States.[45]

At the same time, the durability of Western interests – and Western leverage – in the Middle East has become increasingly clear. While Western states' foreign-policy and security preferences do not always align with those of Arab states, they are con-

China does not provide or enhance security

sequential in ways that China's are not and do not seek to be. In addition, Western states remain engaged with regional partners on foreign-policy and security matters, giving them an opportunity to influence, if not wholly shape, Western positions. We have seen this abundantly on policy towards the war in Gaza, where there has been sustained and meaningful engagement on ending the fighting, providing humanitarian relief and planning for the post-conflict environment. We have also seen it on regional strategies towards Iran, where there has been open dialogue and quiet coordination on countering Iran's efforts to build and fortify an 'axis of resistance' of militias and other non- and quasi-state actors throughout the Middle East.

Furthermore, Western states are more than just vital security partners. The capital they are willing to invest, and the local talent they are willing to help develop, distinguishes them from China. While many Middle Eastern governments have said they never contemplated forgoing close Western ties, the unique benefits of those ties are becoming more evident.

To maximise the benefits of Middle Eastern states' enduring but increasingly qualified affinities for the West, Western states need to focus on three things. The first is gauging what success looks like. No country in the Middle East sees the current geopolitical situation as a new cold war. No country is seeking to fall into a Chinese orbit, and China has no interest in creating an orbit into which they could fall even if they wanted to. These states see themselves in a dynamic market in which they are constantly sensing demand signals and looking to enhance their own worth. There is no escaping this reality. Accordingly, Western governments need to do a better job of deciding and agreeing on what matters. Middle Eastern states will have close relations with China, as virtually all Western governments do, but growing ties by themselves are not a sign of Western failure.

No country is seeking to fall into a Chinese orbit

Secondly, the West cannot lose sight of its inherent advantages. However much most Middle Eastern states want to build Chinese ties, they recognise that their future is much more reliant on a close relationship with the West. Not only are Western economies collectively larger than the Chinese economy, but the 'software' they need – human capital, management skills, scientific know-how and organisational sophistication – have deep roots in Western societies. China has drawn from that, and Middle Eastern states are confident they can too, by making much the same deal that China has. At the same time, Western states should develop a sharper sense of what Middle Eastern states see in China. Obscure value propositions, slow and plodding bureaucracies and onerous requirements are characteristics of tired monopolies, not competitive enterprises. The competition is not going away, and Western governments should take the cue to do better.

Thirdly, Western governments need to better articulate the benefits of a closer alignment, the consequences of a looser one and the criteria by which closeness is judged. This is no easy matter. They themselves do not agree on red lines for Chinese engagement, particularly on issues of technology, infrastructure and military hardware. They should not try to list comprehensively every activity they frown upon, implicitly encouraging partners to come right up to the line of what is permitted and what is forbidden. Instead, they should clearly outline principles and examples, pushing partner states themselves to judge what is consistent with acceptable boundaries and what is outside of them while ensuring that there are consequences to states' behaviour.

In terms of acceptability, the most vexing issue for Western states to address may be the incompatibility between the broad desire to move the world towards systems that embrace human rights and the rule of law, and China's hostility to linking morality with international affairs. That cleavage – which both China and the West are compelled to sustain – is likely to accrue persistently to China's advantage. Yet it need not be debilitating to the West, especially if its goal is approached with humility. Countries as different as Chile, the Czech Republic and South Korea have taken very different paths towards greater democratisation, and countries such as Peru and Myanmar that once seemed to be democratising apace have experienced significant backsliding. Massive efforts to promote democratisation in Iraq and Afghanistan have fallen profoundly short of their aims. Rather than seeking to be the referees of other countries' political and economic journeys or the principal catalysts for change in foreign lands, Western initiatives should account for both the complexity and the substantial time it takes to foster positive change. Ensuring that Western societies stand as positive political examples may be the most important part of this effort, and the hardest.

Tests of this approach will come early. Gaza's reconstruction will almost certainly become a preoccupying concern of the United States and its allies and partners for years to come. Not only will millions of Gazans need to be rehoused, fed and employed, but security – for Gazans and Israelis alike – will need to be nurtured, and a political entity will need to emerge that will simultaneously recognise Palestinian aspirations without threatening Gaza's neighbours. Democracy's role in this will be treacherous, because few Palestinians think democracy has advanced their interests. Hamas won a narrow plurality of votes in Palestine's 2006 legislative elections but took a comfortable majority of seats, ultimately leading to the split between Gaza and the West Bank. Meanwhile, Palestinian Authority President Mahmoud Abbas still clings to power 19 years after his election, 15 years after the supposed expiry of his term, despite an approval rating that hovers near 10%.

As Western powers seek to advance stability in Gaza, a simple formula of 'democracy first' not only will not suffice, but it could prolong Hamas's durability in Gaza. At the same time, it is hard to imagine that any dispensation could be even moderately successful without a sustained international effort that has buy-in from both Arab states and Israel. Western powers will need to play a strong role in coercing and cajoling the parties, in addition to mounting their own direct efforts. China has shown little interest in or aptitude for this sort of 'high touch', long-term effort.

While Western results in the Middle East often have been chequered, decades of experience extending from East Timor to the Balkans to Indochina are likely to make Western powers necessary partners in Gaza's reconstruction. Perceptions of success would enhance their reputations in the Middle East, while perceptions of a badly botched effort would tarnish them. China will almost certainly sit back, seeking to be included in diplomatic processes and playing an economic role, but avoiding much of the difficult diplomacy that will surround these efforts. In other words, China will seek to be involved but not to lead, which Beijing hopes will advance its international reputation while limiting its downside risk.

*   *   *

China is not poised to displace the West from the Middle East, nor are Middle Eastern states about to turn their backs on the West. Developments in the last six months, since Hamas's attack on 7 October 2023 triggered the Gaza war, have made this reality even clearer. But China and Middle Eastern states are united in their desire that the West face greater competition in the Middle East. This is not a bad thing in itself.

At the same time, the Middle East has drivers of dynamism quite apart from China. The energy transition will upend economies in energy-exporting and labour-exporting states alike, and it will reshape how the world relates to the region in the next two or three decades. Managing the region's security challenges – emanating from the reconstruction of Gaza and framing the political future of Palestinians, as well as unsettled civil wars and Iran's efforts to assume a central role in regional affairs – will also demand attention.

China's rise means its Middle East relationships will grow increasingly complex, as they already are between China and all of the Western states. Those states see China as both a competitor and a potential adversary, and as an indispensable – and often their largest – trading partner. Western governments must embrace that complexity in the Middle East and steer it to their advantage, while ensuring that their regional goals are aligned with their global interests. More than merely competing with China in the Middle East, the West needs to do so wisely.

Notes

1   Quoted in Vivian Nereim, 'China and Saudi Arabia Sign Strategic Partnership as Xi Visits Kingdom', *New York Times*, 8 December 2022, https://www.nytimes.com/2022/12/08/world/middleeast/china-saudi-arabia-agreement.html.

2   Xi Jinping, 'Carrying Forward Our Millennia-old Friendship and Jointly Creating a Better Future', *Al-Riyadh*, 8 December 2022, reprinted in English by Xinhua, https://english.news.cn/20221208/cc10b8d41b3749a78ec981ceeda6b26b/c.html.

3   See Fahad Abuljadayel and Abeer Abu Omar, 'Saudi Arabia Says $50 Billion Investments Agreed with China', Bloomberg, 11 December 2022, https://www.bloomberg.com/news/articles/2022-12-11/saudi-arabia-says-50-billion-investments-agreed-at-china-summit.

4   White House, 'Remarks by President Biden on His Meetings in Saudi Arabia', 15 July 2022, https://www.whitehouse.gov/briefing-room/speeches-remarks/2022/07/15/remarks-by-president-biden-on-his-meetings-in-saudi-arabia/.

5   Francis Fukuyama, 'The End of History?', *National Interest*, no. 16, Summer 1989, p. 3.

6   This includes Iran. President Mohammad Khatami's surprise electoral victory as a reformist in 1997 seemed to portend a decisive shift, and Khatami himself advanced the idea of a 'dialogue of civilisations' to help reduce tensions between the Middle East and the West. In an effort to grow the relationship, in early 2000 the Clinton administration lifted bans on the import of Iranian carpets, pistachios and dried fruit, which Iranian interlocutors had advised would have strong symbolic value.

7   S. Jaishankar, *The India Way: Strategies for an Uncertain World* (Gurugram: HarperCollins India, 2020), p. 21. Jaishankar used the same formulation with a specifically Middle Eastern focus in a closed-door meeting in 2019.

8   See Naguib Mahfouz, 'China for Us', *Al-Ahram Weekly*, 31 January–6 February 2002.

9   Mohamed Bin Huwaidan, 'Arabs and the Chinese Model', *Al-Bayan*, 6 March 2008.

10   Joseph Fewsmith, 'Debating "the China Model"', *China Leadership Monitor*, no. 35, Summer 2011, https://www.hoover.org/sites/default/files/research/docs/CLM35JF.pdf.

11   Francis Fukuyama, 'US Democracy Has Little to Teach China', *Financial Times*, 17 January 2011, https://www.ft.com/content/cb6af6e8-2272-11e0-b6a2-00144feab49a.

12   See Yuen Yuen Ang, 'The Real China Model', *Foreign Affairs*, 29 June 2018, https://www.foreignaffairs.com/articles/asia/2018-06-29/real-china-model.

13   Xi Jinping, 'Working Together to Build a Better World', keynote address at the CPC Dialogue with World Political Parties High-level Meeting, 1 December 2017, printed in *China Insight*, December 2017, p. 2, https://www.bjreview.com/2017pdf/Chinainsight13.pdf.

14   Ministry of Foreign Affairs of the People's Republic of China, 'Speech by H.E. Xi Jinping President of the People's Republic of China at the Opening Ceremony of the Belt and Road Forum for International Cooperation', 14 May 2017, https://www.fmprc.gov.cn/mfa_eng/wjdt_665385/zyjh_665391/201705/t20170527_678618.html.

15   *Ibid.*

16   'Xi Jinping's Speech at the General Debate of the 75th Session of the United Nations General Assembly', CGTN, 23 September 2020, https://news.cgtn.com/news/2020-09-23/Full-text-Xi-Jinping-s-speech-at-General-Debate-of-UNGA-U07X2dn8Ag/index.html.

17   Elizabeth Economy, 'Exporting the China Model', Testimony before the US–China Economic and Security Review Commission, 13 March 2020, p. 2, https://www.uscc.gov/sites/default/files/testimonies/USCCTestimony3-13-20%20(Elizabeth%20Economy)_justified.pdf.

18   See Charles Edel and David Shullman, 'How China Exports Authoritarianism', *Foreign Affairs*, 16 September 2021, https://www.foreignaffairs.com/articles/china/2021-09-16/how-china-exports-authoritarianism.

19   Hal Brands, 'Democracy vs Authoritarianism: How Ideology Shapes Great-power Conflict', *Survival*, vol. 60, no. 5, October–November 2018, p. 62.

20   Wang Jisi, 'The Plot Against China?', *Foreign Affairs*, vol. 1, no. 4, July/August 2021, pp. 48–57.

21   *Ibid.*

22   See The World Bank and The Development Research Center of the State Council, 'Four Decades of Poverty Reduction in China: Drivers, Insights for the World, and the Way Ahead', World Bank Group, 2022, p. ix, https://openknowledge.worldbank.org/server/api/core/bitstreams/e9a5bc3c-718d-57d8-9558-ce325407f737/content.

23   See, for example, Rayham Ahmad Khafaji, 'Al-wujūd al-sīnī fī al-sharq al-awsat: al-ālīyāt wal-hudūd' [China's presence in the Middle East: mechanisms and limits], *Al-Mustaqbal al-Arabi*, vol. 45, no. 522, August 2022, pp. 22–37.

24 While much of this evidence is anecdotal, it is consistent and strong. The Arab Barometer project conducted a 2021 survey that asked respondents in Algeria, Iraq, Jordan, Lebanon, Libya, Morocco and Tunisia which country has a reputation for 'building the highest quality'. Germany led in every country, the United States and China were equal in Iraq, Jordan, Lebanon and Tunisia, and the United States prevailed in the remainder. See Arab Barometer, 'Fragile Popularity: Arab Attitudes Towards China', 15 December 2021, https://www.arabba rometer.org/2021/12/fragile-popu larity-arab-attitudes-towards-china/.

25 World Bank, 'Employment in Industry – China, Egypt, Arab Rep.', https:// data.worldbank.org/indicator/SL.IND. EMPL.ZS?locations=CN-EG.

26 See Mohamed El Dahshan, 'Egyptian Exceptionalism in a Chinese-led World', Chatham House, 10 February 2021, https://www.chathamhouse. org/2021/02/egyptian-exceptionalism-chinese-led-world.

27 'China's Wisdom Prevails in the Middle East: Former Egyptian Diplomat', *Global Times*, 1 July 2022, https://www.globaltimes.cn/ page/202207/1270694.shtml.

28 Author interview with businessperson with academic and government background, Cairo, Egypt, 16 March 2022.

29 Author interview with businessperson, Cairo, Egypt, 17 March 2022.

30 Author interview with senior government official involved in economic development, Cairo, Egypt, 17 March 2022.

31 Author interview with businessperson, Cairo, Egypt, 17 March 2022;

and interview with senior government official involved in economic development, Cairo, Egypt, 17 March 2022.

32 See 'Chinese Company to Construct Cairo's Sixth Metro Line', *Egyptian Streets*, 2 January 2016, https:// egyptianstreets.com/2016/01/02/ chinese-company-to-construct-cairos-sixth-metro-line/.

33 See Alicja Siekierska, 'Bombardier Signs Agreement with Egypt to Develop Proposal for New Cairo Metro Line', *Financial Post*, 12 July 2017, https://financialpost.com/ transportation/bombardier-ssigns-agreement-with-egypt-to-develop-pro posal-for-new-cairo-metro-line/wcm/ e02a9b95-99a1-4ce1-b2fe-7aa142d6b1a3.

34 Author interview with businessperson, Cairo, Egypt, 17 March 2022.

35 Author interview with businessperson with academic and government background, Cairo, Egypt, 16 March 2022.

36 Author interview with businessperson, Cairo, Egypt, 17 March 2022.

37 Wilson B. Bishai, 'Review of Ragaei el-Mallakh, Saudi Arabia: Rush to Development', *Annals of the American Academy of Political and Social Science*, vol. 468, July 1983, p. 249.

38 *Ibid*, p. 257.

39 See Martin Hvidt, 'The Dubai Model: An Outline of Key Development-process Elements in Dubai', *International Journal of Middle Eastern Studies*, vol. 41, no. 3, August 2009, pp. 397–418.

40 See Jill Crystal, *Kuwait: The Transformation of an Oil State* (Boulder, CO: Westview Press, 1992), pp. 19–20.

41 Author interview with Dubai think-tank scholar, 4 November 2021.

42 Author interview with senior Arab League official, 16 March 2022.

43 Robert Zoellick, 'Whither China: From Membership to Responsibility?', Remarks to the National Committee on US–China Relations, US Department of State, 21 September 2005, https://2001-2009.state.gov/s/d/former/zoellick/rem/53682.htm.

44 Author interview with US military veteran, 24 January 2023.

45 See Jon B. Alterman, 'What the Red Sea Crisis Reveals About China's Middle East Strategy', *Foreign Policy*, 14 February 2024, https://foreignpolicy.com/2024/02/14/red-sea-crisis-china-middle-east-strategy-egypt-yemen/.

A Delicate Balance: Iraq's Security Culture Between Iran and the United States

Ellen Laipson and Douglas Ollivant

Iraq's security system is in transition. The country's leaders have worked to modernise its national-security structures and improve the effectiveness of its armed forces and law-enforcement agencies. Still, the process of ensuring that the state has a monopoly on the use of force is far from complete. Links between Iraq's political class and subnational armed groups remain a source of tension with the country's professional military. Iraq's nascent democratic culture has brought new voices and competing views into national-security policymaking, and there is no clear consensus about the long-term role for subnational armed groups, including in the Kurdish region, or about the country's national-security strategy.

Iraq has survived insurgency, civil war and a brutal campaign against the Islamic State (ISIS), and is a functioning if flawed democracy with contested elections. In the years since Saddam Hussein's ouster in 2003, no elected prime minister has been removed from power through violence, nor has a strongman emerged to reinstate authoritarianism or regional adventurism. Iraq's partners in the West have been encouraged by the state's gradual evolution and management of core security functions.

At one level, Iraq's political, military and social tensions continue to be of concern. The initially promising 'Tishreen' youth-protest movement of 2019

Ellen Laipson directs the International Security Program at George Mason University. She was the president of the Stimson Center, and before this served in the US government for 25 years. **Douglas Ollivant** is a Senior Fellow at the Foreign Policy Research Institute (FPRI) and Managing Partner at Mantid International. He previously served as Director for Iraq at the US National Security Council and is a retired US Army officer with two tours in Iraq.

Survival | vol. 66 no. 2 | April–May 2024 | pp. 99–114   https://doi.org/10.1080/00396338.2024.2332063

seems to have had little long-term effect after being put down by violence. One major Shia faction in Iraq – the Sadrists – have removed themselves from politics, both withdrawing their winning parliamentarians from the current national government and refusing to participate in the recent provincial elections. Major Sunni politicians, including the former speaker of the House, Mohamed al-Halbousi, have been banned from politics by court order. Iraq continues to suffer from routine military violations of its sovereignty, as Iran, Turkiye and the United States use missiles (and in the Turkish case, ground forces) to attack sub-state groups. Meanwhile, Mustafa al-Kadhimi, the former prime minister who had been the United States' preferred candidate, now lives in exile under a cloud of plausible accusations of his involvement in the $2.5 billion theft of Iraq tax receipts in what has been called the 'heist of the century'.[1]

Yet Iraq's continuing stabilisation has improved its standing in the region. It has gradually reopened diplomatic relations with Gulf Arab states, and facilitated talks between Iran and Saudi Arabia in 2021 and 2022, a process that bore fruit at a later stage with China in the mediator's role.[2] In 2021 and 2022, key Arab states, Iran and Turkiye attended the Baghdad Conference for Cooperation and Partnership, a short-lived effort by France to facilitate Iraq's reintegration in the region. In 2023, Iraq hosted the Arabian Gulf Cup in Basra that showcased for its neighbours its social and economic recovery.

Iraq's partial success story has now been called into question, however. The conflict in Gaza has sharpened the stakes for Iraq's leaders, who have been compelled to rethink the careful balancing act underlying the country's national-security strategy, which seeks to manage what is likely to be a perpetual competition between Washington and Tehran. On 3 March 2024, Prime Minister Mohammed Shia' Al Sudani told a think-tank audience in Baghdad: 'Iraq is the only country in the region that maintains excellent relations with both Iran and the United States, working on multiple fronts to foster rapprochement.'[3]

The upheaval in Gaza has mobilised the most radical Iraqi militias, which operate independently of the formal security apparatus. As of spring 2024, it seemed more likely than not that US forces would be asked to leave the country. In the words of an adviser to Prime Minister Sudani: 'Iraq doesn't want to be the backyard of any conflict nor an arena for settling scores.'[4] A departure of American and allied forces would reduce Iraq's exposure to outbreaks of violence stemming from tensions between Washington and Tehran.

The 2,500 US troops still present in Iraq perform only training and counter-terrorism functions, and do not have the authority to conduct conventional military operations. They operate under standard rules of engagement with respect to force protection. More than 150 violent encounters between radical, pro-Iranian Iraqi militias and US forces in Iraq, Jordan and Syria have taken place since 7 October 2023. The US has responded with lethal attacks against senior militia leaders in Baghdad. These episodes have reminded the Iraqi public of the violation of their country's sovereignty that occurred in January 2020, when the US killed Iranian official Qasem Soleimani, leader of the Quds Force of the Islamic Revolutionary Guard Corps (IRGC), and Abu Mahdi al-Muhandis, the commander of Iraq's Hashd al-Shaabi forces.

The widening of the regional crisis that began with Hamas's attack on Israel on 7 October, along with US support for Israel's military campaign against Hamas, is entangling Iraq in the conflict between the US and the Iran-aligned Islamic resistance movement. While Iraq has eschewed any deep involvement in the Israel–Palestine question for decades, public interest in the plight of the Palestinians has heightened, and the expression of anti-Israel and anti-Western views has increased.[5] Attacks on US bases and facilities in Iraq, which invite US military responses, are threatening the delicate balance Iraq has maintained in its relations with Washington and Tehran. Any appearance that Iraq is repudiating its relationship with Washington would foster perceptions that Iran and the 'axis of resistance' it leads are winning the regional struggle for primacy.

Evolution of Iraq's security sector since 2003

The United States' 2003 invasion of Iraq continues to profoundly affect Iraq's security players and institutions. Some would argue that any flaws in contemporary Iraq's security structures and practices can be traced to the invasion, when US occupiers made critical choices to disband the Saddam-era army, Ministry of Defence and intelligence agencies. The goal was to create a new political system representing all of Iraq's sectarian and ethnic groups, and to rely more on law enforcement and newly created intelligence and counter-terrorism organisations than on the once-privileged military of the *ancien régime*.[6]

The gradual and uneven evolution of Iraq's national-security community has been an important priority for the US and NATO over the past two decades, but this interest has not always been welcomed by Iraq's political parties, militia organisations or civil society. Understanding the country's security culture and decision-making is critical to assessing whether and when Iraq might be fully restored to its traditional status as one of the power centres of the Middle East, with a strong professional military that is capable of defending its territory and deterring would-be adversaries from preying on its land, people and resources.

The presence of US troops in Iraq has been a point of friction since United Nations Security Council Resolution 1790, which authorised the presence of multinational forces, expired at the end of 2008.[7] The United States and Iraq held negotiations on a successor agreement throughout 2008, and after several rejected drafts, a mutually agreed text was adopted in November of that year.[8] The agreement extended the presence of US troops by three years, to the end of 2011. Americans tended to refer to this final text as 'SOFA' (status-of-forces agreement), but it was more properly the 'Withdrawal Agreement', based on the requirement that US forces withdraw at the end of the three years.[9] The agreement was adhered to by the Maliki and Obama administrations, and all US forces left Iraq by the end of 2011.

Those who had predicted negative consequences from the withdrawal may have felt some vindication in June 2014, when the Islamic State came seemingly from nowhere to capture Mosul – Iraq's second-largest city – before sweeping further south and east to capture Kirkuk, threatening both Baghdad and Erbil. At the height of the Islamic State's power, about 30% of the country was occupied by the radical group, which was composed primarily of Iraqis and Syrians, along with other Sunni Arabs. The failure of the Iraqi Army and police forces to prevent this humiliating loss of territory to a non-state group called into question the viability of the US training enterprise. While the Iraqi Army's embarrassing performance shocked

Washington, Baghdad and Tehran took action to prevent the total collapse of the state.[10]

Iraq quickly formed, with the blessing of Shia religious leader Grand Ayatollah Ali al-Sistani, a new security organisation, the Hashd al-Shaabi or Popular Mobilisation Units/Forces, operating independently from the Ministry of Defence to immediately protect Baghdad. Consisting of volunteers drawn primarily from Iraq's Shia south, the Hashd incorporated cadres from Iraq's religious establishment and militia groups that had formed to oppose either the Ba'ath regime or the American occupation. These groups were largely organised and coordinated by Iran's IRGC and its Hizbullah allies in Lebanon.

The United States belatedly returned to Iraq in autumn 2014 to assist in the training and equipping of the Iraqi Army, as well as the country's counter-terrorism forces and the Kurdish Peshmerga. The US did not engage directly with the Hashd. While the details of the 2014 agreement (still in force today) between the United States and Iraq have not been made public, it is widely rumoured that US forces are there under a government-to-government agreement that can be revoked by either side, though there is reportedly a clause that gives the US one year to complete a withdrawal so that this is accomplished in an orderly manner. Table 1 provides estimated personnel levels for each Iraqi security service.

The return of the United States in late 2014 essentially created two parallel and competing security-sector reform efforts. One, led by the US with help from its coalition, focuses on the Ministry of Defence, the Counter Terrorism Service and the Peshmerga. The US assists all three institutions through advising, training, participation in the foreign-military sales process, and financial assistance for the purchase of military hardware via

Table 1: **Estimated personnel levels of Iraqi defence institutions as of 2024**

Institution	Personnel
Iraqi Army	190,000
Kurdish Peshmerga	150,000
Counter Terrorism Service	10,000–13,500 (2016)
Hashd	100,000–160,000

Sources: CIA, 'Iraq', World Factbook, https://www.cia.gov/the-world-factbook/countries/iraq/; and David Witty, 'The Iraqi Counter Terrorism Service', Center for Middle East Policy, Brookings Institution, p. 26, n. 238. Note that estimates of Iraqi personnel levels may vary.

foreign-military financing and the Counter-ISIS Train and Equip fund. In addition, all three forces are able to send officers and soldiers to military schools in the United States via the International Military Education and Training programme.

The second effort, led by the Iranians with assistance from Hizbullah, focuses on the Hashd. While the United States and others prefer to think of the Hashd as a temporary force that will eventually be drawn under the control of the Ministry of Defence, it seems clear that its fighters do not see themselves that way. The Hashd, in the wake of the army's failure, seems intent on preventing any future large-scale violations of Iraq's sovereignty. Its members appear to believe that the army and Ministry of Defence cannot be trusted with that responsibility, and therefore Hashd fighters are the true defenders of the state.

In the north, the two major Kurdish parties, the Kurdish Democratic Party and the Patriotic Union of Kurdistan, had nominally merged their militia forces under the Ministry of Peshmerga Affairs, which promised to provide a unified security force reporting to the Kurdistan Regional Government. However, no neutral observer believes that the Peshmerga have ever truly taken orders from the ministry, deferring instead to the party leaders that formed them in the first place. Despite major US and NATO efforts to encourage integration, Peshmerga forces have retained these party loyalties.

The Counter Terrorism Service (CTS) had been trained by US and allied special forces since their founding in 2003 and 2004 as two distinct units that were merged into a brigade force in May 2004. The relationship between what were originally called the Iraqi Special Operations Forces (ISOF) and their US Special Forces counterparts became extremely close. During the occupation period, American special-forces units tended to return for repeated tours to advise the same ISOF units (one of the authors personally observed this in 2004), and ISOF leaders were often selected by US Special Forces commanders

While the CTS would achieve some notoriety in 2011–14 as the 'Dirty Brigade' that enforced then-prime minister Nuri al-Maliki's policies, its role in the ISIS campaign elevated it, as well as its field commander, General Abdul-Wahab al-Saadi, to near-mythical status in the Iraqi public eye. The CTS was in a slightly better position than other Western-sponsored forces during this interim period, as support continued via the office of security cooperation at the US Embassy, as well as – reportedly – from the CIA.[11]

Competing priorities

The evolution of Iraq's security apparatus since 2003 has produced a system characterised by overlapping and redundant institutions. The Ministry of Interior and Ministry of Defence continue to perform duties comparable to similar institutions in other ministerial systems, with the former providing oversight for local police, and directly commanding the Department of Border Enforcement and the National Police. The Ministry of Defence administers the army, air force and navy. By post-2003 tradition, the Iraqi defence minister is a Sunni Arab and the interior minister a Shia Arab.

The CTS works outside the ministerial system, reporting directly to the prime minister. It had achieved this 'quasi-ministerial status' by 2007.[12] The Kurdish Peshmerga are not represented in the federal ministerial system either, though there is a minister of Peshmerga affairs within the Kurdistan Regional Government. As noted, the Peshmerga's primary loyalties lie with party leaders rather than the minister.

The Hashd, like the CTS, reports directly to the prime minister's office. As a result, both the Hashd and the CTS suffer from a lack of ministerial or parliamentary oversight. Moreover, like the Peshmerga, the primary loyalty of Hashd forces is to the political parties that originally formed them, and not necessarily to the leadership of the Hashd Commission. Thus, a member of the Badr Organization will be most loyal to Hadi al-Amiri, a member of Asaib Ahl al-Haq to Qais Khazali, and a member of the Peace Brigades to Moqtada al-Sadr.

A distinctive feature of some Hashd groups is that they see themselves as having a mandate outside the territorial borders of Iraq as members of the Islamic resistance, a mandate which is independent of any Iraqi government.[13] A substantial minority of the Shia Hashd see an extraterritorial mission to defend the worldwide Shia community as a core interest, though it is not always clear how seriously any given faction takes this rhetoric. In some cases, this mission needs to be balanced with the necessity of being part of the Iraqi state apparatus, whether for reasons of patriotism, power or resources.

A similar pattern of competing interests is discernible within Iran's security architecture. Observers have identified two parallel security efforts, one in which the IRGC supports the pro-Iranian Hashd factions with which it feels closely aligned ideologically, and a second, led by the Iranian presidency and Foreign Ministry, which is a more mainstream, state-to-state security effort in which the stability of Iraq is viewed as the higher good.[14]

It is possible that a desire among Iran's pre-revolutionary institutions to support security structures in Iraq stems in part from its resentment of the IRGC's role in Iran. This does not mean that traditional Iranian institutions do not support Hashd groups – they absolutely do. But many Iranian actors appear to favour the integration of the Hashd into traditional state institutions, again likely reflecting their wishes about the IRGC. Iranians holding these views have lent their support to groups aligned with Grand Ayatollah Sistani, seeing them as most closely linked to the state and therefore most likely to produce a stable outcome.

Since the October 2023 Hamas attack on Israel and subsequent Israeli attacks on Gaza, the two most dedicated Islamic resistance groups, Kataib Hezbollah and the Nujaba movement (both designated by the US as terrorist groups), have conducted attacks on US assets in both Iraq and Syria. However, Asaib Ahl al-Haq ('Leagues of the Righteous' or AAH), traditionally seen as aligned with these groups, has not. AAH is notorious for its sophisticated abduction, and eventual murder, of US soldiers from an Iraqi police station in Karbala in early 2007, and its kidnapping of a British hostage, Peter Moore, in May 2007, who was held for more than two years. However, AAH – via its political wing, Al-Sadiqoun – is now a part of the Shia Coordination Framework and therefore of Iraq's governing coalition. Whether because being part of the government has moderated its stance, or because it wishes to safeguard opportunities for financial gain, AAH has not seen fit to follow fellow resistance members in, well, resistance.[15]

A key unanswered question about Iraq's security apparatus is whether other groups that are part of the 'state within a state' will change their orientation should they find a power base within the state itself. Is it possible that doing so is a more attractive political option than maintaining a nebulous status that is neither fully in nor fully out? Or will groups follow what one study sees as the example set by the Badr Organization, which 'oscillates between a "state-within-state" vision and acceptance of a functioning Iraq state (with the Badr organization as a key actor)'?[16]

New crisis in US–Iraq relations

The Gaza war has exacerbated pre-existing tensions about the presence of US and coalition forces in Iraq. At their peak in 2007, there were more than 100,000 American personnel in Iraq. This dropped to 50,000 in 2009–11, with some tens of thousands present during the anti-ISIS campaign. There is now a residual force of 2,500 in Baghdad, Erbil and Al-Asad air base in Anbar. Some have asked why these troops remain given that ISIS was defeated in 2017. This unease came to a head in the wake of the January 2020 killings of Soleimani and Muhandis. The Iraqi parliament immediately passed a resolution calling for the ejection of US forces from Iraq – but without action by the council of ministers, the action was non-binding, much like a 'sense of the Congress' resolution would be in the US. The resolution did communicate deep frustration with a force that was seen to have violated the terms of its mandate by participating in the killing of an Iraqi security official.

The urgency of the issue seemed to diminish over time, until the onset of the war in Gaza. That conflict has produced a dramatic increase in attacks on US targets in the Middle East: according to one tabulation, an attack on Tower 22 in Jordan on 26 January that killed three US servicemembers was the 166th such attack since 7 October 2023. Virtually all of the attacks are assessed to have been conducted by the pro-Iran Kataib Hezbollah or the Nujaba movement.

These attacks placed the government of Prime Minister Sudani in an awkward position. Sudani has made it clear that he wants a good relationship with the United States – he has been invited to the White House and is rumoured to be planning a trip for April 2024. But until the Tower 22 attack, Sudani appeared unable to prevent these militia actions. After that attack, Kataib Hezbollah expressed remorse, declaring that it would suspend its operations against 'occupation forces'. The group's secretary-general explained that the decision had been made 'in order to prevent embarrassment of the Iraqi government'.[17] This suspension had endured for more than six weeks by the time this article went to press, smoothing the path for Sudani's Washington visit.

While the US presence is deeply unpopular, the prime minister's primary fear is of a widening conflict on Iraqi soil. Both Iraqi and American casualties are deeply destabilising for the country's society and government. Sudani – along with most of his government – understands the reassuring signal that the US presence provides to the international community. When American forces come under constant attack, however, this inverts the signal by giving the impression of lawlessness.

The process of negotiating the removal of the residual American forces appears to be under way. On 25 January 2024, a Higher Military Commission between the US Department of Defense and the Iraqi Ministry of Defence was announced that 'fall[s] within the spirit of our 2008 Strategic Framework Agreement'.[18] Should this move be interpreted as the beginning of the end of the US presence, it may have the effect of extending the renewed truce between the US and Iraqi militias during the negotiations. If it doesn't, it may be necessary for the Sudani government to accept the diplomatic rift that would accompany an abrupt revocation of the invitation for the US forces.

The fallout from any Iraqi insistence on the withdrawal of US forces would play out on several levels. Security officials in both countries would see a genuine vulnerability arising from a serious rupture in the security partnership. Iraq might face the curtailing, though probably not the full denial, of its access to US training programmes. More strategically, Iraqi leaders would worry about damaging the careful balance they have maintained between Washington and Tehran, and of losing the psychological and military value of the American presence. A key regional casualty of a US withdrawal would be American support for the Syrian Democratic Forces, comprising mainly Syrian Kurds, as the last bastion against the Islamic State and the threat it poses to the government in Damascus. Finding alternative means of supporting the US–Syrian mission could be challenging, but ironically, this would reflect a shared interest of the US and the Iraqi militias, to the extent it counters the Islamic State.

Implications of Iraq's security challenges

The current approach to security in Iraq – with its formal and informal characteristics – may be minimally acceptable to national leaders as being consistent with the country's complexities. It is less clear if there is a similar consensus among Iraq's diverse political factions, which still harbour mistrust of the central government and often default to personalised and communal politics. In an overlapping yet distinct concern, minority communities worry about radical Shia groups that are not under the direct control of the government, and fears of domestic conflict linger. Some may support a greater effort to consolidate security functions within the state, while others may see subnational militias as necessary to defend their communities from the Shia majority. Others, including former president Barham Salih, have promoted constitutional reforms that would strengthen the office of the president to mitigate the power of patronage and corruption in the current system.[19]

Iraq's delicate balancing act between Washington and Tehran has been put to the test many times, but no test has been as acute as the regional fallout from the Gaza war, which has brought into sharp relief the contradictions of Iraq's security system. The government in Baghdad now faces a difficult choice between mitigating the threat to its sovereignty by ending the US military presence in the country or insisting that Iraqi militias abide by the country's national-security strategy. Either option carries risks for the country's stability. As formal negotiations begin with Washington, it seems likely that Iraq's leaders will spend the next year or more trying to navigate internal pressures for reducing the US footprint, Washington's demands for more forceful action to rein in the militias and, presumably, demands from Iran to allow Shia groups to be part of the anti-Israel and anti-Western resistance. Security professionals and senior elected officials may prefer the status quo ante, but the pressures to demonstrate new approaches are strong. Political and military leaders who would like to keep doors open to Washington hope for a nuanced outcome that maintains cooperation, albeit in a different form.

Iraq's security partners in Washington and other Western capitals – which have spent two decades engaging with Iraq's military, intelligence and counter-terrorism agencies – will be watching this process closely. They will be loath to forfeit the progress that has been achieved, and the institutional investments that have been made. There has been recent improvement in the government's commitments to anti-corruption, and long-awaited infrastructure enhancements with direct and indirect implications for the country's security. Support remains within Iraqi ministries for a continued partnership, even if it has to be restructured. Officials in Baghdad will be expected to find ways to curb the activism of militias, even if a full-scale crackdown or a forced integration into the armed forces is more than the political market will bear. In particular, Washington must understand the political dynamics that allow the Hashd to operate as an independent security institution.

Some of Iraq's neighbours and friends among the world's middle and great powers see today's Iraq as relatively stable, or stable enough, despite the recent stresses. The country's Shia majority dominates national politics while carrying legal and political obligations to Sunni and Kurdish power centres, representing roughly 30% and 15% of the total Iraqi population respectively. So long as Iraq has no ambitions to engage militarily in any of the region's festering conflicts, its neighbours, including Iran, can maintain friendly relations, including varying degrees of security cooperation.

Not all of Iraq's neighbours are invested in its stability, however. Turkiye and Iran in particular have used coercion and other means to compel Iraq's leaders and subnational groups to acquiesce to their demands to pursue their national interests on Iraqi territory. Although a stable Iraq would be advantageous to both these regional powers in the long term, neither puts its strategic interest in Iraqi stability ahead of the short-term national interests that play out on Iraqi soil.

Meanwhile, the effects of the conflict in Gaza have been acutely felt in Iraq. It has become one of the main territories in which groups loosely identified as 'resistance forces' have upped the ante, conducting lethal attacks against the US as Israel's security guarantor. The suspension of these attacks suggested that some combination of Washington counter-attacks, Sudani's political capital and Iranian interest in avoiding further escalation had produced a shift in Hashd policy, however temporary.

The more strategic concern is whether any of Iraq's armed groups will emerge as regional threats comparable to Lebanon's Hizbullah or Yemen's

Houthis. Working in Iraq's favour is the fact that it enjoys a more cohesive and effective central government than either Lebanon or Yemen, and that the Hashd groups are more diverse and decentralised than their resistance counterparts. Still, the burden is on Baghdad to cultivate the nationalism of subnational groups and to encourage them to align their activities with state priorities.

Iraq's leaders aspire to a more prominent role in managing and containing these groups at the regional level, given the country's legacy as one of the great civilisations of the ancient Middle East, and its more recent status as a regional powerhouse by virtue of its energy wealth and military prowess. During the Saddam era, Iraq was often at the centre of regional power struggles between conservative monarchies and secular military regimes, but its excesses at home and abroad made it a pariah among Arab states by the time it invaded Kuwait in August 1990.

Iraq's oil production should enhance its clout

In recent years, Iraq's leaders have demonstrated considerable diplomatic skill in facilitating Saudi–Iranian rapprochement. Iraq's geography makes it a regional centre of gravity. It is well suited to act as a bridge between the Shia and Sunni worlds, and is equally well positioned to play a key diplomatic role between Ankara and Damascus.

Iraq has other assets with which to rebuild its regional brand. It has a potentially important economic role to play as a major oil producer and as a transit country for new supply routes. It still has work to do to recapitalise and upgrade its oil infrastructure, which has been damaged by war and corruption. Its oil and gas production should, over time, enhance its regional clout, as should plans for east–west transportation corridors that could provide an alternative to the Suez Canal for trade between Asia and Europe. At present, Iraq's efforts to attract regional attention and support, as exemplified by the Baghdad Conference for Cooperation and Partnership, have been stymied by the Gaza war. Meanwhile, regional momentum has shifted in favour of the Gulf states, the young leaders of which, while content to welcome Iraq back into the Arab family, are not prepared to defer to it as a major power that sets the agenda for the region.

Iraq will have a role to play in determining whether the Middle East remains in turmoil or finds a new equilibrium after the Gaza war. It has a stake in working to mitigate regional tensions, as it has proven to be vulnerable to geopolitical shocks (notably ISIS and Gaza). In times of relative stability, Iraq has opportunities to build, but in the Middle East, such moments can be fleeting. It is unlikely to emerge as a major driver of broader regional trends, but is gradually maturing into a democratising, multi-ethnic state with a complex but increasingly effective security system. Long-term assessments of Iraq need to capture its uneven, fitful and contingent progress. Iraq is, through this lens, a textbook case of a transition from authoritarian rule. The textbook would tell us not to be surprised if the future holds setbacks as well as successes.[20]

Notes

1 See Simona Foltyn, '"Heist of the Century": How $2.5bn Was Plundered from Iraqi State Funds', *Guardian*, 20 November 2022, https://www.theguardian.com/world/2022/nov/20/heist-century-iraq-state-funds-tax-embezzlement.

2 It is worth noting that Iraq was never tempted by the Abraham Accords, the Trump-era project to encourage normalisation of security and economic relations between Israel and major Arab states, particularly in the Gulf, and it has not been involved in any talks (currently on hold) to expand the accords to Saudi Arabia.

3 Media Office of the Prime Minister of Iraq, 'Prime Minister Mohammed S. Al-Sudani Participates in Al-Rafidain Forum For Dialogue 2024', 3 March 2024.

4 Farhad Alaaldin, 'Iraq Doesn't Want to Be an Area for Settling Scores', *National*, 8 February 2024, https://www.thenationalnews.com/opinion/comment/2024/02/08/iraq-war-isis-terrorism-security/#Echobox=1707375003.

5 Iraq remains in a formal state of war with Israel and recently passed legislation criminalising any discussion of normalising relations in the absence of a resolution to the Palestine question.

6 Safa al-Sheikh Hussein, 'Iraq's Security Sector: Twenty Years of Dashed Hopes', Chatham House, 17 April 2023, https://www.chathamhouse.org/2023/03/iraq-20-years-insider-reflections-war-and-its-aftermath.

7 The majority of troops assigned to what is technically a combined and joint task force (with a British deputy commander) are American.

8 Rick Brennan, Jr, et al., *Ending the U.S. War in Iraq: The Final Transition, Operational Maneuver, and Disestablishment of United States*

Forces–Iraq (Santa Monica, CA: RAND Corporation, 2013), pp. 62–4.

9   The full text of the 'Withdrawal Agreement' is available at https://graphics8.nytimes.com/packages/pdf/world/20081119_SOFA_FINAL_AGREED_TEXT.pdf.

10   This paragraph is taken from Douglas Ollivant, 'Why Iraq Is Calling for the Withdrawal of U.S. Forces', Dispatch, 16 January 2024, https://thedispatch.com/article/why-iraq-is-calling-for-the-withdrawal-of-u-s-forces/.

11   David Witty, 'The Iraqi Counter Terrorism Service', Center for Middle East Policy at Brookings, 2016, pp. 24–5.

12   *Ibid.*, p. 11.

13   This is not true of all Hashd groups, however. The Christian, Shabak and Sunni brigades within the Hashd lack this orientation by definition. Those closely associated with the religious establishments in Najaf and Karbala are also unlikely to be closely aligned with the IRGC. Likewise, the Sadrist elements of the Hashd, despite being fiercely anti-US and anti-Israel, keep a critical distance from the IRGC and its training efforts.

14   See Christian Høj Hansen and Troels Burchall Henningsen, 'Whose Proxy War? The Competition Among Iranian Foreign Policy Elites in Iraq', *Small Wars & Insurgencies*, vol. 33, no. 6, 2002, pp. 973–98, https://doi.org/10.1080/09592318.2022.2064152.

15   According to Inna Rudolph: 'The behavior of the Islamic resistance factions on the ground and their readiness to interfere in the national decision-making process depend more strongly on their domestic agenda as well as on their interpretation of the contours of power.' Inna Rudolph, 'Iraq's Popular Mobilization Units', in Assaf Moghadam, Vladimir Rauta and Michel Wyss (eds), *Routledge Handbook of Proxy Wars* (Abingdon: Routledge, 2023), p. 359.

16   Hansen and Hennningsen, 'Whose Proxy War?', p. 983.

17   Max Matza, 'Kataib Hezbollah: Iran-backed Group Suspends Attacks Against US After Drone Strike', BBC News, 31 January 2024, https://www.bbc.com/news/world-us-canada-68150359.

18   US Department of Defense, 'Senior Defense, Military and State Department Officials Hold a U.S.–Iraq Higher Military Commission Background Briefing', 25 January 2024, https://www.defense.gov/News/Transcripts/Transcript/Article/3656654/senior-defense-military-and-state-department-officials-hold-a-us-iraq-higher-mi/. The text of the 'Strategic Framework Agreement for a Relationship of Friendship and Cooperation Between the United States of America and the Republic of Iraq' signed on 17 November 2008 is available at https://2009-2017.state.gov/documents/organization/122076.pdf.

19   Barham Salih, '20 Years After Liberation, Iraq Needs Root-and-branch Reform', *Foreign Policy*, 24 April 2023, https://foreignpolicy.com/2023/04/24/iraq-war-liberation-saddam-political-system-constitution-reform/.

20   See Gillermo O'Donnell and Philippe C. Schmitter, *Transitions from Authoritarian Rule: Tentative Conclusions About Uncertain Democracies* (Baltimore, MD: Johns Hopkins University Press, 1986).

Red Sea Tensions, Tanker War Lessons?

Ethan J. Lee

The Red Sea is the gateway for 15% of global seaborne trade.[1] Shortly after the start of the Gaza war that followed Hamas's brutal 7 October 2023 attack on Israel, Yemen's Iran-backed Houthi rebel movement began to target Israel and international shipping transiting this waterway to pressure Israel to stand down in Gaza. American, British, Egyptian, French, Israeli and Saudi forces successfully intercepted some Houthi attacks, while China, India, Iran and Italy increased their naval presence in the region. On 12 January 2024, the United States and the United Kingdom began a military campaign to degrade the Houthis' ability to threaten commerce. As of early March, however, the Houthi threat to maritime shipping – which has substantially disrupted the flow of trade – had shown little sign of stopping.

Some critics of US President Joe Biden urged his administration to confront the Houthis, other Iran-backed groups and Tehran itself more aggressively. They invoked as precedent the Reagan administration's military action against Iran during the Iran–Iraq War of 1980–88. Both Iran and Iraq targeted merchant shipping in what became known as the 'Tanker War'. It peaked following Iran's mine attack on an American frigate in April 1988, when the US Navy retaliated against Iranian forces in *Operation Praying Mantis*. On 3 July 1988, the USS *Vincennes* also mistakenly shot down an

Ethan J. Lee is assistant editor and David M. Rubenstein Editorial Fellow at *Foreign Affairs*.

Survival | vol. 66 no. 2 | April–May 2024 | pp. 115–126   https://doi.org/10.1080/00396338.2024.2332064

Iranian commercial airliner, killing all 290 civilians aboard. A little over a month later, Tehran accepted a ceasefire ending the Iran–Iraq War.

In December 2023, William Luti, a former senior Pentagon and National Security Council official, characterised the operation as a 'case study in strengthening deterrence'.[2] Former supreme allied commander of NATO James Stavridis added on 3 January 2024 that in 1988, 'Iran got the message. Perhaps it is time to send it again.'[3] Former CIA officer Reuel Marc Gerecht argued that without an 'updated version' of *Operation Praying Mantis* Iran would continue its proxy war.[4]

Facile interpretations of the Tanker War's history, however, can contribute to misguided comparisons and expectations. In both conflicts, Iran was the source of attacks on maritime commerce, and the United States attempted to tightly manage the use of force to counter them and control escalation. But the US is currently in an asymmetric conflict against Iran-backed non-state armed groups rather than conventional Iranian forces in the Gulf, and strategically constrained from bringing American military power to bear in a decisive and straightforward manner. In the 1980s, moreover, Iran's primary concern was major war with Iraq, which threatened the clerical regime's grip on power and reduced its military capacity to challenge US forces. At present, Iran has no comparable distraction.

Is past prologue?

The Iran–Iraq War was a protracted, brutal conflict that resulted in millions of casualties. Iraqi leader Saddam Hussein wanted to prevent the spread of the Iranian Revolution, fearing Tehran's incitement of discord between Iraq's Shia majority and its Sunni-led government. Baghdad also wanted to dominate the Persian Gulf and establish effective control over Iran's oil-rich Khuzestan province. In September 1980, Iraq invaded Iran with approximately 200,000 troops, expecting an easy victory due to Iran's post-revolution turmoil and lack of international support. But the Iraqi advance stalled after three months and, by mid-1982, Iran had recaptured almost all lost territory and launched its own offensive into Iraqi territory.[5]

Bolstered by both Western and Soviet-aligned states' military assistance – including in developing and using chemical weapons – Iraq began attacking

Iranian cities and maritime infrastructure in 1984. Baghdad aimed to provoke Tehran into taking drastic actions that would convince external powers, particularly the United States, to intervene. Washington had warned Tehran that the US would step in if Iranian forces attempted to blockade the Strait of Hormuz. Tehran initially responded to Baghdad's maritime expansion of the conflict with limited reprisals, attacking only Iraqi shipping while keeping the strait open to other maritime traffic, on which Iran's economy also relied. But by 1986, both countries were attacking non-combatant ships to deprive each other of trade.

Kuwait appealed for international help to safeguard its shipping. Moscow offered it by chartering Kuwaiti tankers, whereupon Washington began to escort reflagged Kuwaiti oil tankers in what became the biggest convoy operation since the Second World War. In May 1987, Iraqi missiles hit the guided-missile frigate USS *Stark* while it traversed international waters, killing 37 sailors. Iraq blamed Iran for the circumstances surrounding the incident, and Ronald Reagan stated that the United States had never considered Iraq hostile.[6] In April 1988, the USS *Samuel B. Roberts*, a guided-missile frigate, struck a mine and nearly sank while transiting the Persian Gulf. Additional mines recovered from the area matched those seized aboard an Iranian mine-laying ship the year before. The incident prompted the Reagan administration to greenlight *Operation Praying Mantis*, which was intended as a limited operation targeting Iran's military presence in the Persian Gulf to compel Tehran to stop threatening maritime commerce. Three American surface-action groups were tasked to sink one of the Iranian Navy's pre-revolution *Alvand*-class frigates and destroy three oil platforms used by Iran's Islamic Revolutionary Guard Corps as military and surveillance outposts.[7]

The American operation began with a naval attack on two of the oil platforms, prompting Iran to launch an air and sea counter-attack against US forces and commercial traffic in the Persian Gulf. Within a few hours, US warships and aircraft had destroyed half of Iran's naval forces.[8] Before the US Navy struck the third oil platform, Washington ended offensive operations, even as Iran continued fighting by launching ground-based, anti-ship *Silkworm* cruise missiles against American ships – none of which hit – and preparing for a follow-on strike with attack aircraft.[9] Iran was significantly outgunned and faced the prospect of heavy losses, and its seemingly unreasonable reaction to a limited American operation puzzled US officials. To prevent further escalation while protecting the United States' reputation for resolve – Washington had issued repeated deterrent threats against the use of *Silkworm* missiles – American officials equivocated on the existence of the attacks and refrained from retaliating. They recognised that a US counter-attack against *Silkworm* launch and storage sites could escalate to full-scale war, and doubted that limited strikes would neutralise the threat these missiles posed.[10]

The Tanker War lasted four years and ultimately resulted in damage to more than 500 commercial ships and the deaths of more than 400 civilian sailors.[11] In the end, it did not substantially affect oil exports from the Gulf, nor did it lead to prolonged increases in the price of oil. Estimates suggest that Iranian and Iraqi actions disrupted no more than 2% of the shipping traffic in the Gulf.[12] Iran sought peace by July 1988, a decision attributable to what the Iranian leadership saw as a series of coordinated developments: *Operation Praying Mantis*, which shifted the balance of power in the Gulf towards Iraq; lack of international sympathy for Iran after the USS *Vincennes* incident; and, most importantly, Iraq's decisively retaking all its lost territory, capturing dozens of Iranian towns and threatening a renewed large-scale invasion further into Iran and additional chemical-weapons attacks against Iranian cities.

Strait expectations

The United States and Iran's long-standing mutual hostility is central to the conflict in Yemen. Building on lessons learned from its experiences in Afghanistan, Iraq, Lebanon, the Persian Gulf and Syria, Tehran has heeded the advice that 'there are two ways to fight the United States: asymmetrically or stupidly'.[13] It has consolidated a military doctrine of forward defence, seeking to confront the United States and other adversaries with proxy groups in neighbouring countries with an eye to pushing the US out of the Middle East and deterring American and Israeli military action against Iranian interests.[14] Iran provides funding, weapons and training to members of a so-called 'axis of resistance', which includes Hamas and

Palestinian Islamic Jihad in the occupied territories, Hizbullah in Lebanon, the Popular Mobilisation Units and Kataib Hezbollah in Iraq, and the Houthi movement in Yemen. The Houthis have, of course, effectively resisted the Saudi-led military intervention in Yemen's civil war to support Yemen's internationally recognised government. Even before Hamas's 7 October attack, Houthi rebels attempted to carry out over two dozen attacks on maritime commerce.[15]

Between the beginning of the Gaza war and March 2024, the Houthi movement had attempted more than 100 attacks on Israeli territory and commercial ships associated with 35 countries, including a helicopter hijacking that resulted in a hostage crisis that was ongoing as this article went to press.[16] Houthi leaders have repeatedly stated that their attacks will continue until Israel ends the war and Gaza receives adequate humanitarian assistance.[17] The Houthi attacks have disrupted global trade more severely than the Tanker War: over half of the commercial traffic bound for the Red Sea region has rerouted around Africa, significantly impacting the Suez Canal's $10 billion annual contribution to the debt-ridden Egyptian economy while doubling or tripling war-risk insurance premiums for maritime commerce.[18] Other geo-economic complications exacerbate the problem. The Panama Canal's capacity has been reduced due to low water levels, necessitating the rerouting of Asia-to-America shipping to the Suez Canal and, now, around Africa. Europe's reliance on Middle Eastern oil has grown due to sanctions on Russian energy. Red Sea disruptions have thus far failed to trigger the worst potential market shocks, but J.P. Morgan Research predicts that global core-goods inflation will rise by 0.7% in the first half of 2024, with the Organisation for Economic Co-operation and Development warning that a doubling of seaborne-freight rates could lead to nearly a 5% increase in import prices.[19] Smaller disruptions will ripple through global supply chains, likely producing noticeable increases in delivery times, higher consumer costs and heightened economic discontent.

Citing declassified American intelligence, the White House asserted in mid-December that Iran was 'deeply involved' in planning Houthi attacks.[20] Tehran, which publicly acknowledges its support for armed groups such as the Houthi movement, claimed that its proxies' recent attacks were of their own accord, maintaining plausible deniability.[21] To address the Houthi maritime threat, Washington assembled a 20-country naval task force to escort ships in December 2023, with at least eight countries in the task force opting to remain anonymous in light of the Israel–Hamas war's political sensitivities.[22] After a series of attacks against a commercial vessel on 31 December, a US helicopter sank three assaulting Houthi boats, killing ten. On 9 January, Houthi rebels attempted a large-scale attack on a US carrier strike group and a UK destroyer that was ultimately intercepted, contradicting Washington's earlier assertions that Houthi forces were not directly attacking US forces.[23] Two days later, US Navy SEALs raided a dhow off the coast of Somalia, resulting in the dhow's sinking, the capture of its crew and the drowning of two SEALs. Only after several days had passed did the Pentagon acknowledge that the dhow was transporting missile components from Iran to Houthi forces.[24] By then, the United States, the United Kingdom, and other key allies had issued a joint statement to compel an end to Houthi attacks.[25] The United Nations Security Council passed a resolution demanding a halt to the attacks and the release of captured vessels and crews.[26] On 12 January, US and UK aircraft and warships and an American attack submarine launched hundreds of cruise missiles and precision-guided munitions at more than 60 targets in Yemen.[27]

A critical comparison

The Iran–Iraq War was a Cold War-era inter-state conflict between neighbours over territory, with both the West and the Soviet Union backing Iraq to 'engineer a stalemate', and only Libya, North Korea and Syria exclusively siding with Iran.[28] Iran and Iraq used their naval forces to target each other's seaborne trade – particularly oil exports – as part of what both understood to be total war. Both countries' economies relied on their trade flowing through the Strait of Hormuz, and Washington's primary objective was to maintain the flow of oil.

Today's crisis is markedly different. Russia and China broadly support an increasingly assertive Iran, which greenlit its armed proxies' latest round of attacks against Israel and US assets. Iran has capitalised on the war in Gaza to rally public support across the region against the United States and Israel. Washington is reluctant to re-immerse itself in the region, and this time Washington has been unable to avoid targeting on-shore missile launchers. In addition, the Houthis' attacks in the Red Sea region have been relatively indiscriminate, with targets ranging from a tanker transporting Russian oil to an Iran-bound grain ship.[29] During the Tanker War, the US typically escorted only a handful of Kuwait's fleet of 11 tankers, and even that comparatively limited operation posed significant challenges, having been preceded by the Iraqi missile attack on the USS *Stark*.

The Houthi rebels' offensive weapons pose stiffer challenges than the mixture of small boats, mines, aircraft and ground-based anti-ship cruise missiles 40 years ago. Houthi attacks have relied heavily on ground-based drones and included the first instances of ballistic missiles being used to strike ships in a real-world setting. By compelling carriers to change their routes, the Houthi movement is exercising military power in a manner traditionally consigned to the air and naval forces of states, imposing lopsided costs on countries defending the commerce in jeopardy. For instance, the US Navy relies on interceptor missiles costing several million dollars each to defend against the Houthis' Iranian-built drones costing about $20,000 per unit.[30] Targeting drone and missile launchers in Yemen is also more complex than striking naval vessels in the Persian Gulf: fighters can move and conceal these weapons systems in western Yemen's mountainous terrain and urban centres until moments before launch.

Houthi-rebel attacks are ostensibly intended to force Israel to end the war in Gaza. Indeed, military support for the Palestinians has been a fixture of Yemeni politics and is deeply rooted in the Houthis' founding ideology. But belligerents often use compellent signals for purposes other than coercive bargaining, such as mobilising for war, legitimising the use of force and conveying a sense of last resort. In spite of international pressure and Washington's preferences, Israeli military action against Hamas probably will not end soon. It is also unlikely that the Houthis, who have a history of recruiting child soldiers and based their slogan 'Death to America, death to Israel, curse the Jews and victory to Islam' on a popular chant in Iran, will moderate their behaviour. The significant international attention to their movement increases its legitimacy as the dominant political force in Yemen, feeding into its own and Tehran's propaganda and enabling the Houthis to better compete with other armed groups for funding and support.[31] Iran, for its part, probably will not ask the Houthis to stand down, as the attacks sustain Iran's credibility as leader of the Shia resistance and ease the burden on other Iranian proxies to do so while avoiding the escalatory risk of direct Iranian action. The Houthi attacks also help to identify US military vulnerabilities to the benefit of all Iran-backed groups in the region.[32]

American and British military operations are attempting to compel an end to the pattern of Houthi attacks in the Red Sea region through a strategy of denial. A strict application of the Tanker War's history might suggest that such a strategy would work against the Houthis, as it did against Iran in the 1980s.[33] But the US and UK face a challenge more akin to the one Saudi Arabia encountered when it intervened in Yemen, with the Houthis continuing attacks against seaborne trade and US and UK forces counter-attacking concealed and hardened weapons-storage facilities, mobile drone and missile launchers, and radar and air-defence sites spread across western Yemen that are difficult to neutralise. Inhibiting allied operations are embedded advisers from Iran's Quds Force and Lebanon's Hizbullah, whom the US and UK are trying to avoid targeting due to escalation concerns. As of March, maritime trade in the region had not returned to normal levels. Washington and London now face classic dilemmas of asymmetric warfare: attacking civilians is easier than defending them, and the non-state actor wins by not losing.

*   *   *

The most informative aspects of the comparison of the two situations appear to be their differences rather than their similarities. Iran's decision not to continue escalating in 1988 was largely attributable to the consuming nature of its war with Iraq and the annihilation of its naval forces. Neither of these circumstances is present now: war does not existentially threaten the Iranian regime, and allied strikes have failed to decisively stop the Houthi movement from critically threatening international trade. Accordingly, the United States and its partners should be less than sanguine about their ability to control escalation in attempting to counter and deter Houthi attacks or directly retaliate against Iranian forces.

Tehran's Quds Force commanders likely maintain control over their proxies' strategies – the Houthis' in particular – and are probably averse to significant escalation since current dynamics yield benefits at acceptable risk. Greater uncertainty arises at the operational and tactical levels, where the Quds Force cannot restrain or specifically calibrate Houthi behaviour in the fog of war. Though part of the axis of resistance, the Houthi movement is still more autonomous than other Iranian proxies.[34] If Houthi attacks go too far and exceed Iranian guidance, Tehran would face the choice of distancing itself from or embracing the movement's actions. Tehran might well choose the latter course to preserve the cohesion of its axis of resistance and the viability of its forward-defence doctrine.

In the late 1980s, the consuming nature of the Iran–Iraq War was the key ingredient that enabled US military operations to halt Iranian maritime attacks and deter further escalation. A similar element is missing in the present circumstances, contributing to distinct contingencies and risks. To facilitate the safe passage of commerce while avoiding unsought escalation, Washington and London need to strike a delicate balance between offensive and defensive measures. Yet one or the other could increase domestic political pressure in Iran or the United States for retaliation, inadvertently leading to broader conflict. For the current crisis in the Red Sea, the Tanker War's essential lesson is its own limitation.

Notes

1   See Wailin Wong et al., 'Red Sea Tensions Spell Trouble for Global Supply Chains', NPR, 2 January 2024, https://www. npr.org/2024/01/02/1197959330/ red-sea-tensions-global-shipping.

2   William J. Luti, 'How We Deterred Iran in the Gulf Last Time', *Wall Street Journal*, 25 December 2023, https://www. wsj.com/articles/how-we-deterred-iran-

in-the-gulf-last-time-reagan-navy-opera tion-praying-mantis-580b3c95.

3   James Stavridis, 'Hit the Houthis – and Iran – Where It Counts', Bloomberg, 3 January 2024, https://www.bloomberg. com/opinion/articles/2024-01-03/ us-can-strike-houthi-and-iranian-targets-to-protect-red-sea-shipping.

4   Nick Schifrin and Dan Sagalyn, 'US Blames Iran-backed Militia for Deadly

Attack, Leaving Middle East on Edge', PBS NewsHour, 31 January 2024, https://www.pbs.org/newshour/show/u-s-blames-iran-backed-militia-for-deadly-attack-leaving-middle-east-on-edge.

5 See Efraim Karsh, *The Iran–Iraq War: 1980–1988* (Oxford: Osprey, 2002), pp. 12–59.

6 See Lou Cannon, 'Reagan Pays Tribute to Victims, Says Iran Is "the Real Villain"', *Washington Post*, 19 May 1987, https://www.washingtonpost.com/archive/politics/1987/05/20/reagan-pays-tribute-to-victims-says-iran-is-the-real-villain/c1d9607f-6f5a-4a8f-8f0e-238ef5f492e2/.

7 See Harold Lee Wise, 'One Day of War', *Naval History Magazine*, vol. 27, no. 2, March 2013, https://www.usni.org/magazines/naval-history-magazine/2013/march/one-day-war.

8 See Michael A. Palmer, *Command at Sea: Naval Command and Control Since the Sixteenth Century* (Cambridge, MA: Harvard University Press, 2007), pp. 308–14.

9 See Lee Allen Zatarain, *America's First Clash with Iran: The Tanker War, 1987–88* (Havertown, PA: Casemate Publishers, 2010), pp. 525–7.

10 See *ibid.*, pp. 631–91.

11 'Time to Step Back from Tanker War Two', *Lloyd's List*, 15 May 2019, https://lloydslist.com/LL1127507/Time-to-step-back-from-Tanker-War-Two.

12 See Martin S. Navias, 'Oil and Water: The Tanker Wars', *History Today*, vol. 69, no. 9, 8 August 2019, https://www.historytoday.com/archive/feature/oil-and-water-tanker-wars.

13 Attributed to Conrad Crane in H.R. McMaster, 'Preserving the Warrior Ethos', Hudson Institute, 1 November 2021, https://www.hudson.org/national-security-defense/preserving-the-warrior-ethos.

14 See Alex Vatanka, 'Whither the IRGC of the 2020s? Is Iran's Proxy Warfare Strategy of Forward Defense Sustainable?', *New America*, 15 January 2021, https://www.newamerica.org/future-security/reports/whither-irgc-2020s/.

15 See Håvard Haugstvedt, 'Red Sea Drones: How to Counter Houthi Maritime Tactics', *War on the Rocks*, 3 September 2021, https://warontherocks.com/2021/09/red-sea-drones-how-to-counter-houthi-maritime-tactics/; and Caleb Weiss, 'Analysis: Houthi Naval Attacks in the Red Sea', *Long War Journal*, 17 August 2019, https://www.longwarjournal.org/archives/2019/08/analysis-houthi-naval-attacks-in-the-red-sea.php.

16 See Chris Gordon, 'US, Allies Take On Over 100 Attacks by Houthis with New "Operation Prosperity Guardian"', *Air & Space Forces Magazine*, 18 December 2023, https://www.airandspaceforces.com/operation-prosperity-guardian-houthi-attacks/.

17 See Brad Lendon, 'Drones vs. Warships: How US Military Hardware Is Combatting Houthi Attacks on Maritime Shipping', CNN, 27 December 2023, https://www.cnn.com/2023/12/27/middleeast/red-sea-attacks-us-navy-warships-intl-hnk-ml/index.html.

18 See Alex Longley, Ruth Liao and Yongchang Chin, 'Shipping Insurance for Red Sea Transit

Soars After Mounting Attacks', Bloomberg, 20 December 2023, https://www.bloomberg.com/news/articles/2023-12-20/shipping-insurance-for-red-sea-transit-soars-as-attacks-persist; 'Commercial Suez Canal Traffic Down Almost 60% Since Houthi Attacks Began', SupplyChainBrain, 4 January 2024, https://www.supplychainbrain.com/articles/38789-commercial-suez-canal-traffic-down-almost-60-since-houthi-attacks-began; and Adam Taylor, 'Houthi Attacks on Shipping Threaten Global Consequences', *Washington Post*, 19 December 2023, https://www.washingtonpost.com/world/2023/12/19/houthi-red-sea-global-shipping-effects/.

19 See Sambit Mohanty, 'Red Sea Turmoil Has So Far Spared Oil Supplies, but Buyers Have Reasons to Worry', S&P Global, 7 February 2024, https://www.spglobal.com/commodityinsights/en/market-insights/blogs/oil/020724-red-sea-turmoil-spared-oil-supplies-buyers-reasons-to-worry; Jenni Reid, 'Red Sea Tensions Risk Significantly Higher Inflation, OECD Warns', CNBC, 5 February 2024, https://www.cnbc.com/2024/02/05/red-sea-tensions-risk-significantly-higher-inflation-oecd-warns-.html; and 'What Are the Impacts of the Red Sea Shipping Crisis?', J.P. Morgan, 8 February 2024, https://www.jpmorgan.com/insights/global-research/supply-chain/red-sea-shipping.

20 Quoted in Felicia Schwartz, 'US Says Iran "Deeply Involved" in Houthi Red Sea Shipping Attacks', *Financial Times*, 22 December 2023, https://www.ft.com/content/87325ffa-e1a7-4480-804b-a1cc42f8f141.

21 See Helene Cooper, Eric Schmitt and Julian E. Barnes, 'A U.S.–Iranian Miscalculation Could Lead to a Larger War, Officials Say', *New York Times*, 29 November 2023, https://www.nytimes.com/2023/11/29/us/politics/israel-iran-gaza-us-attacks.html.

22 See US Department of Defense, 'Statement from Secretary of Defense Lloyd J. Austin III on Ensuring Freedom of Navigation in the Red Sea', 18 December 2023, https://www.defense.gov/News/Releases/Release/Article/3621110/statement-from-secretary-of-defense-lloyd-j-austin-iii-on-ensuring-freedom-of-n/.

23 See Lolita C. Baldor, 'Who Are the Houthis and Why Hasn't the U.S. Retaliated for Their Attacks on Ships in the Middle East?', PBS NewsHour, 12 January 2024, https://www.pbs.org/newshour/politics/who-are-the-houthis-and-why-hasnt-the-u-s-retaliated-for-their-attacks-on-ships-in-the-middle-east.

24 See Lolita C. Baldor, 'US Military Revises Account of What Happened to 2 SEALs Who Died Trying to Board Yemen-bound Ship', AP News, 31 January 2024, https://apnews.com/article/seals-navy-deceased-weapons-raid-yemen-2e1ce5eb4fda2ca789fa88f25cf8e9ba; and Julian E. Barnes and Eric Schmitt, 'Two SEAL Team Members Missing After Incident Off Somalia Coast', *New York Times*, 13 January 2024, https://www.nytimes.com/2024/01/13/us/politics/navy-seal-team-somalia-coast.html.

25 See White House, 'A Joint Statement from the Governments of the

United States, Australia, Bahrain, Belgium, Canada, Denmark, Germany, Italy, Japan, Netherlands, New Zealand, Republic of Korea, Singapore, and the United Kingdom', 3 January 2024, https://www.whitehouse.gov/briefing-room/statements-releases/2024/01/03/a-joint-statement-from-the-governments-of-the-united-states-australia-bahrain-belgium-canada-denmark-germany-italy-japan-netherlands-new-zealand-and-the-united-kingdom/.

26 See United Nations, 'Adopting Resolution 2722 (2024) by Recorded Vote, Security Council Demands Houthis Immediately Stop Attacks on Merchant, Commercial Vessels in Red Sea', 10 January 2024, https://press.un.org/en/2024/sc15561.doc.htm.

27 See Jon Gambrell et al., 'US Military Strikes Another Houthi-controlled Site After Warning Ships to Avoid Parts of Red Sea', AP News, 13 January 2024, https://apnews.com/article/yemen-houthis-us-ship-attacks-bombing-red-sea-iran-cc06d9186a00d1f22bea6b9c14dda12a.

28 Bob Woodward, *Veil: The Secret Wars of the CIA, 1981–1987* (New York: Simon & Schuster, 2007), p. 507.

29 See Patrick Wintour, 'Houthis Strike Iran-bound Grain Ship in First Red Sea Attack in Six Days', *Guardian*, 13 February 2024, https://www.theguardian.com/world/2024/feb/13/houthis-strike-iran-bound-grain-ship-in-first-red-sea-attack-in-six-days; and 'Houthis Mistakenly Target Tanker Carrying Russian Oil, Security Firm Says', Reuters, 12 January 2024, https://www.reuters.com/world/middle-east/houthis-mistakenly-target-tanker-carrying-russian-oil-ambrey-report-2024-01-12/.

30 See Laura Seligman and Matt Berg, 'A $2M Missile vs. a $2,000 Drone: Pentagon Worried over Cost of Houthi Attacks', *Politico*, 20 December 2023, https://www.politico.com/news/2023/12/19/missile-drone-pentagon-houthi-attacks-iran-00132480.

31 See Justin Conrad and William Spaniel, *Militant Competition: How Terrorists and Insurgents Advertise with Violence and How They Can Be Stopped* (Cambridge: Cambridge University Press, 2021); and Asher Orkaby, 'The Perils of Red Sea Piracy and Propaganda', *Diplomatic Courier*, 15 December 2023, https://www.diplomaticourier.com/posts/red-sea-piracy-propaganda.

32 See James Stavridis, 'US-led Naval Force Might Not End Houthi Ship Attacks', Bloomberg, 19 December 2023, https://www.bloomberg.com/opinion/articles/2023-12-19/can-us-led-naval-force-protect-ships-oil-in-red-sea-persian-gulf?.

33 See David B. Crist, 'Gulf of Conflict: A History of U.S.–Iranian Confrontation at Sea', Policy Focus no. 95, Washington Institute for Near East Policy, June 2009, https://www.washingtoninstitute.org/media/3423.

34 See Daniel Sobelman, 'Houthis in the Footsteps of Hizbullah', *Survival*, vol. 65, no. 3, June–July 2023, pp. 129–44.

Harnessing the Power of Cyber Defence

Peter Campbell and Michael J. Donahoo

The costs of malign behaviour on the internet are enormous. It is estimated that cyber crime will cost the global economy $10.5 trillion by 2025 – more than twice the GDP of Japan or Germany, the third- and fourth-largest economies in the world.[1] However, criminals are not the only ones profiting from the use of tools like ransomware and malware. States are building illicit revenue streams through the internet. North Korea has employed cyber attacks to steal $2 billion from banks and cryptocurrency exchanges to fund its weapons programmes.[2] In July 2021, NATO accused China of engaging in extensive cyber intrusions, most notably of the Microsoft Exchange Server.[3] Russia penetrated the Democratic National Committee (DNC) in 2016 in order to influence the US presidential election. More recently, Russian hackers broke into the information-technology firm SolarWinds, through which they gained access to the sensitive data of multiple US government agencies and departments.[4] It's nothing new.[5] The success of these intrusions has led many to denigrate remaining on the defensive in cyber and advocate unleashing offensive cyber operations. The executive and legislative branches of the US government have promoted a more aggressive approach to threats emanating from cyberspace. The Trump administration emphasised 'defending forward'. The McCain Act gave the US military

Peter Campbell is an associate professor of political science at Baylor University and author of *Military Realism: The Logic and Limits of Force and Innovation in the US Army* (University of Missouri Press, 2019). **Michael J. Donahoo** is a professor in the School of Engineering and Computer Science at Baylor University.

Survival | vol. 66 no. 2 | April–May 2024 | pp. 127–142   https://doi.org/10.1080/00396338.2024.2332065

the power to penetrate foreign adversaries' networks as a normal part of ensuring national security.[6] The second pillar of the Biden administration's National Cybersecurity Strategy is to 'disrupt and dismantle threat actors' in cyberspace using 'all the instruments of national power'.[7]

While the language employed has been defensive in tone, it often entails offensive action. For instance, US Cyber Command characterises 'defend forward' as follows: 'if a device, a network, an organization, or adversary nation is identified as a threat to US networks and institutions, or is actively attacking them in or through cyberspace – it can expect the United States to impose costs in response.' Stating that costs will be imposed not only on those actively attacking 'US networks and institutions' but also those considered 'a threat to US networks and institutions' implies that defend forward is not passive, but has offensive elements. The same goes for 'persistent engagement', which Cyber Command argues shifts its 'posture in cyberspace from reactive to proactive' and includes efforts to 'degrade the capabilities and networks of adversaries'.[8]

We define an action in cyberspace as offensive if it involves gaining unauthorised access to a computer network and then using that access to extract information, cause destruction or plant malicious code. This includes cyber espionage and intelligence operations. Under this definition, 'defend forward' and 'persistent engagement' are offensive. These actions may have defensive purposes, such as uncovering the offensive capabilities of an adversary to protect one's own networks. But they are not defensive in the sense of merely seeking to strengthen a network against intrusions and responding to intrusions only when they occur.

Before shifting resources into offensive cyber operations, it would be prudent to consider, and to the extent possible harness, the advantages of being on the defensive. Defensive modes of warfare tend to attract less scholarly interest than their offensive counterparts.[9] Our aim is to provide a more balanced assessment of the power of defensive measures, which can help moderate calls for a highly aggressive approach to cyber security. We argue that, properly assessed, cyber defence is strong and getting stronger. We tilt towards scholars such as Thomas Rid and Erik Gartzke, who have sought to reduce alarmism about cyber capabilities among policymakers and the public.[10]

The growing power of the defence

The offence–defence literature assesses whether it is easier to attack or to defend in war, how technology and geography alter the balance between the offence and the defence, and the effects of this balance on international relations, especially as a cause of war. An offence-dominant world is more war-prone because even non-aggressive actors are tempted to strike first.[11] A number of scholars have tried to assess the strengths, weaknesses and implications of the balance between offence and defence in cyberspace.[12] Ben Buchanan argues that the nature of cyber capabilities produces a cyber-security dilemma that explains the calls to unleash the cyber offence to secure the state. He notes that even states without hostile intentions must engage in offensive network penetrations to ready their cyber defences against an adversary's hidden offensive capabilities.[13] Others have argued that the relative weakness and impermanence of cyber attacks mean that offensive actions in cyber can actually ease security dilemmas. For example, resorting only to cyber attacks in response to a crisis could forestall crisis escalation and produce reassurance by signalling a country's intention not to extend warfare beyond cyberspace.[14]

Of course, the offence–defence balance can be misperceived, with disastrous consequences. Just prior to the First World War, the great powers had considerable faith in the superiority of the offence, which helped precipitate war.[15] Policymakers are now underrating the advantages of the defence, this time in cyber. According to Richard Clarke and Robert Knake, in the early days of the internet, the attacker had a distinct advantage because the internet's defences were so porous.[16] As recently as a decade ago, according to a former US National Security Agency (NSA) cryptanalyst, cyber attackers could infiltrate industrial-control systems relatively easily.[17] Today, however, the balance has begun to shift towards the defender.[18] Dave Aitel, a veteran hacker who worked for the NSA and then private cyber-security firms, told Clarke and Knake that intrusion-detection capabilities 'actually work', which is 'a huge change'. This makes the job of the attacker much more difficult. 'For the nation-state offense', Aitel said, 'you put such a premium on not getting caught that you really don't have a huge advantage'.[19] In some ways this is unsurprising. Cyber security is one of the top ten fastest-growing fields, according to the US Bureau of Labor Statistics, with a projected growth rate of 35% over the next ten years, much higher than the projected growth rate of jobs in other fields.[20] The more resources that the government and private sector invest in cyber security, the more difficult it becomes for attackers to find soft targets.[21] The advantages of cyber defence over offence were among the findings of the report of the Cyberspace Solarium Commission in 2020.[22]

While technological shifts affect the balance between attack and defence in conventional warfare, the built-in advantages of the defence eventually tend to reassert themselves. New technologies can initially favour the attacker, but when these technologies diffuse to the defender, and the defender combines them with its inherent advantages, the attacker's initial edge often slips away. In 1940, when the German army crushed France's in six weeks, it appeared that German panzers, which seemed unstoppable, had decisively shifted the balance to the attacker's advantage. However, when the defender armed itself with the same weapons and adjusted its tactics, the balance shifted back to the defence. Later in the war, the Germans themselves demonstrated how technology had empowered the defence. In resisting the Allied advance after D-Day, the Germans used their panzers to strengthen defence-in-depth and inflicted major losses on the Allied attackers. In July 1944, for instance, during *Operation Goodwood*, the Germans destroyed more than a third of the British tanks brought onto the continent after the Normandy landings.[23] The difficulties Ukraine encountered in its recent counter-offensive reflected the effectiveness of Russia's prepared defence.[24] A similar arc is playing out in cyberspace.

Despite the general recognition that defence is the stronger form of cyber warfare, investment in defensive capabilities and techniques has lagged because of the costs of implementation. That too is now changing. Defence is getting cheaper and stronger, driving up the costs of engaging in offence and strengthening deterrence. Not only are advances in network technology and security making cyber defence even stronger, but these innovations are also reducing the cost of deploying resilient cyber defence-in-depth, which some network defenders are already deploying. Some have argued that, given unlimited time and resources, the cyber attacker will always get through, affording the offence a long-term advantage.[25] But the mere fact that an attacker can gain access to a defender's computer network does not mean it will defeat the defender. The fight does not stop at the network's border. Indeed, given the speed and frequency of cyber attacks, preventing every network penetration and exploitation is impossible, and resilience is key to functionality. But many of the advantages enjoyed by the defender do not arise until after the attacker has actually gained unauthorised access to the network. With a properly organised cyber defence, networks can become more resilient, continuing to function despite penetration, while frustrating attackers' attempts to exploit their intrusion.

Conventional war vs cyber war

Some tactical advantages of the defence in conventional ground warfare are straightforward. The defender usually fires at the oncoming attacker from behind cover. The attacker must break cover and move towards the defender to dislodge it. Consequently, the attackers must expose themselves to deadly fire to engage the defenders, who will inflict more casualties on exposed attackers than they themselves suffer.[26] These defensive advantages yield the rule of thumb that three attackers are required to subdue one defender, a ratio some have increased to six-to-one owing to the greater lethality and accuracy of new weapons.[27]

In conventional warfare, the defender is also typically more familiar with the terrain that the attacker must traverse and has often prepared it for defence.[28] The defender will employ natural and built obstacles to channel the attacker into areas of the battlefield where it is most vulnerable to the defender's fires. Through such preparations, the defender can seize the initiative. When an attacker penetrates a well-prepared defence-in-depth, it is often following to the defender's script. In that case, the defender, not the attacker, can dictate the terms of engagement. Moreover, a stalwart defence-in-depth can produce victory by so frustrating an attacker that it breaks off the attack. During the Cold War, the US Army – a force steeped in the virtues of the offence but then insuperably outnumbered by Soviet conventional forces in Europe – rediscovered the virtues of the defensive, crystallising them in its doctrines of Active Defense and AirLand Battle.[29]

In the cyber realm too, defenders typically have better knowledge of the terrain – the network they are defending – than attackers. Today, this awareness is increased through the use of artificial intelligence (AI) to map the network's terrain and detect anomalous behaviour.[30] Employing AI in cyber defence is essential because the sheer volume and speed of attacks mean that individual cyber defenders cannot possibly detect and address each one.[31] The terrain of cyberspace, however, is different from the natural battlespace that is shaped by the defender in ground combat. Cyberspace has far greater plasticity than physical space, offering the defender more options in preparing the battlespace.[32]

> *Defenders typically have better knowledge of the terrain*

Gaining unauthorised access to a network is only the first step for the attacker. It must still find what it is looking for, which calls for mapping the network. This is why hackers often spend so much time inside a network before moving to exploitation. Russian hackers were inside the network of the DNC for months before they exfiltrated the batch of internal email communications that caused such a stir.[33] Once in the network, of course, the attacker is on the defender's terrain. However, a computer network is not like a terrain feature on a battlefield. It would be impossible for a conventional defender to make forests spring up where once there were plains or to render valleys smooth and bring mountains low. The defender in cyberspace, however, can do something comparable, altering the digital ground under the attacker's feet by changing the configuration of its network, thus preserving its superior situational awareness.[34] Such techniques can frustrate the attacker into breaking off its attack. Even if they don't, when the defender of a network periodically alters the configuration of the network, attackers that have managed to avoid detection and are assiduously mapping the network for exploitation will find that their data has become outdated. The harder it is to map a network, the longer the attacker must stay in the system, increasing the likelihood that it will be discovered.

Furthermore, if the attacker has manipulated part of the network to hide its presence, reconfiguring the network can expose its hideout when it fails to change with the rest of the network.

Cyber defenders are already using some of these defensive tactics. For instance, the health-insurance company Aetna's cyber defenders routinely change aspects of its network so that attackers are never certain about their position within it, retaining their home-court advantage.[35] Intentional network manipulation is also getting easier by virtue of cloud-infrastructure virtualisation. Devices are virtualised and typically provided as services, which means that there is nothing physical to purchase, house, wire, power or cool. A cloud provider such as Amazon maintains the virtual device, and users simply configure it to their specifications. The elements physically exposed to the internet are owned, operated and defended by the cloud provider. The flexibility this affords to shape the terrain is immense. In fact, virtualisation allows the cyber defender to change the shape of the terrain during an attack to frustrate the attacker.[36] The network that can change its configuration is a more resilient network, which is especially important for military forces that need to fend off virtual attackers while simultaneously fighting physical adversaries.

Few companies have a cyber-defence budget the size of Aetna's, and in the past few could mount an elaborate defence. But now that the components of a network are owned, operated and defended by the likes of Amazon, economies of scale make the resources and expertise necessary to mount a formidable cyber defence-in-depth within reach of an expanding range of national governments, local governments and private companies.

Finally, even if a cyber attack is successful, virtualisation facilitates quick recovery. It is much easier to load a pre-attack version of a virtual machine, patch its vulnerabilities and return it to service than it is to restore a physical computer to an earlier state. Virtualisation may also mean that defenders have access to a wider array of online resources to deal with distributed denial-of-service attacks.

Cyber attackers, of course, can also manipulate the virtual terrain of the network they have infiltrated. But defenders are still countering from their own territory, and their superior control and knowledge of the network means that they know the inventory and can detect changes through relatively simple means, such as white lists. Defenders can also embed responses triggered when behaviour outside of the network's established norms occurs that morphs the network and isolates the attacker. The defender still enjoys significant home-field advantages.

Observing the attacker

In ground combat, the defender can observe the approach of an attacker while remaining concealed, gathering information on capabilities and intentions.[37] The defender of a computer network can do the same. The informational advantages increase when the network defender also reconfigures the network. In facilitating the defender's search for technical signatures, these defensive advantages can also help it overcome one of the thorniest problems in cyberspace: the attacker's anonymity. With these advantages in mind, the cyber-security firm MITRE has decided that it would not make its primary objective to eject attackers from the network. Instead, it isolates and observes attackers in its system to learn about the tools they are using and to waste the time of the attacker, which often has no idea that it is under observation or that it has lost the initiative.

The intelligence-gathering capacity of the defender increases dramatically when it exploits the malleability of the virtual landscape by establishing fake machines, known as 'honey pots', or entire fictitious networks, called 'honey nets', on its network. To draw another conventional-warfare analogy, in the Second World War, the Germans would leave the first few defensive positions that they constructed empty. Unaware of this, the attacker would deploy to breach these phantom positions. Concealed German scouts would observe this action and communicate tactical intelligence about artillery, air support and other factors to the defenders in the inhabited positions. Likewise, the cyber defender can build fake computers and networks populated with fake data to fool the attacker, and even malicious code to infect it.[38] Moreover, because honey nets are quiet networks with very little traffic, the defender can identify any intrusion as the work of a malicious actor. At no time would the actual home network be in danger. The intruder, for its part, would remain ignorant of the fact that the stalwart defence it is confronting is not there to protect the defender's actual network. Perhaps the most important resources that the attacker wastes in breaching a honey net are exploitation tools. Once it uses one, the defender can patch against that tool in its home network, inoculating it against that exploit. In addition, honey nets can potentially contribute to cyber resilience. If the attacker diverts resources to a honey net, it is not in the real network disrupting its normal operations, reducing the degradation of the network and allowing normal operations to continue despite the presence of an intruder.

The extensive information obtained in defending a false network can also empower AI tools being used in a detection and defence role in the defender's real network. In order for AI to learn what to defend against, it needs data on previous attacks, and it is vital that this data be constantly updated. AI can work from the data generated from the defence of the honey net to defend the real network, detect intrusion attempts against it, and identify the intruder based on the kinds of exploitation tools it uses and other signatures. AI might even be able to predict the next move of the attacker.[39]

Finally, many, perhaps most, decisions about cyber security in both the private and public sectors are financial. If the projected losses from intrusions are lower than the cost of providing security, then governments and countries will forgo the security upgrade. For instance, prior to the 2016 election, a cyber-security consultant told the DNC that its computer network was vulnerable. Rather than spend resources on a cyber-security upgrade, the DNC decided to allocate the resources that would have required to increasing voter turnout – a decision they would come to regret.[40] The virtualisation of computer networks has reduced the cost of building honey nets, and this service is now provided by several cyber-security firms.[41]

The offence–defence balance and the cyber-security dilemma

Sometimes the only way to stop a persistent attacker is to counter-attack and disrupt its ability to keep attacking. Offensive as well as defensive cyber capabilities will unavoidably be part of any major conflict. But it's important to remember that defence is not entirely inactive. As Carl von Clausewitz noted almost 200 years ago, 'the defensive form of war is not a simple shield, but a shield made up of well-directed blows'.[42] The information that the cyber defender gathers about the attacker's techniques and modes of operation can inform a more effective counter-attack. Such cyber counter-attacks, called response actions, are part of US doctrine for defensive cyber operations. The relevant doctrinal publication defines them as 'external to the defended network or portion of cyberspace without the permission of the owner of the affected system … normally in foreign cyberspace'. Some response actions may involve the 'physical damage or destruction of enemy systems'.[43] Through the use of honey pots and honey nets, for instance, the defender might introduce disguised malicious code, which the attacker unwittingly extracts and incorporates into its own network. Response actions aim to 'kill the archer' instead of just 'catching arrows'.[44] They are central to the more offensive aspects of 'defend forward' and 'persistent engagement'.

The use and scale of response actions depends upon the context of the attack, and the degree of actual and potential damage inflicted. The most important consideration, however, is 'the degree of certainty in attribution of the threat'.[45] Cyber attackers make Herculean efforts to hide their identity to reduce the likelihood of retaliation.[46] To avoid escalation and diplomatic discord, it is crucial that the counter-attacker determine that its target is the actual attacker. Here the advantages of cyber defence for counter-attack come into focus. A capable cyber defender gathers extensive information on the attacker, including its methods and intentions, which, with human and other technical intelligence, can be used to arrive at the attacker's identity. The longer the cyber defender observes the attacker, the better the overall intelligence package. In cyberspace, the best offence may emerge from a stalwart defence.

AI and quantum computing are sometimes seen as shifting the balance in cyber warfare decisively to the offence. This seems far from certain. AI is likely be as effective on defence as it is on offence. AI is being used, for example, to develop intrusion-detection systems that 'outperform other techniques because of their flexibility, adaptability, rapid calculations, and quick learning'.[47] While quantum computing will make it harder for defenders to encrypt their networks, cyber-security experts have begun designing essentially quantum-proof encryption.[48]

Ben Buchanan argues that there is a security dilemma in the cyber domain that will drive states to engage in offensive cyber operations. The logic is that states must offensively penetrate their potential adversaries' networks to discover what offensive capabilities they possess; they, in turn, could interpret these intrusions as precursors to an attack or the attack itself, eliciting a cyber counter-attack and potentially triggering an escalatory spiral.[49] Yet full consideration of the advantages of the cyber defence can dampen this logic. One key reason nation-states might engage in offensive cyber intrusions is that they think that their identity will remain hidden. But a defender who mobilises the advantages of cyber defence can use the information it gains to identify the potential attacker. Beyond that, the defender can use the information about the attacker's capabilities to launch a precisely targeted counter-attack. This capability constitutes a substantial deterrent.

Again, offensive capabilities are a necessary part of cyber national security, and penetrating networks will prove essential in any conflict spanning multiple domains. But defenders do not always need to attack opposing networks to develop and hone their offensive cyber capabilities. This can be done through red-teaming, which has become a common practice in network defence in cyberspace. Companies like MITRE and FireEye develop offensive cyber tools to stress-test the networks of their customers. Structurally, as cyber defence becomes stronger, offensive intrusions will require more and more resources, decreasing their efficiency over time. Money and time – the latter being a resource we can never recover – will be better spent on cyber defence. Without doubt, incentives will remain to engage in intrusions, albeit in the name of defence, but undertaking them will become increasingly risky and inefficient, and the incentives for doing so correspondingly diminished. Accordingly, the intensity of the cyber-security dilemma is likely to decrease.

*   *   *

We have painted a rather optimistic picture of the future of cyber defence, and we acknowledge that it is hardly guaranteed. As in conventional war, the offence–defence balance is not static. For now, however, advances in cyber-security technology have made it easier to harness the advantages of cyber defence. The balance has shifted towards the defender and is likely to shift still further in its favour. Policymakers therefore should not assume that offensive cyber operations are the most effective tools for assurance and de-escalation.[50] A key objective of a strategy is to convince adversaries that their own strategies cannot succeed.[51] Advertising and mobilising the advantages of the cyber defence could affect their perceptions, helping to convince them that the offensive game is not worth the candle.

Furthermore, as Clausewitz argued, there are advantages to being on the defensive at the strategic as well as the tactical level. It is plausible that the tactical advantages of cyber defence could be scaled up to protect a strategic network of networks. There has been much hand-wringing about the havoc that minor-power adversaries such as Iran and North Korea could wreak in cyberspace. But minor-power US allies can also punch above their weight in cyberspace, and they have a vested interest in securing it. Jared Cohen and Richard Fontaine have intriguingly proposed a virtual alliance among technologically advanced democracies.[52] Properly organised and coordinated, they could collectively employ the tactical advantages of cyber defence to establish a formidable network of networks, prioritising defensive measures, sharing information gathered on attackers and strengthening cyber security across the board. This would be a powerful means of consolidating the defenders' advantages and deterring those who would seek to achieve cyber security through cyber attack.

Acknowledgements

The authors would like to thank Peter Wostenberg, a PhD candidate in Baylor University's Department of Political Science, for his assistance with research and revisions.

Notes

1   Steve Morgan, 'Cybercrime to Cost the World $10.5 Trillion Annually by 2025', *Cybercrime Magazine*, 13 November 2020, https://cybersecurityventures. com/hackerpocalypse-cybercrime-report-2016/.

2   Michelle Nichols, 'North Korea Took $2 Billion in Cyberattacks to Fund Weapons Program: U.N.

Report', Reuters, 5 August 2019,
https://www.reuters.com/article/
idUSKCN1UV1ZX/.

3   See NATO, 'Statement by the North
Atlantic Council in Solidarity
with Those Affected by Recent
Malicious Cyber Activities Including
the Microsoft Exchange Server
Compromise', Press Release 120, 19
July 2021, https://www.nato.int/cps/
en/natohq/news_185863.htm.

4   See Christopher Bing, 'Suspected
Russian Hackers Spied on U.S.
Treasury Emails – Sources',
Reuters, 13 December 2020,
https://www.reuters.com/article/
idUSKBN28N0PH/; and Marcus
Willett, 'Lessons of the SolarWinds
Hack', Survival, vol. 63, no. 2, April–
May 2021, pp. 7–26.

5   See John Arquilla, 'Cyberwar Is
Already Upon Us', Foreign Policy, 27
February 2012, https://foreignpolicy.
com/2012/02/27/cyberwar-is-already
upon-us/; Richard A. Clarke and
Robert K. Knake, Cyber War: The Next
Threat to National Security and What to
Do About It (New York: Ecco, 2012);
Richard A. Clarke and Robert K.
Knake, The Fifth Domain: Defending
Our Country, Our Companies, and
Ourselves in the Age of Cyber Threats
(New York: Penguin Press, 2019);
and Martin C. Libicki, Conquest in
Cyberspace: National Security and
Information Warfare (Cambridge:
Cambridge University Press, 2007).

6   See Clarke and Knake, The Fifth
Domain, pp. 195–6; and Brandon
Valeriano and Benjamin Jensen,
'The Myth of the Cyber Offense: The
Case for Restraint', Policy Analysis
862, Cato Institute, 15 January 2019,

https://www.cato.org/policy-analysis/
myth-cyber-offense-case-restraint.

7   White House, 'National Cybersecurity
Strategy', March 2023, p. 14,
https://www.whitehouse.gov/
wp-content/uploads/2023/03/National-
Cybersecurity-Strategy-2023.pdf.

8   US Cyber Command, 'CYBER 101
– Defend Forward and Persistent
Engagement', 25 October 2022, https://
www.cybercom.mil/Media/News/
Article/3198878/cyber-101-defend-
forward-and-persistent-engagement/.

9   See Antonio Calcara et al., 'Will
the Drone Always Get Through?
Offensive Myths and Defensive
Realities', Security Studies, vol. 31, no.
5, October 2022, pp. 791–825.

10   See Erik Gartzke, 'The Myth
of Cyberwar: Bringing War in
Cyberspace Back Down to Earth',
International Security, vol. 38, no. 2, Fall
2013, pp. 41–73; Erik Gartzke and Jon
R. Lindsay, 'Weaving Tangled Webs:
Offense, Defense, and Deception in
Cyberspace', Security Studies, vol.
24, no. 2, April 2015, pp. 316–48;
Thomas Rid, Cyber War Will Not Take
Place (Oxford: Oxford University
Press, 2013); and Samuel Zilincik and
Isabelle Duyvesteyn, 'Strategic Studies
and Cyber Warfare', Journal of Strategic
Studies, vol. 46, no. 4, February 2023,
pp. 836–57.

11   See Karen Ruth Adams, 'Attack and
Conquer? International Anarchy and
the Offense–Defense–Deterrence
Balance', International Security, vol.
28, no. 3, Winter 2003/04, pp. 45–83;
Stephen Biddle, 'Rebuilding the
Foundations of Offense–Defense
Theory', Journal of Politics, vol. 63, no.
3, August 2001, pp. 741–74; Charles L.

Glaser and Chaim Kaufmann, 'What Is the Offense–Defense Balance and How Can We Measure It?', *International Security*, vol. 22, no. 4, Spring 1998, pp. 44–82; Robert Jervis, 'Cooperation Under the Security Dilemma', *World Politics*, vol. 30, no. 2, January 1978, pp. 167–214; and Keir A. Lieber, 'Grasping the Technological Peace: The Offense–Defense Balance and International Security', *International Security*, vol. 25, no. 1, Summer 2000, pp. 71–104.

12 See Ben Garfinkel and Allan Dafoe, 'How Does the Offense–Defense Balance Scale?', *Journal of Strategic Studies*, vol. 42, no. 6, September 2019, pp. 736–63; Gartzke and Lindsay, 'Weaving Tangled Webs', pp. 316–48; Keir A. Lieber, 'The Offense–Defense Balance and Cyber Warfare', in Emily O. Goldman and John Arquilla (eds), *Cyber Analogies* (Monterey, CA: Naval Postgraduate School, 2015), pp. 96–107; William J. Lynn III, 'Defending a New Domain: The Pentagon's Cyberstrategy', *Foreign Affairs*, vol. 89, no. 5, September/October 2010, pp. 97–108; Rebecca Slayton, 'What Is the Cyber Offense–Defense Balance? Conceptions, Causes, and Assessment', *International Security*, vol. 41, no. 3, Winter 2016/17, pp. 72–109; and Valeriano and Jensen, 'The Myth of the Cyber Offense'.

13 See Ben Buchanan, *The Cybersecurity Dilemma: Hacking, Trust and Fear Between Nations* (Oxford: Oxford University Press, 2016).

14 See Erica D. Lonergan and Shawn W. Lonergan, 'Cyber Operations, Accommodative Signaling, and the De-escalation of International Crises', *Security Studies*, vol. 31, no. 1, January 2022, pp. 32–64. Some scholars have criticised Erica and Shawn Lonergan's arguments as being incomplete. See, for example, Brandon K. Yoder, 'Can Cyberattacks Reassure? Half Measures as a De-escalation Strategy', *Security Studies*, vol. 31, no. 4, August 2022, pp. 757–63.

15 See Jervis, 'Cooperation Under the Security Dilemma'; Margaret MacMillan, *The War that Ended Peace: The Road to 1914* (New York: Random House, 2014); and Jack Snyder, *The Ideology of the Offensive: Military Decision Making and the Disasters of 1914* (Ithaca, NY: Cornell University Press, 2013).

16 See Clarke and Knake, *Cyber War*.

17 See Dale Peterson, 'Offensive Cyber Weapons: Construction, Development, and Employment', *Journal of Strategic Studies*, vol. 36, no. 1, February 2013, pp. 120–4.

18 See Clarke and Knake, *The Fifth Domain*, pp. 4–5, 13, 35–9.

19 *Ibid.*, pp. 35–6.

20 US Bureau of Labor Statistics, Office of Occupational Statistics and Employment Projections, 'Occupational Outlook Handbook', September 2022.

21 See James E. McGhee, 'Liberating Cyber Offense', *Strategic Studies Quarterly*, vol. 10, no. 4, Winter 2016, pp. 46–63; and Max Smeets, 'Building a Cyber Force Is Even Harder than You Thought', *War on the Rocks*, 12 May 2022, https://warontherocks.com/2022/05/building-a-cyber-force-is-even-harder-than-you-thought/.

22 See US Cyberspace Solarium Commission, 'Final Report',

March 2020, https://drive.google.com/file/d/1ryMCIL_dZ3oQyjFqFkkf1oMxIXJGT4yv/view.

23 See Stephen D. Biddle, *Military Power: Explaining Victory and Defeat in Modern Battle* (Princeton, NJ: Princeton University Press, 2004), pp. 108–31.

24 See Stephen Biddle, 'Back in the Trenches', *Foreign Affairs*, vol. 102, no. 5, September/October 2023, pp. 153–64.

25 See Austin Long, 'A Cyber SIOP? Operational Considerations for Strategic Offensive Cyber Planning', *Journal of Cybersecurity*, vol. 3, no. 1, March 2017, pp. 19–28.

26 See B.A. Friedman, *On Tactics: A Theory of Victory in Battle* (Annapolis, MD: Naval Institute Press, 2017), pp. 106–7.

27 See Peter Campbell, *Military Realism: The Logic and Limits of Force and Innovation in the US Army* (Columbia, MO: University of Missouri Press, 2019), p. 140.

28 See Carl von Clausewitz, *On War*, ed. Michael Howard and Peter Paret, (Princeton, NJ: Princeton University Press, 1989), p. 360.

29 See Campbell, *Military Realism*, chapter 4.

30 See Thanh Cong Truong, Quoc Bao Diep and Ivan Zelinka, 'Artificial Intelligence in the Cyber Domain: Offense and Defense', *Symmetry*, vol. 12, no. 3, March 2020, pp. 3–4.

31 See *ibid.*, pp. 3, 18.

32 See Clarke and Knake, *The Fifth Domain*, p. 94; and Gartzke and Lindsay, 'Weaving Tangled Webs', pp. 320–1.

33 See David E. Sanger, *The Perfect Weapon: War, Sabotage, and Fear in the Cyber Age* (New York: Crown, 2018), pp. 192–3.

34 See Clarke and Knake, *The Fifth Domain*, p. 42.

35 See *ibid.*, pp. 41–2.

36 See T. Aditya et al., 'The Future of Networking: Embracing Software-defined Solutions', *International Journal of Advanced Research in Science, Communication and Technology*, vol. 3, no. 2, February 2023, pp. 503–11; Seung Hun Jee, Ji Su Park and Jin Gon Shon, 'Security in Network Virtualization: A Survey', *Journal of Information Processing Systems*, vol. 17, no. 4, August 2021, pp. 801–17; and Yu Zheng et al., 'Dynamic Defenses in Cyber Security: Techniques, Methods and Challenges', *Digital Communications and Networks*, vol. 8, no. 4, August 2022, pp. 422–35.

37 See Gartzke and Lindsay, 'Weaving Tangled Webs', pp. 320–1, 340–1; and Kristin E. Heckman et al., 'Active Cyber Defense with Denial and Deception: A Cyber-wargame Experiment', *Computers & Security*, vol. 37, September 2013, pp. 72–7.

38 See Gartzke and Lindsay, 'Weaving Tangled Webs', pp. 340–1; and Heckman et al., 'Active Cyber Defense with Denial and Deception'.

39 See Truong, Diep and Zelinka, 'Artificial Intelligence in the Cyber Domain'.

40 See Sanger, *The Perfect Weapon*, pp. 171–2.

41 They include Rapid7 (https://www.rapid7.com/products/insightidr/features/deception-technology/); SentinelOne (https://www.sentinelone.com/surfaces/identity); and Acalvio (https://www.acalvio.com/products/advanced-threat-defence/).

42 Clausewitz, *On War*, p. 357.

43 US Chairman of the Joint Chiefs of Staff, 'Cyberspace Operations', Joint

Publication 3-12, 8 June 2018, p. II–4, https://irp.fas.org/doddir/dod/jp3_12.pdf.

44 Brett T. Williams, 'The Joint Force Commander's Guide to Cyberspace Operations', *Joint Force Quarterly*, vol. 73, 2nd Quarter 2014, p. 16, https://nsarchive.gwu.edu/sites/default/files/documents/6379791/National-Security-Archive-Maj-Gen-Brett-T.pdf.

45 *Ibid.*

46 See Florian Skopik and Timea Pahi, 'Under False Flag: Using Technical Artifacts for Cyber Attack Attribution', *Cybersecurity*, vol. 3, no. 1, March 2020, p. 8.

47 Truong, Diep and Zelinka, 'Artificial Intelligence in the Cyber Domain', p. 8.

48 See Sophie Bushwick, 'New Encryption System Protects Data from Quantum Computers', *Scientific American*, 8 October 2019, https://www.scientificamerican.com/article/new-encryption-system-protects-data-from-quantum-computers/.

49 See Buchanan, *The Cybersecurity Dilemma*.

50 See Michael P. Fischerkeller, 'Cyber Signaling: Deeper Case Research Tells a Different Story', *Security Studies*, vol. 31, no. 4, December 2022, pp. 772–82; and Yoder, 'Can Cyberattacks Reassure?'

51 See, for example, Michael J. Mazaar, 'Understanding Deterrence', *Perspective*, RAND Corporation, 19 April 2018, p. 7, https://www.rand.org/content/dam/rand/pubs/perspectives/PE200/PE295/RAND_PE295.pdf.

52 See Jared Cohen and Richard Fontaine, 'Uniting the Techno-democracies', *Foreign Affairs*, vol. 99, no. 6, November/December 2020, pp. 112–22.

US Security Assurances and Nuclear Tripolarity

Linde Desmaele

The persistent threat of nuclear proliferation, setbacks in arms control and disarmament, the disruptive potential of technological advancements in the nuclear domain, and a resurgence of overt nuclear brinkmanship suggest the advent of a new nuclear age.[1] One of its key features is the risk of sharp nuclear competition among Washington, Moscow and Beijing.[2] While analysts and scholars have begun exploring the implications for US nuclear deterrence, they have devoted less attention to American nuclear-security assurances.[3] The challenges are not new and have been much debated.[4] Tripolarity, whereby three major nuclear-armed powers compete for advantage, imposes a new layer of complexity and compels revisiting them.[5]

A new landscape

In previous decades, although there were multiple nuclear-armed states, their nuclear arsenals were significantly smaller and less sophisticated than those of the United States and Russia. Other states with nuclear weapons also lacked the economic and military characteristics of a superpower. During the Cold War, they were generally either aligned with or strongly leaned toward one of the two superpowers. As a consequence, much of US nuclear

Linde Desmaele is a post-doctoral fellow in the Security Studies Program at the Massachusetts Institute of Technology and a senior associate researcher at the Centre for Security, Diplomacy and Strategy at Vrije Universiteit Brussel.

Survival | vol. 66 no. 2 | April–May 2024 | pp. 143–156   https://doi.org/10.1080/00396338.2024.2332066

strategy, including its approach to nuclear assurances, was premised on bipolar competition between the United States and the Soviet Union.

Today, however, the US is engaged in several separate but interconnected nuclear rivalries. Although multiple rivalries are simultaneously under way, the 2022 US Nuclear Posture Review primarily centres on those involving China and Russia.[6] These countries, like the United States itself, are engaged in extensive, long-term modernisation programmes driven in part by their perceptions of the capabilities of the other two countries. The United States maintains the most advanced and survivable arsenal among the three. Russia also has a substantial arsenal and has made significant investments in so-called non-strategic nuclear weapons. China has accelerated the modernisation of its nuclear arsenal, though its current one is much smaller and less sophisticated than the United States' or Russia's. While the US has tenser relationships with Russia and China than they have with each other, they still closely monitor each other's nuclear activities.[7]

Assurances are commitments made through declarations or less explicit signals to undertake or refrain from taking specific actions in the future. While deterrence relies on the threat of force, assurance is based on the assessment that, in certain circumstances, greater stability results from providing others with a greater sense of security.[8] Currently, policy discussions in Washington revolve predominantly around the credibility of allied assurance.[9] The 2022 US Nuclear Posture Review underlines the centrality of allied assurance to the US nuclear posture and explicitly commits to strengthening it.[10] Yet assurances also play an important role in the relationship between the United States and its nuclear-armed adversaries. If an actor expects punishment regardless of whether it challenges a deterrent commitment, it lacks the incentive to avoid doing so.[11] Deterrence can fail if assurance is insufficiently credible. A further complicating matter is the United States' pledge not to 'use or threaten to use nuclear weapons against non-nuclear weapons states that are party to the NPT [Nuclear Non-Proliferation Treaty] and in compliance with their nuclear non-proliferation obligations'.[12] These are negative assurances, committing the United States to refrain from taking actions against a target state.

Tripolar competition raises three sets of challenges with respect to US nuclear-security assurances. Firstly, the United States needs to synchronise its efforts to assure allies, responding effectively to the diverse concerns and requirements of multiple allies across different geographic theatres.[13] Secondly, there is the problem of ambiguity. A higher number of nuclear-armed competitors makes it harder for the United States to strike a balance between deterrence and assurance in individual bilateral relationships, and increases the risk of accidental crises or wars due to miscalculations and misperceptions.[14] Thirdly, the proliferation problem becomes more acute as more nuclear-weapons states appear to normalise nuclear weapons as appropriate means of pursuing national-security goals. Here there is persistent tension. While providing extended nuclear deterrence and assurance to allies requires the United States to maintain a sufficiently large nuclear arsenal ready for potential deployment, doing so makes assurances to non-nuclear states that nuclear weapons will not be used against them less credible.[15] Vertical proliferation among the established nuclear powers may therefore inadvertently foster horizontal proliferation.[16]

Allied assurance and the synchronisation challenge

The United States' commitment to using nuclear weapons to deter and defend against attacks on its allies – alternately referred to as its nuclear umbrella or extended nuclear deterrence – has played a pivotal role in US security policy for nearly eight decades.[17] What Glenn Snyder calls the 'alliance dilemma' has made it a vexing commitment. Allied states fear both abandonment and entrapment. Abandonment can take various forms, such as failing to provide expected support in critical situations, reneging on commitments or aligning with adversaries. Entrapment involves being drawn into conflicts over an ally's interests that may not fully align with one's own. It occurs when the value of preserving the alliance outweighs the costs of fighting for the ally's particular cause.[18] These considerations are particularly salient in the nuclear domain because of the unique destructive capability of nuclear weapons. The core challenge for Washington is to assure allies that its nuclear deterrent is reliable and offers protection, but that it will not recklessly provoke nuclear war.

The credibility of US assurances is in the eye of the beholder.[19] As Heather Williams has put it, 'assurance for one is not assurance for all, and what looks like assurance to one may look like entrapment to another'.[20] This underscores the need for the United States to tailor its strategies to multiple allies with diverse concerns and requirements, and to understand and shape their perceptions through dialogue and consultation.[21]

The United States must now synchronise its assurances to allies in both Europe and Asia.[22] While the challenge of coping with the reverberations of US strategy in Asia for Europe and vice versa is nothing new, the shift away from a relatively Eurocentric extended-deterrence framework presents distinct challenges. Allies who tend to fear abandonment may fear it even more in the context of tripolarity. Allies recognise that US military resources and policymakers' attention are finite.[23] During the Cold War, US nuclear strategy prioritised a single primary nuclear-armed competitor, the Soviet Union, in both Europe and East Asia. Insofar as adjustments one side made to its policy in one region were likely to compel the other side to respond, there was no major risk of neglecting one region in favour of the other.[24] But with two nuclear major-power adversaries in separate regions, changes to the US commitment in one region will have a more immediate opportunity cost for its commitment to the other, since resources allocated in one area cannot be easily relocated to the other.[25]

Tripolarity may also amplify allies' worries about entrapment, as they now face the additional risk of becoming embroiled in an extra-regional conflict. As Iain Henry notes,

> if a state fears that its ally will abandon it if conflict breaks out with an adversary, it is unlikely to fear its ally entrapping it into a conflict with this adversary. However, it may be fearful of its ally entrapping it into a conflict with a different adversary.[26]

While such entrapment could assume various forms, it is reasonable to expect any nuclear conflict, whether in Europe or Asia, to have spillover effects into other regions.

Allied concerns about abandonment and entrapment are shaped by the types of missions for which nuclear weapons could be used. Current US strategy for both Europe and Asia designates nuclear weapons to deter and defend against a broad range of potential nuclear and non-nuclear threats, placing a significant burden on resources and refraining from establishing a sole-purpose commitment.[27] The United States is also committed to a doctrine that focuses on counterforce – that is, targeting an adversary's nuclear forces.[28] This approach is relatively resource intensive because it tethers the configuration of the US nuclear arsenal to that of its adversaries.[29] A counterforce approach requires nuclear forces of greater quantity and precision than a counter-value strategy centred on nuclear threats to an adversary's society and infrastructure.[30] Proponents of the current counterforce approach have called for a nuclear build-up to prepare for potential nuclear conflicts with both Russia and China.[31] Counter-value advocates point out that it places lower demands on resources and may entail fewer immediate resource trade-offs.[32]

The more missions the United States assigns to its nuclear weapons, the more difficult it will be for it to allay allies' fears of abandonment across multiple regions. Allies may also find the status quo itself escalatory, and fear entrapment instead. Different allies' demands for assurance may also change, complicating Washington's efforts to tailor its assurances.

Adversary assurance and the ambiguity challenge

There is a case to be made that more nuclear weapons for more players could actually make adversary assurance easier and have a stabilising effect. If the United States and multiple adversaries are mutually vulnerable, arguably they should all be deterred and incentivised to show restraint.[33] Under this rationale, the possibility of a response not only from an intended target but also from other nuclear-weapons states would strengthen strategic stability.[34] US policymakers have signalled concern about an 'opportunistic third party' that could exploit a potential nuclear conflict to enhance its own position.[35] Given that the cost of nuclear war may be even higher in a situation involving more nuclear players – or at least more uncertain – states have compelling reasons to avoid initiating one.[36]

This logic may not hold in practice. Nuclear-armed states can inadvertently stumble into crises they wish to avoid owing to ambiguity about the status quo or miscalculation about how adversaries will perceive their actions.[37] A single crisis could encompass multiple issues, with each participant defending a specific aspect of the status quo. Third parties can further complicate matters, making it unclear which side is acting defensively.[38] Since the perception of assurance varies from one party to another, having more players can open additional pathways to inadvertent war due to misperceptions or miscalculations. One example of this dynamic is the United States' deployment in South Korea of a regional missile-defence system. Its stated purpose was to defend South Korea against North Korean missiles. China, however, argued that it was part of a broader US scheme to develop a first-strike capability against China. US efforts to target one adversary may increase tensions in relations with others, fuelling arms races and ultimately weakening assurances provided to adversaries.[39]

Long-standing questions about the compatibility between adversary assurance and allied assurance also endure. Some have argued that the two cannot be logically reconciled in situations of mutually assured destruction.[40] If, for example, country A invades an ally of country B, and B's defence of its ally increases the risk of nuclear escalation, it would appear irrational, thus not credible, for B to undertake that defence.[41] However, if B enjoyed escalation dominance because of something akin to a credible first-strike capability, threats against B's ally could probably be more effectively deterred. Following this logic, scholars have argued that Cold War efforts to stabilise deterrence between the superpowers undermined the credibility of US extended nuclear deterrence. Conversely, US alliance commitments incentivised the US to develop war-winning strategies to assure allies and reinforced the possibility of a destabilising arms race.[42]

Other have pointed out, however, that Thomas C. Schelling's famous 'threat that leaves something to chance' can help harmonise these seemingly conflicting objectives, and that the incompatibility problem is exaggerated.[43] His point is that a country need not always convey a definitive commitment that it will act in a given circumstance; threats that it merely could act can still be effective deterrents. The key insight here is that the final decision to carry out such threats may not be entirely within the control of the party making the threat due to accidents, flaws in decision-making processes, mechanical errors and so on.[44] From this perspective, the challenge for Washington is not so much to establish escalation dominance but rather to keep the risk of all-out nuclear war at a level slightly above zero. Deterrence is thus conceived as a 'competition in risk-taking', not solely dependent on battlefield success. It is about showing the resolve to take risks that could lead to high costs that neither side desires, thus leveraging the mutual interest in avoiding nuclear war. From this standpoint, the requirements of assuring allies do not seem too different from those of assuring adversaries.

The fact of the matter is that the United States has in practice adopted a nuclear war-fighting strategy. Relatedly, some US allies in Europe and East Asia have opposed US proposals to reduce the role of nuclear weapons in their alliance posture, including US plans to adopt a 'sole purpose' policy.[45] If history offers any guide to the future, this suggests that Washington may well continue an approach in which efforts to bolster allied assurance tend to undermine adversary assurance and vice versa. But tripolar nuclear competition increases both the number of audiences involved and the associated risks.

Assuring third parties and the proliferation challenge

Since 1978, Washington has repeatedly indicated that it

> will not use nuclear weapons against any non-nuclear-weapon state party
> to the NPT or any comparable internationally binding commitment not
> to acquire nuclear explosive devices, except in the case of an attack on the
> United States, its territories or armed forces, or its allies, by any state allied
> to a nuclear-weapon state or associated with a nuclear-weapon state in
> carrying out or sustaining the attack.[46]

While these negative assurances are not part of the NPT text, they were reaffirmed in 1995 as an integral part of the treaty's indefinite extension.[47] Under United Nations Security Council Resolution 255, the United States has also pledged to come to the aid of a non-nuclear-weapons state threatened or attacked with nuclear weapons.[48] The difference between these assurances and the positive nuclear commitments made to US treaty allies essentially comes down to the fact that, in the latter case, the United States commits to using its own nuclear weapons to support its allies if necessary.[49]

The United States' extended-deterrence commitments cut against the spirit of negative assurances to non-nuclear states.[50] Notes Jeffrey Knopf: 'Promises not to threaten or use nuclear weapons against non-nuclear states become more convincing if nuclear weapon states reduce the numbers of nuclear weapons they possess, and the missions and roles assigned to those.'[51] Accordingly, non-nuclear-weapons states have grown dissatisfied with attempts to advance the NPT's ultimate goal of nuclear disarmament. This frustration was a major driver of the 2017 Treaty on the Prohibition of Nuclear Weapons.[52] Tripolar nuclear competition may make matters worse by triggering horizontal proliferation through the normalisation or legitimisation of a reliance on nuclear weapons for national-security goals. Negative assurances, which limit the role of nuclear weapons, tend to align better with efforts to delegitimise these weapons.[53] Positive security assurances, such as extended nuclear deterrence, signal that nuclear weapons are valuable tools of statecraft. While such assurances are often credited with preventing nuclear proliferation within the US umbrella, this is not the case for those countries and actors that fall outside it. Moreover, some now argue that positive assurance can backfire by reinforcing the perception that allied security depends on nuclear weapons, boosting pro-nuclear factions in allied countries.[54]

At bottom, the capacity of nuclear assurances to bolster non-proliferation is context-dependent. Convincing one actor to refrain from developing nuclear weapons might induce another to acquire them. Vertical and horizontal nuclear proliferation therefore cannot be treated as two fully separate challenges.

*   *   *

Washington has identified nuclear tripolarity as a central feature of the future strategic landscape. With respect to US nuclear-security assurances, this focus raises the challenges of synchronisation, ambiguity and proliferation. The United States must credibly assure allies in different theatres that its nuclear umbrella is reliable against more than one adversary. At the same time, it must avoid making nuclear weapons appear appropriate and useful means for non-nuclear-weapons states, allies and adversaries alike to enhance their security. There is no easy solution to these challenges, as each choice involves trade-offs and political considerations. Both deterrence and assurance fundamentally involve influencing perceptions and intentions, and this is very hard to do. Since its inception, nuclear strategy has been as much an art as a science. That much has not changed.

Notes

1   See Andrew Futter and Benjamin Zala, 'Strategic Non-nuclear Weapons and the Onset of a Third Nuclear Age', *European Journal of International Security*, vol. 6, no. 3, February 2021, pp. 257–77.

2   See US Department of Defense, '2022 Nuclear Posture Review', p. 4, available at https://armscontrolcenter.org/2022-nuclear-posture-review/.

3   See Center for Global Security Research, 'China's Emergence as a Second Nuclear Peer: Implications for U.S. Nuclear Deterrence Strategy', Spring 2023, https://cgsr.llnl.gov/content/assets/docs/CGSR_Two_Peer_230314.pdf; and Heather Williams et al., 'Project Atom 2023: A Competitive Strategies Approach for U.S. Nuclear Posture Through 2035', Center for Strategic and International Studies, September 2023, https://csis-website-prod.s3.amazonaws.com/s3fs-public/2023-09/230929_Williams_ProjectAtom_2023.pdf.

4   See Jeffrey W. Knopf (ed.), *Security Assurances and Nuclear Nonproliferation* (Stanford, CA: Stanford University Press, 2012).

5   See Caitlin Talmadge, 'Multipolar Deterrence in the Emerging Nuclear Era', in Vipin Narang and Scott D. Sagan (eds), *The Fragile Balance of Terror* (Ithaca, NY: Cornell University Press, 2023), pp. 12–38.

6   See US Department of Defense, '2022 Nuclear Posture Review', p. 4.

7   See Talmadge, 'Multipolar Deterrence in the Emerging Nuclear Era'.

8   See Jeffrey W. Knopf, 'Varieties of Assurance', *Journal of Strategic Studies*, vol. 35, no. 3, April 2012, pp. 375–99.

9   See Heather Williams et al., 'Alternative Nuclear Futures: Capability and Credibility Challenges for U.S. Extended Nuclear Deterrence', Center for Strategic and International Studies, May 2023, https://csis-website-prod.s3.amazonaws.com/s3fs-public/2023-05/230508_Williams_AlternativeNuclearFutures.pdf.

10 See US Department of Defense, '2022 Nuclear Posture Review', pp. 3, 8, 11, 14. See also Alexander Mattelaer, 'Rethinking Nuclear Deterrence: A European Perspective', CSDS Policy Brief 13/2022, Centre for Security, Diplomacy and Strategy, 23 May 2022, https://brussels-school.be/sites/default/files/CSDS%20Policy%20brief_2213.pdf; and Adam Mount, 'The US and South Korea: The Trouble with Nuclear Assurance', *Survival*, vol. 65, no. 2, April–May 2023, pp. 123–40.

11 See Thomas C. Schelling, *Arms and Influence*, revised ed. (New Haven, CT: Yale University Press, 2008), pp. 4, 74. See also Matthew D. Cebul, Allan Dafoe and Nuno P. Monteiro, 'Coercion and the Credibility of Assurances', *Journal of Politics*, vol. 83, no. 3, July 2021, pp. 975–91; and Thomas J. Christensen et al., 'How to Avoid a War Over Taiwan', *Foreign Affairs*, 13 October 2022, https://www.foreignaffairs.com/china/how-avoid-war-over-taiwan.

12 US Department of Defense, '2022 Nuclear Posture Review', p. 9.

13 See Williams et al., 'Alternative Nuclear Futures', in which the term 'synchronisation challenge' was coined.

14 See Talmadge, 'Multipolar Deterrence in the Emerging Nuclear Era'.

15 See Knopf, 'Varieties of Assurance'; and Knopf, *Security Assurances and Nuclear Nonproliferation*.

16 On the distinction between horizontal and vertical proliferation, see Benoît Pélopidas, *Repenser les choix nucléaires* (Paris: Presses de Sciences Po, 2022).

17 See M. Eliane Bunn, 'Extended Nuclear Deterrence and Assuring Allies', in Charles Glaser, Austin Long and Brian Radzinsky (eds), *Managing U.S. Nuclear Operations in the 21st Century* (Washington DC: Brookings Institution Press, 2022), pp. 166–94.

18 See Glenn H. Snyder, 'The Security Dilemma in Alliance Politics', *World Politics*, vol. 36, no. 4, July 1984, pp. 461–95.

19 See Robert Jervis, 'Deterrence and Perception', *International Security*, vol. 7, no. 3, Winter 1982–83, pp. 3–30.

20 Heather Williams, *Tailored Assurance: Balancing Deterrence and Disarmament in Responding to NATO–Russia Tensions* (Paris: Institut français des relations internationales, 2018), p. 14. See also Iain Henry, *Reliability and Alliance Interdependence* (Ithaca, NY: Cornell University Press, 2022), p. 173.

21 See Bunn, 'Extended Nuclear Deterrence and Assuring Allies'.

22 See Tongfi Kim and Luis Simón, 'A Reputation Versus Prioritization Trade-off: Unpacking Allied Perceptions of US Extended Deterrence in Distant Regions', *Security Studies*, vol. 30, no. 5, December 2021, pp. 725–60.

23 See Tongfi Kim and Luis Simón, 'Power and Perceptions: How Allies View America's Reputation and Prioritisation After Ukraine', CSDS Policy Brief 16/2023, Centre for Security, Diplomacy and Strategy, 31 May 2023, https://csds.vub.be/wp-content/uploads/2023/09/CSDS-Policy-brief_2316.pdf.

24 This does not necessarily apply to conventional capabilities. See, for example, Ronald R. Krebs and Jennifer Spindel, 'Divided Priorities: Why and When Allies Differ Over Military Intervention', *Security Studies*, vol. 27, no. 4, July 2018, pp. 575–606.

25 See Kim and Simón, 'Power and Perceptions'; and Evan Braden Montgomery, 'Primacy and Punishment: US Grand Strategy, Maritime Power, and Military Options to Manage Decline', *Security Studies*, vol. 29, no. 4, August 2020, pp. 769–96.

26 Henry, *Reliability and Alliance Interdependence*, p. 17.

27 See Ankit Panda and Vipin Narang, 'Sole Purpose Is Not No First Use: Nuclear Weapons and Declaratory

Policy', *War on the Rocks*, 22 February 2021, https://warontherocks. com/2021/02/sole-purpose-is-not-no-first-use-nuclear-weapons-and-declaratory-policy/.

28 See Hans M. Kristensen and Matt Korda, 'United States Nuclear Forces, 2020', *Bulletin of the Atomic Scientists*, vol. 76, no. 1, January 2020, pp. 46–60; and Keir A. Lieber and Daryl G. Press, 'The New Era of Counterforce: Technological Change and the Future of Nuclear Deterrence', *International Security*, vol. 41, no. 4, Spring 2017, pp. 9–49.

29 See Dallas Boyd, 'Challenging Nuclear Bromides', *Survival*, vol. 65, no. 5, October–November 2023, pp. 75–94.

30 See *ibid.*; and Charles L. Glaser, James M. Acton and Steve Fetter, 'The U.S. Nuclear Arsenal Can Deter Both China and Russia', *Foreign Affairs*, 5 October 2023, https://www.foreignaffairs.com/united-states/us-nuclear-arsenal-can-deter-both-china-and-russia.

31 See Center for Global Security Research, 'China's Emergence as a Second Nuclear Peer'.

32 See Glaser, Acton and Fetter, 'The US Nuclear Arsenal Can Deter Both China and Russia'.

33 See Scott D. Sagan and Kenneth Waltz, *The Spread of Nuclear Weapons: A Debate Renewed* (New York: W. W. Norton & Co., 2002).

34 See Talmadge, 'Multipolar Deterrence in the Emerging Nuclear Era', p. 23.

35 US Department of Defense, '2022 Nuclear Posture Review', p. 6. See also Brad Roberts, 'Tripolar Stability: The Future of Nuclear Relations Among the United States, Russia, and China', IDA Paper P-3727, Institute for Defense Analyses, September

2002, https://apps.dtic.mil/sti/tr/pdf/ADA409682.pdf; and Talmadge, 'Multipolar Deterrence in the Emerging Nuclear Era', p. 23.

36 See Talmadge, 'Multipolar Deterrence in the Emerging Nuclear Era'.

37 See Brendan R. Green, *The Revolution that Failed: Nuclear Competition, Arms Control, and the Cold War* (Cambridge: Cambridge University Press, 2020), pp. 21–3; and Talmadge, 'Multipolar Deterrence in the Emerging Nuclear Era', p. 25.

38 See Paul Avey, 'Just Like Yesterday? New Critiques of the Nuclear Revolution', *Texas National Security Review*, vol. 6, no. 2, Spring 2023, pp. 9–31.

39 See Linton Brooks and Mira Rapp-Hooper, 'Extended Deterrence, Assurance, and Reassurance in the Pacific During the Second Nuclear Age', in Ashley J. Tellis, Abraham Denmark and Travis Tanner (eds), *Strategic Asia 2013–14: Asia in the Second Nuclear Age* (Seattle, WA: National Bureau of Asian Research, 2014); and Talmadge, 'Multipolar Deterrence in the Emerging Nuclear Era', p. 25.

40 See Richard Betts, *Nuclear Blackmail and Nuclear Balance* (Washington DC: Brookings Institution Press, 1987); Keir A. Lieber and Daryl G. Press, *The Myth of the Nuclear Revolution: Power Politics in the Atomic Age* (Ithaca, NY: Cornell University Press, 2020); Earl C. Ravenal, 'Counterforce and Alliance: The Ultimate Connection', *International Security*, vol. 6, no. 4, Spring 1982, pp. 26–43; and Erich Weede, 'Some (Western) Dilemmas in Managing Extended Deterrence',

Journal of Peace Research, vol. 22, no. 3, September 1985, pp. 223–38.

41 See Mark Bell, *Nuclear Reactions: How Nuclear-armed States Behave* (Ithaca, NY: Cornell University Press, 2023), pp. 144–5; and Francis Gavin, *Nuclear Weapons and American Grand Strategy* (Washington DC: Brookings Institution Press, 2020), p. 95.

42 See 'Book Review Roundtable: The Meaning of the Nuclear Revolution 30 Years Later', *Texas National Security Review*, 30 April 2020, https://tnsr.org/roundtable/book-review-roundtable-the-meaning-of-the-nuclear-revolution-30-years-later/; Brendan Green and Austin Long, 'The MAD Who Wasn't There: Soviet Reactions to the Late Cold War Nuclear Balance', *Security Studies*, vol. 26, no. 4, October 2017, pp. 606–41; Matthew Kroenig, *The Logic of American Nuclear Strategy: Why Strategic Superiority Matters* (Oxford: Oxford University Press, 2018); Lieber and Press, *The Myth of the Nuclear Revolution*; and Weede, 'Some (Western) Dilemmas in Managing Extended Deterrence'.

43 See 'Book Review Roundtable'.

44 See Thomas C. Schelling, *The Strategy of Conflict* (Cambridge, MA: Harvard University Press, 1960).

45 See Anna Clara Arndt, Liviu Horovitz and Lydia Wachs, 'The US "Sole Purpose" Debate: A Backgrounder', SWP Working Paper no. 3, Stiftung Wissenschaft und Politik, December 2021; and Brad Roberts, 'On Creating the Conditions for Nuclear Disarmament: Past Lessons, Future Prospects', *Washington Quarterly*, vol. 42, no. 2, Summer 2019, pp. 7–30.

46 See George Bunn and Roland M. Timerbaev, 'Security Assurances to Non-nuclear-weapons States', *Nonproliferation Review*, vol. 1, no. 1, Fall 1993, p. 13. See also Virginia Foran (ed.), *Security Assurances: Implications for the NPT and Beyond* (Washington DC: Carnegie Endowment for International Peace, 1995); and US Department of State, 'Secretary Anthony J. Blinken's Remarks to the Nuclear Non-Proliferation Treaty Review Conference', 1 August 2022, https://www.state.gov/secretary-antony-j-blinkens-remarks-to-the-nuclear-non-proliferation-treaty-review-conference/.

47 See Joseph F. Pilat, 'Reassessing Security Assurances in a Unipolar World', *Washington Quarterly*, vol. 28, no. 2, Spring 2005, pp. 159–70.

48 See George Bunn, 'The Legal Status of U.S. Negative Security Assurances to Non-nuclear Weapon States', *Nonproliferation Review*, vol. 4, no. 3, Spring–Summer 1997, pp. 1–17; and Pilat, 'Reassessing Security Assurances in a Unipolar World'.

49 See Pilat, 'Reassessing Security Assurances in a Unipolar World'.

50 See Stephan Frühling and Andrew O'Neil, 'Alliances and Nuclear Risk: Strengthening US Extended Deterrence', *Survival*, vol. 64, no. 1, February–March 2022, pp. 77–98; and Knopf, 'Varieties of Assurance', p. 389.

51 Knopf, 'Varieties of Assurance', p. 389.

52 See Paul Meyer and Tom Sauer, 'The Nuclear Ban Treaty: A Sign of Global Impatience', *Survival*, vol. 60, no. 2, April–May 2018, pp. 61–72.

53 See Knopf, *Security Assurances and Nuclear Nonproliferation*.

54 See Mount, 'The US and South Korea'; and Lauren Sukin and Toby Dalton,

'Reducing Nuclear Salience: How to Reassure Northeast Asian Allies', *Washington Quarterly*, vol. 44, no. 2, Summer 2021, pp. 143–58. For a related argument, see Ariel E. Levite, 'Never Say Never Again: Nuclear Reversal Revisited', *International Security*, vol. 27, no. 3, Winter 2002/03, pp. 59–88.

Review Essay

The Rise of Economic Nationalism

Hanns W. Maull

EU and US Foreign Economic Policy Responses to China: The End of Naivety
Joachim Schild and Dirk Schmidt. Abingdon: Routledge, 2023.
£130.00. 272 pp.

The 'unipolar moment' began in 1990 and lasted about two decades. This moment came with its own ideology – neo-liberalism, 'the disenchantment of politics by economics'[1] – which seemed to replace the centrality of national security with the imperative of economic efficiency. The hidden assumption was that this would help cement US dominance in the global order.[2] Economic statecraft withered while globalisation boomed, driven by the foreign-economic policies of America, China and the European Union. Geopolitics and economic statecraft have since returned with a vengeance to international affairs.

Two major developments ignited this resurgence. The first was the global financial crisis in 2008–09, triggered by the bankruptcy of the US investment bank Lehman Brothers.[3] Its repercussions undermined the credibility of neo-liberalism. The second was the rise of China. This had started much earlier, but was accelerated by the crash. China had never bought into the neo-liberal canon, but exploited it to bolster its own national security,

Hanns W. Maull is Senior Distinguished Fellow at Stiftung Wissenschaft und Politik (SWP) and an adjunct professor for international relations and strategic studies at the Johns Hopkins School of Advanced International Studies (SAIS) Europe. He is co-author (with Alexandra Sakaki, Kerstin Lukner, Ellis Krauss and Thomas Berger) of *Reluctant Warriors: Germany, Japan, and Their U.S. Alliance Dilemma* (Brookings Institution Press, 2019).

Survival | vol. 66 no. 2 | April–May 2024 | pp. 157–164   https://doi.org/10.1080/00396338.2024.2332067

wealth and power. In doing so, it followed the East Asian tradition of the 'developmental state', first conceived by Japan, which involved mercantilism and cleverly crafted industrial policy.[4] Variants of the developmental state were behind the East Asian 'economic miracle' in the second half of the last century.[5] Perceived threats to national security drove aspirations to create 'rich countries, strong armies'.[6] While the first-wave economic powers in East Asia were either allies of the United States or non-aligned middle powers that could be easily integrated into the existing international order, China was different. For the first time, a rising power represented a potential adversary of the West and the United States.

The essence of China's rise is captured by 'Made in China 2025', China's blueprint for building a globally dominant high-tech manufacturing sector, issued in 2013. China has channelled enormous amounts of money and imposed an array of sophisticated policy regulations with an eye to dominating virtually all global high-tech industries, from aeronautics through biotechnology to quantum computing and space exploration, by the middle of this decade.[7] Made in China 2025 and the Belt and Road Initiative (BRI), a programme to connect the Global South and much of the rest of the world with China's economy through international commerce, also announced in 2013, outlined a new Chinese grand strategy.[8] Made in China 2025 was to provide the muscle, BRI the sinew.

Responses to Chinese economic statecraft

Economic statecraft – the coupling of economic means with the purposes of national power and national security – has thus come back into fashion, reviving interest in classic works such as those of Albert Hirschman, David Baldwin and Klaus Knorr.[9] It seeks to strengthen a country's own national military power and economic base through industrial policies, an example being China's 'civil–military fusion'.[10] It mobilises 'carrots' such as loans or bribes, and 'sticks' such as boycotts or embargoes, to influence the behaviour of other states, blocs or organisations. Economic statecraft also aims to weaken the military power of opponents and their economic bases. Finally, it may be deployed to restructure international economic exchanges and the rules that govern them, as Western financial sanctions against Russia after its invasion of Ukraine restricted Russia's access to the international financial system.

In the shift towards geo-economics, China has been the primary challenge to America and Europe. How they have responded, why they have responded as they have, and how and why their responses have differed are the three questions that Joachim Schild and Dirk Schmidt endeavour to answer in *EU and US Foreign Economic Policy Responses to China: The End of Naivety*. The book represents the first comprehensive, in-depth and comparative assessment of these issues. In their first substantive chapter, the authors detail China's push for economic power and its mercantilist logic. They employ a liberal framework that includes the key principles of 'reciprocity' and a 'level playing field'. Yet, from Beijing's point of view, China's interaction with the global economy centred not on implementing those principles but on laying the economic foundations for a great-power role in world affairs. The Chinese Communist Party leadership cleverly used market mechanisms, but also deployed extensive state ownership and intervention to exploit the opportunities offered by globalisation. Membership in the World Trade Organization (WTO) was tactically useful to China, but somewhat indigestible for the rest of the world. While Schild and Schmidt manage to highlight the deep chasm between Chinese and Western economic policies, in confining their analysis to economic policy they elide the comprehensive nature of China's grand strategy, which strives to connect economic and political means and ends seamlessly.

The subsequent two chapters provide detailed, in-depth assessments of European and American policy responses, including tariffs and anti-dumping measures, foreign inward and outward direct-investment screening, export controls, supply-chain regulation, government-procurement provisions and industrial policies in support of high-tech manufacturing and innovation, such as the CHIPS and Science Act and the Inflation Reduction Act in the United States and the Chips Act in the EU.

These essentially empirical chapters are preceded by a sophisticated and somewhat lengthy theoretical framework, and followed by a comparative analysis of European and American policies. The authors point to a paradigm shift in foreign-economic policies on both sides of the Atlantic, away from an essentially liberal framework – characterised as 'ad hoc globalization' in the US and 'managed globalization' in the EU – towards a mercantilist emphasis on sovereignty, autonomy, resilience and security.

Differences in American and European responses

While both America and Europe are now focusing on economic security, they are doing so in different ways. The US defines and pursues defensive and offensive economic goals vis-à-vis China to secure its dominant position in world affairs, whereas the EU continues to emphasise multilateralism rather than strategic competition. America's new approach seeks to contain China's rise by targeting its material capabilities and denying it access to key cutting-edge technologies, such as semiconductors and the tools needed to produce them. Both the Trump and Biden administrations have pursued what Schild and Schmidt call a 'zero-sum "whole of society" competition in a global struggle for power and status between the two major powers in the international system' (p. 235). Europe's 'de-risking' approach, by contrast, aims to diminish its high dependence on China as a supplier and thus level the playing field between the two sides. At the same time, Europe wants to protect its profitable commercial relations with China.

Military security casts a very long shadow over America's policies, but it is largely absent from the EU's. While US responses reflect, in the judgement of the authors, 'a comprehensive form of economic nationalism', the EU continues to cling to the idea of free trade, which is 'deeply engrained' in its DNA (p. 237). America sees itself in an existential, great-power contest with China for national security and primacy in world affairs, while Europe does not. Schild and Schmidt also note that European policy changes have been more incremental than those of the US, which they characterise as 'sweeping, punctuated and disruptive' (p. 243), reflecting a much higher degree of politicisation.

The differences in American and European responses are most obviously explained by the nature of the respective beasts: while the US is a sovereign nation-state and a great power whose executive branch dominates foreign relations, the EU is a unique political entity with much more complicated political decision-making. The authors consider other factors as well, such as the influence of vested interests in foreign-economic policymaking. Here, they find that in both America and Europe, demands for protection against import competition from China have grown as the Chinese economy moved from largely complementary to competitive in its foreign-trade patterns with the West. This meant China was now advancing on the commanding heights of advanced Western industries, prompting ever more intense calls for protection.

*　　　*　　　*

Schild and Schmidt concentrate on what they define as foreign-economic policies. As their analysis shows, however, it is increasingly difficult to separate 'foreign' from 'domestic' and 'economic' from 'security'. The consensus is that for America to blunt China's challenge to its dominant position in the global order, it will have to start at home, initiating far-reaching changes to bring its economy and society up to speed for a new global contest.[11] Furthermore, economic statecraft will itself change the country that applies it, its intended target and the international context in ways that may be unintended and unpredictable. America and China have each adopted policy measures that the other perceives in its own way and for its own purposes. Ironically, this may make America and China more alike in some respects and produce mirror-imaging that increases their antagonism.[12] America's and China's economic nationalism, which the authors see gathering further momentum in the future, is a case in point. Others will follow their example and further undermine the already fragile international trade order centred on the WTO. Geopolitically, this will likely leave Europe caught somewhere in between America and China in their struggle for global dominance, and its ideals of multilateralism and functioning international institutions marginalised in favour of security alliances, hedging and transactional relationships. Whether Europe will be able to hold its own in this new world is a critical question.

The authors do not discuss the shift in China's economic policy under President Xi Jinping in recent years that both anticipated and accounted for American and European responses. Encapsulated in the catchphrase 'dual circulation', it turns on reducing China's dependence on the world economy – what America and Europe call de-risking.[13] More time will be needed to permit a thorough evaluation of the results of American, Chinese and European economic statecraft. Sanctions, for instance, are a particularly prominent and popular tool of economic statecraft, but one of highly uncertain effectiveness.[14] The imposition of heavy sanctions on Russia after the annexation of Crimea in 2014 and, even more severely, since the attack on Ukraine in 2022 justifies scepticism.[15] Broader doubts about the efficacy of economic statecraft are warranted. Will it make its practitioners more secure, resilient, powerful and autonomous? Can China be contained through economic statecraft combined with military deterrence? Will China forsake its economic dynamism, opting instead for a new, more insular mode of economic statecraft? Whatever the answers, the authors persuasively conclude that the trend towards economic nationalism is unlikely to be reversed any time soon.

Notes

1   William Davies, *The Limits of Neoliberalism: Authority, Sovereignty and the Logic of Competition*, rev. ed. (Thousand Oaks, CA: Sage, 2017), p. xiv.

2   See Helen Thompson, *Disorder: Hard Times in the 21st Century* (Oxford: Oxford University Press, 2022); and Martin Wolf, *The Crisis of Democratic Capitalism* (New York: Penguin Press, 2023).

3   See Adam Tooze, *Crashed: How a Decade of Financial Crises Changed the World* (New York: Penguin Press, 2019).

4   Earlier European and American thinking and practice – notably that of Friedrich List and Alexander Hamilton, respectively – inspired the concept. See Chalmers Johnson, *MITI and the Japanese Miracle: The Growth of Industrial Policy, 1925–1975* (Stanford, CA: Stanford University Press, 1982); and Robert Wade, *Governing the Market: Economic Theory and the Role of Government in East Asian Industrialization* (Princeton, NJ: Princeton University Press, 1990). For a fascinating comparison between contemporary China and imperial Germany, see Markus Brunnermeier, Rush Doshi and Harold James, 'Beijing's Bismarckian Ghosts: How Great Powers Compete Economically', *Washington Quarterly*, vol. 41, no. 3, Fall 2018, pp. 161–76.

5   See Nancy M. Birdsall et al., *The East Asian Miracle: Economic Growth and Public Policy* (Oxford: Oxford University Press for the World Bank, 1998).

6   The formulation 'rich country, strong army' originated in ancient

China during the period of the warring states and was later taken up by imperial Japan as well as communist China. See Oliver Corff, '"Rich Country, Strong Army": China's Comprehensive National Security', Security Policy Working Paper No. 17/2018, Federal Academy for Security Policy, 2018, https://www.baks.bund.de/en/working-papers/2018/rich-country-strong-army-chinas-comprehensive-national-security; and Richard J. Samuels, 'Rich Nation, Strong Army': National Security and the Technological Transformation of Japan (Ithaca, NY: Cornell University Press, 1994).

7   For details, see Jost Wübbeke et al., 'Made in China 2025: The Making of a High-tech Superpower and Consequences for Industrial Countries', Mercator Institute for China Studies (MERICS) Papers on China, no. 2, December 2016, https://espas.secure.europarl.europa.eu/orbis/system/files/generated/document/en/MPOC_No.2_MadeinChina_2025.pdf.

8   See Rush Doshi, The Long Game: China's Grand Strategy to Displace American Order (Oxford: Oxford University Press, 2021); and Aaron L. Friedberg, A Contest for Supremacy: China, America and the Struggle for Mastery in Asia (New York: W. W. Norton & Co., 2011).

9   See David A. Baldwin, Economic Statecraft (Princeton, NJ: Princeton University Press, 1985); Albert O. Hirschman, National Power and the Structure of Foreign Trade (Berkeley, CA: University of California Press, 1945); and Klaus Knorr, Power and

Wealth: The Political Economy of International Power (New York: Basic Books, 1973).

10   Richard A. Bitzinger, Yoram Evron and Zi Yang, 'China's Military–Civil Fusion Strategy: Development, Procurement, and Secrecy', Asia Policy, vol. 16, no. 1, January 2021, pp. 1–64.

11   This has also become a key theme in the China policy of the Biden administration. See Kurt M. Campbell and Jake Sullivan, 'Competition Without Catastrophe: How America Can Both Challenge and Coexist with China', Foreign Affairs, vol. 98, no. 5, September/October 2019, pp. 96–110; and White House, 'Remarks by National Security Advisor Jake Sullivan on Renewing American Economic Leadership at the Brookings Institution', 27 April 2023, https://www.whitehouse.gov/briefing-room/speeches-remarks/2023/04/27/remarks-by-national-security-advisor-jake-sullivan-on-renewing-american-economic-leadership-at-the-brookings-institution/.

12   See Hanns W. Maull, Angela Stanzel and Johannes Thimm, 'United States and China on a Collision Course: The Importance of Domestic Politics for the Bilateral Relationship', Stiftung Wissenschaft und Politik, SWP Research Paper 5, May 2023, https://www.swp-berlin.org/10.18449/2023RP05/.

13   See 'China's "Dual-circulation" Strategy Means Relying Less on Foreigners', The Economist, 5 November 2020, https://www.economist.com/china/2020/11/05/chinas-dual-circulation-strategy-means-relying-less-on-foreigners. See also Barry Naughton and Briana

Boland, 'CCP Inc.: The Reshaping of China's State Capitalist System', Center for Strategic and International Studies, January 2023, https://csis-website-prod.s3.amazonaws.com/s3fs-public/2023-01/230131_Naughton_Reshaping_CCPInc_0.pdf.

14 See Özgür Özdamar and Evgeniia Shahin, 'Consequences of Economic Sanctions: State of the Art and Paths Forward', *International Studies Review*, vol. 23, no. 4, December 2021, pp. 1,646–71.

15 See 'Are Sanctions on Russia Working?', *The Economist*, 25 August 2022, https://www.economist.com/leaders/2022/08/25/are-sanctions-working.

Book Reviews

United States
David C. Unger

**The Anti-oligarchy Constitution: Reconstructing the
Economic Foundations of American Democracy**
Joseph Fishkin and William E. Forbath. Cambridge, MA:
Harvard University Press, 2022. £34.95/$41.00. 640 pp.

Judicial review appears nowhere in the US Constitution; it was invented by
the Supreme Court itself. Yet today's Americans have come to believe that the
Supreme Court is the sole interpreter of what the Constitution permits or requires.

In this important and readable book, law professors Joseph Fishkin and
William Forbath marshal a historically grounded challenge to that conventional wisdom. Their sweeping reinterpretation of US political and legal
history is aimed at demonstrating that the court's rulings have assumed such
a definitive aura only in recent decades. They show that, from the earliest days
of the American republic through the 1940s, constitutional interpretation had
been shaped and reshaped by back-and-forth dialogues between the political
and judicial branches of government. They urge us to understand constitutional interpretation as an ongoing and inherently political process, a battle
over competing normative visions of what purposes the American republic is
meant to serve.

Their own vision is one they call the 'Democracy of Opportunity' tradition
– a formulation taken from Franklin D. Roosevelt's speech accepting the 1936
Democratic presidential nomination. This tradition sees the Constitution's overriding purpose as being expressed in its Article 4 guarantee of a 'Republican Form
of Government'. Fishkin and Forbath argue that making good on that guarantee
imposes three affirmative duties on America's political and judicial branches:

Survival | vol. 66 no. 2 | April–May 2024 | pp. 165–172   https://doi.org/10.1080/00396338.2024.2332068

1) erecting and maintaining 'restraints against oligarchy'; 2) assuring 'a political economy that sustains a robust middle class'; and 3) applying and expanding 'a constitutional principle of inclusion' that transcends race, sex and other potential lines of exclusion (p. 3).

Fishkin and Forbath argue that these three principles, rather than textual literalism or originalism, should guide constitutional interpretation in a process not confined to the court alone, but engaged in by the elected branches as well, and ultimately decided by the sovereign people. In other words, without a numerically dominant middle class operating in an open and competitive economy, sufficiently freed from the fear of want to take part in political life, and inclusive of all Americans, republican government as conceived by the Framers cannot survive. The authors argue that for most of American history, the biggest threats to achieving those conditions have been oligarchy, economic depression and racism.

The chief opposing constitutional tradition they discuss is one that has become known as 'Lochnerism' after the landmark 1905 Supreme Court decision in the case of *Lochner v. New York*. In that case, the court struck down a New York state maximum-hours law for bakers, ruling that it violated the 14th Amendment's guarantee of freedom of private contract. More broadly, the authors see the *Lochner* decision's reasoning as embodying a constitutional tradition built around the Madisonian supremacy of property and contracts, not the Jeffersonian ideal of egalitarian citizenship.

Tracing the history of these two competing constitutional traditions through Reconstruction and the New Deal to the present, Fishkin and Forbath conclude that the three guiding principles of the Democracy of Opportunity tradition must stand or fall together – in other words, that an anti-oligarchic, middle-class interpretation prospers when it embraces inclusion and falters when it does not. The evidence from American history is ambiguous. The two periods that saw the strongest efforts to broaden inclusion – the first Reconstruction era of the 1860s and 1870s, and what has been called the 'second reconstruction' of the 1960s – both gave way to America's first and second Gilded Ages, periods in which oligarchy and plutocracy triumphed in the judicial and political arenas.

What It Took to Win: A History of the Democratic Party
Michael Kazin. New York: Farrar, Straus and Giroux, 2022.
$20.00. 432 pp.

It is no small challenge to write a coherent history of the US Democratic Party, from its Jacksonian origins as a white man's party upholding slavery, states' rights and the ethnic cleansing of America's native population to today's 'woke' party of rainbow coalitions, multiculturalism and activist federal government. Michael Kazin, who teaches history at Georgetown University and who formerly edited the democratic-left journal *Dissent*, successfully takes up this challenge in *What It Took to Win*. The six previous books Kazin authored or co-authored on various strands of the Democratic Party's left wing prepared him well for this larger task, broadening his historical perspective and illustrating how a wide range of ideologies and constituencies managed simultaneously to find homes within broader Democratic electoral coalitions. It helps too that Kazin is a clear and graceful writer who artfully draws on his research to enliven his narrative with colourful stories of individual Democrats and their not-always-successful efforts to shape party policies.

Kazin creates a unifying theme by noting the Democrats' consistent portrayal of themselves as 'the Democracy' – the party of the common people against special interests, and of the disempowered many against the powerful few. Using this narrative device allows him to trace continuities between Democrats as different as Andrew Jackson, William Jennings Bryan, Woodrow Wilson, Franklin Roosevelt, Harry Truman, Lyndon Johnson and Jesse Jackson. It proves somewhat more of a strain to extend that continuity to such recent Democratic presidents as Jimmy Carter and Bill Clinton.

Kazin does not gloss over the uglier parts of Democratic Party history. He calls out the Jim Crow prejudices and practices of Woodrow Wilson, the decisive role played by the Ku Klux Klan at the Democrats' 1924 convention, the Jim Crow carve-outs Roosevelt made to New Deal programmes to make them more palatable to segregationist southern Democrats, the serial incompetence of Carter, and the social and electoral costs of Clinton's 'triangulation' of Republican ideas and neo-liberal initiatives from the Democratic Leadership Council. Kazin faults Barack Obama for his frustrating political passivity once in office, arguing that he forfeited the best chance in many years to rebuild the Democrats' demographic base beyond minorities and college-educated professionals, and thereby overcome the Republicans' structural small-state advantages in the electoral college and US Senate. Writing in 2022, Kazin sees Joe Biden repeating some of these same political mistakes, albeit in the absence of Obama's stronger electoral mandate and personal charisma. The author looks, hopefully, to the grassroots energies of a revving American labour movement to pick up some slack.

Illusions of Progress: Business, Poverty, and Liberalism in the American Century
Brent Cebul. Philadelphia, PA: University of Pennsylvania Press, 2023. $39.95. 432 pp.

The economic-development strategies now labelled neo-liberal date back long before the 1970s, as Brent Cebul shows in this important revisionist history of government-sponsored urban- and rural-development initiatives throughout the twentieth century. 'Supply-side liberals' (as Cebul calls them) in the federal government have partnered with 'supply-side state builders' in the private sector at least since the days of Franklin Roosevelt's New Deal, leveraging public and private sources of capital, and shaping local spending of federal dollars.

As Cebul's case studies of northwest Georgia (for state-aided rural-development schemes) and the city of Cleveland (for Rust Belt urban-redevelopment programmes) illustrate, such public–private partnerships have consistently reinforced the power of local business establishments. One feature common to programmes in both areas was the incremental marginalisation of African-American interests and voices, reinforcing surviving Jim Crow practices in Georgia and amplifying the political influence of Cleveland's biggest banks, private developers and law firms. By spotlighting Georgia as one of his case studies, Cebul is also able to illustrate the developing political views of Jimmy Carter, first as the state's governor (1971–75) and then as US president (1977–81). Neo-liberal ideas and methods shaped Carter's political career in Georgia long before they became nationally fashionable during his presidency.

Structural forms of neo-liberalism, like public–private partnerships, date back to the New Deal era, but it is only since the mid-1970s that development and redevelopment for their own sakes have displaced empowering the poor as explicit goals of 'New' and 'Third Way' Democrats. Under the Republican administration of Richard Nixon, federally targeted development grants had given way to revenue-sharing block grants that reinforced local power establishments. During the Reagan administration, the federal government sought to withdraw from publicly funded development altogether, over the howls of local power brokers used to federal handouts with few strings attached.

Republicans like Nixon and Ronald Reagan are only one part of this depressing story. Cebul charts supply-side liberal Democrats' steady loss of interest in bargaining on behalf of the poor and marginalised constituencies their party claimed to represent during the New Deal and Great Society eras. That shift in attitudes translated into less determination among Democratic officeholders to involve communities in planning their own futures and a lessened sense of government responsibility for the poor. Meaningful consultation of poor communities peaked, albeit very briefly, during the Great Society years, before Lyndon Johnson quickly heeded the complaints of local power brokers and reined it in. By the 1980s, differently packaged 'trickle-down growth' formulas were all either Democrats or Republicans offered the poor. At least that was the case in Georgia and Cleveland; Cebul doesn't indicate whether the same trends applied elsewhere, though plenty of anecdotal evidence suggests that they did.

Cebul, who teaches history at the University of Pennsylvania, is passionately angry about the story he tells. It's easy to see why.

A Fabulous Failure: The Clinton Presidency and the Transformation of American Capitalism
Nelson Lichtenstein and Judith Stein. Princeton, NJ: Princeton University Press, 2023. £35.00/$39.95. 544 pp.

It takes a frustratingly long time after an American administration leaves office before scholars can do full justice to its record. They must wait until relevant archives are opened, memoirs written and oral histories recorded. Until now, we've had to content ourselves with partial sketches of the Clinton adminis-tration, some depicting the 42nd US president as an archetypical neo-liberal, others as a tactical wizard with infinitely flexible principles, still others as a reinventor of progressive politics for the post-Reagan era – a potentially trans-formative leader whose achievements were cut short by the self-inflicted Lewinsky scandal.

The late Judith Stein, who launched the research project that led to this book, and Nelson Lichtenstein, who completed it after Stein's death in 2017, have now given us the more complete account scholars have been waiting for. *A Fabulous Failure* is the most coherent and insightful study I have yet read on the policies and politics of the Clinton administration.

Stein's research and teaching focused on American social movements and political economy. Lichtenstein has written 18 books spanning labour history, social thought and political economy. Their overlapping skill sets proved useful as they worked their way through the now available primary sources, produc-ing an original, balanced and revisionist account of this pivotal period in which the Democratic Party aligned itself with economic globalisation, welfare-state dismantlement, mass-incarceration anti-crime strategies and financial-market deregulation in ways no Republican administration could have politically carried through. The consequences of these 'New Democrat' policies contin-ued to be felt long after Bill Clinton left office – most notably in the financial meltdown of 2007–08 and the electoral estrangement of former blue-collar Democrats in the Trump era.

Lichtenstein and Stein show how Clinton came to office not as a neo-liberal market fundamentalist but as a different kind of Democrat. His early appointees, such as Robert Reich as labor secretary, Mickey Kantor as chief trade negotiator and Laura Tyson as chair of the White House Council of Economic Advisers, favoured interventionist economic planning and nationalistic trade diplomacy aimed at making American corporations stronger international competitors.

Within his first two years, however, Clinton yielded ground on these and other fronts under the influence of some of his other economic appointees, including Lloyd Bentsen, his first treasury secretary, Robert Rubin, who chaired Clinton's newly created National Economic Council before succeeding Bentsen at the Treasury, and Alan Greenspan, the Reagan-appointed chairman of the Federal Reserve. Whatever survived of early market-interventionist ideas were swept away after the 1994 midterm congressional elections in which the Republicans gained 54 House seats, enabling them to install Newt Gingrich as speaker.

A Fabulous Failure takes readers through successive phases of Clinton's political transformation: the 1993 budget fights over deficits and stimulus; the split in the Democratic Party over the North American Free Trade Agreement (NAFTA); the thwarting of his health-insurance reform proposals by a Democrat-controlled Congress; the fulfilment of Clinton's campaign promise to 'end welfare as we know it'; the punitive racial politics of mass incarceration under the Clinton-championed, Joe Biden-drafted 1994 crime bill; Clinton's sponsorship of China's accession to the World Trade Organization without human-rights conditionality; and his administration's calamitous refusal to regulate exotic financial derivatives, and even more calamitous deregulation of banking and finance.

The political fallout from early battles shaped the political outcome of later ones. Most consequentially, Clinton's alienation of pro-labour Democrats over NAFTA cost him potential votes that might have passed his healthcare reforms. We'll never know what might have happened if he had chosen to take on healthcare first.

By all accounts, Clinton's second-term entanglement with Monica Lewinsky and subsequent impeachment impaired his personal focus. But Lichtenstein and Stein conclude that these did surprisingly little to deflect his administration's post-1994 policy directions. Much as the Watergate scandal strengthened Henry Kissinger's hand in the Nixon administration, Clinton's impeachment reinforced the already decisive influence of Rubin and his acolytes such as Larry Summers, who served as Secretary of the Treasury from 1999 to 2001.

Left Behind: The Democrats' Failed Attempt to Solve Inequality

Lily Geismer. New York: PublicAffairs, 2022. $30.00. 448 pp.

A large new class of Democrats came to office in the elections of the mid-1970s, benefiting from the political fallout from Watergate and the Nixon pardon. Their victories extended the party's base into new demographic turf that was more suburban, socially liberal and fiscally conservative than the labour-oriented urban enclaves that had characterised the previous New Deal Democratic coalition. Many of these newly elected Democrats – men like senator Gary Hart, House members (and future senators) Tim Wirth, Paul Tsongas and Al Gore, and governors Bill Clinton and Michael Dukakis – soon became outspoken critics of old-line liberal Democratic leaders and their New Deal-style policies.

Many of these new Democrats had worked in George McGovern's 1972 presidential campaign (Hart managed it nationally and Clinton helped run its Texas operations). But that year's blowout Democratic defeat, followed by the failed presidential campaigns of Jimmy Carter in 1980 and Walter Mondale in 1984, pushed these newcomers to sound out fresh electoral strategies and policy directions. These new approaches were more market-friendly and less union-friendly than those the Democrats had been running on since the New Deal, their funding less dependent on federal spending, their benefit structures means-tested rather than universal. These policy changes culminated in the founding of the Democratic Leadership Council (DLC) in 1985, which in turn became the launching pad for Clinton's successful 1992 presidential campaign.

The story of the DLC, the policy ideas it nurtured, their application during Clinton's two presidential terms and their real-life consequences for those most directly affected is well told by Lily Geismer, who teaches history at Claremont McKenna College. Drawing from the thinking of the DLC's think tank, the Progressive Policy Institute, Clinton sought to replace New Deal and Great Society-style universal entitlements with public–private initiatives. Through political exhortations, personal networking and fiscal incentives, Clinton sought to replace government-guaranteed benefit programmes with publicly funded, privately run market-based alternatives.

That larger shift underpinned Clinton's tireless promotion of microlending, empowerment zones, charter schools and, most consequentially, welfare reform. It was also reflected in his campaign to 'reinvent government', largely by shrinking it. Geismer tracks the political and intellectual roots of these policies and the early pilot projects that served as their proving grounds, examining what happened when scaled-up versions of the pilots encountered the real world. Many of the resulting programmes were designed for those most able to take advantage of them – in Clinton's frequently repeated phrase, those willing to 'work hard and play by the rules'. Since Clinton was also committed to budget-cutting, many of these were woefully underfunded. And since Clinton was an instinctively silver-tongued politician, many were rhetorically oversold.

As Geismer shows, those unwilling or unable to conform to Clinton's middle-class norms became the 'left behind'. The success or failure of Clinton's programmes often depended on the luck of the economic cycle; even in booms, they shifted a great deal of decision-making from public to private hands. Programmes once intended to buffer the harsh vagaries of the market were replaced by ones that typically reinforced market shocks. Geismer's overall assessment is reflected in the book's subtitle, though the many case studies she presents include individual success stories as well.

In an epilogue, Geismer looks at the devastating social consequences of Clinton's reforms that played out in the years after he left office – from the mass foreclosures of the subprime-mortgage crisis of 2007–08 to the public-sector unpreparedness that worsened the deadly toll of the 2020–22 COVID-19 pandemic. She concludes that 'it is time to stop trying to fuse the functions of the federal government with the private sector' (p. 331).

Middle East
Ray Takeyh

The 1973 Arab–Israeli War
Galen Jackson, ed. Lanham, MD: Rowman & Littlefield, 2023.
£68.00/$89.00. 202 pp.

The 50th anniversary of the 1973 Yom Kippur War has led to a slew of new books. The commemoration comes at a particularly troubling time, with Israel having once more fallen victim to a surprise attack. This time, it was not a coalition of Arab states but the militant Palestinian group Hamas that shocked a complacent Israeli national-security apparatus. As in 1973, Israel finds itself consumed by a large-scale military campaign, with commissions of inquiry sure to follow.

'Intelligence failure' is a phrase often used by politicians seeking to blame spy agencies for their own misjudgements. In 1973, there was plenty of evidence that the Arab states were gearing up for another war to avenge their ignominious defeat during the Six-Day War. As with Hamas's war-planning, it was hard to miss the Arab states' preparations. Yet Israeli officials convinced themselves that the critical Arab state, Egypt, could not mount an attack until it had fully absorbed the Soviet weaponry it had received, something officials believed would take several years. This proved a gross miscalculation, as Risa Brooks demonstrates in her chapter on how Egypt subtly transformed its armed forces into a more effective military machine.

All edited books suffer from certain shortcomings. This volume is no different, and could have focused more on Israel's domestic political scene and the nature of its alliance with the United States. However, this deficiency is more than made up for in careful chapters on Syria's role and the politics of petroleum. Hafez al-Assad stands as one of the more tragic figures in this melodrama, as he really seemed to have gone to war to destroy Israel. His senior partner, Egyptian president Anwar Sadat, was more focused on a symbolic victory to jolt the Americans into launching a peace process. The ploy worked, and eventually the Carter administration negotiated a separate agreement between Israel and Egypt that eliminated the possibility of another inter-state war in the Middle East.

Given the latest conflict in Gaza, there will inevitably be comparisons with the surprise attack of 1973. The differences are more pronounced than the superficial similarities, however. In 1973, Egypt wanted a limited war as a pathway to peace, and after it left the ranks of the Arab radicals, an uneasy truce came to Israel's various frontiers. Hamas is not seeking to revive a peace process, but

Survival | vol. 66 no. 2 | April–May 2024 | pp. 173–179   https://doi.org/10.1080/00396338.2024.2332069

simply to traumatise Israeli society and thwart the Abraham Accords that had normalised relations between Israel and a number of Gulf Arab states. Prior to the attack, it was thought that Saudi Arabia would be the next country to sign a peace pact with the Jewish state.

In the coming months, a reckoning awaits Prime Minister Benjamin Netanyahu, who must eventually explain to his shell-shocked country how he missed all the signs of danger on its southern flank. Commissions of inquiry will make their assessments and the blame game will ensue, but it is hard to see how a politician who prides himself on providing security can withstand the torrent of criticism sure to come his way. The Gaza war is far from over and may yet engulf the entire region. We can hope that cooler heads will prevail, but we are not living in a reasonable age.

Heroes to Hostages: America and Iran, 1800–1988
Firoozeh Kashani-Sabet. Cambridge: Cambridge University Press, 2023. £25.99. 433 pp.

Books about America's relations with Iran are plentiful in the academy and beyond. Most are polemical accounts decrying various aspects of US policy. The trajectory is usually the same: America transformed from what many Iranians believed was a benevolent actor into another imperialist state manipulating Persian politics. This is why *Heroes to Hostages* is such a welcome addition to the literature: it offers a deeply researched and dispassionate account of this thorny relationship.

American curiosity about Persia began with missionaries seeking souls. There were very few converts, but well-meaning Americans staffed plenty of hospitals and schools. All this left a favourable impression as the United States stood aside from the Great Game whereby Britain and Russia carved out their spheres of influence. This game was never a one-way street, as many Persian politicians used their connections to London and Moscow as leverage against their rivals. Indeed, Whitehall had a very cosy relationship with the clerical estate.

The direction of American policy changed as the Second World War ended the United States' splendid isolation. Suddenly, thousands of US troops found themselves in Iran to transport supplies to the beleaguered Russian front through the so-called 'Persian corridor'. America was now represented in Iran by diplomats, generals and spies. Author Firoozeh Kashani-Sabet is fair-minded in chronicling an encounter that was not without its share of misapprehensions. Iran laboured under an occupation that generated shortages and famines as the Allies hoarded food supplies for themselves. In the aftermath of the war, the Soviets refused to withdraw their troops from Azerbaijan, leading to the first crisis of the Cold War. It should never be forgotten that the Truman administration stood by Iran and pressed for the eviction of Soviet forces at the risk of jeopardising the Grand Alliance.

The reign of Shah Mohammad Reza Pahlavi has always presented a challenge for historians, who have regularly sacrificed the presumed objectivity of their craft. CIA complicity in the 1953 coup that displaced the nationalist prime minister Mohammad Mosaddegh has been stripped of its complexity and reduced to a plot by an imperialist state diverting Iran's democratic trajectory. The 1979 revolution is often seen as justified retribution for American sins. Even the hostage-taking of US diplomats in violation of international law has seen its share of justifications.

The author is at her best when navigating this contested terrain. As the Pahlavi dynasty fades into history, a more balanced account of its achievements and shortcomings is finally becoming easier to attain. *Heroes to Hostages* does not limit itself to power politics, but also focuses on the way American culture penetrated certain sectors of Iranian society. This was not always positive, and there was too much borrowing from the West; the sight of unveiled women in miniskirts and young people flocking to Western films offended not just clerics but also intellectuals concerned about a loss of identity. The revolution did away with the old ways, but did not squash the Iranians' quest for a more accountable government.

The Political Ideology of Ayatollah Khamenei: Out of the Mouth of the Supreme Leader of Iran
Yvette Hovsepian-Bearce. Abingdon: Routledge, 2017. £39.99.
398 pp.

Sayyid Ali Khamenei stands as one of the most consequential rulers in the modern Middle East, yet surprisingly little is known about him, and no conventional biography is available. This is an odd shortcoming for a leader who has managed to sustain a revolution at home while helping defeat the United States in the region. *The Political Ideology of Ayatollah Khamenei* will not be the last word on this important figure, but it is the most comprehensive accounting of his ideological perspective so far.

Khamenei was never a conventional cleric. He had an eclectic mind and was interested in Western literature and the radical writings of revolutionary thinkers. He was drawn more to politics than the seminary, and emerged as one of the most influential disciples of Ayatollah Ruhollah Khomeini, leader of the 1979 revolution. He was arrested on six occasions, spending time in prison and internal exile. In the popular recounting of the revolution, he is often overshadowed by larger personalities, but his centrality as a bureaucratic infighter should not be ignored.

Shortly after the triumph of the revolution, Khamenei was put in charge of cleansing Iran of Western culture. Libraries were purged of objectionable books, universities were closed while their curricula were revised, and many writers and intellectuals found themselves out of work. One of this book's more important contributions is to demonstrate how a fixation with cultural purity remains the focus of Khamenei's career. He continues to give speeches about how the most sinister of Western designs is cultural subversion. To Khamenei, Western films are more of a threat than the American armadas that have patrolled Iran's coastlines for the past four decades. It is a losing battle, as Iran's youth are secular in outlook and liberal in cultural disposition. The Supreme Leader likes to deny all this, portraying the country's youth as aligned with his thinking. It's hard to know if he really believes his own rhetoric or is merely dissembling. After all, the young people's rejection of their patrimony would be a terrible blow to the regime.

The Political Ideology of Ayatollah Khamenei is not without its share of problems. It could have used a good editorial scrubbing. There are too many lengthy passages from Khamenei's speeches. The chapters are chronological but choppy. There is little in the way of analysis or assessment. The context is all but missing, and there are few clues as to why Khamenei made the decisions he did, or how both foreign and domestic actors have influenced his thinking. Still, the book offers a deep dive into a treasure trove of material that is indispensable in understanding Iran's philosopher-king.

Today, the 84-year-old Khamenei faces the prospect of succession. As the book makes clear, when Khomeini died in 1989, Khamenei was adamant that any bungling of the regime's first succession process would allow foreigners to exploit the power vacuum to overthrow the government. It remains to be seen whether he has learned important lessons from that episode.

America and the Yemens: A Complex and Tragic Encounter
Bruce Riedel. Washington DC: Brookings Institution Press,
2023. £19.99/$27.00. 104 pp.

Yemen seems synonymous with the word 'tragedy'. An enclave nestled in the Persian Gulf, it has seen its share of invasions, wars and famines. It is a nation often divided against itself, having been formally partitioned at various points in its history. It has flirted with radical ideologies that proved destructive, and strongmen who only looked out for themselves. It has also assumed a centrality hardly merited by its actual importance. Yemen has been a focus of several

American presidents, who have viewed it through either the prism of the Cold War or the cold politics of the Middle East.

In his short and thoughtful book, Bruce Riedel deftly introduces the reader to the many actors and events that have shaped modern Yemen. A practitioner-scholar in the best sense, Riedel brings to his task the experience of a seasoned policymaker who has seen it all, and a scholar with an informed perspective. In the 1960s, the Middle East was fractured between radical Arab states and traditional monarchies. This was the Arab Cold War, and the superpowers lined up behind their respective allies. It was in Yemen that the cold war got hot. The battle between Marxists and monarchists eventually dragged Egypt and Saudi Arabia into the morass of Yemeni politics. When Israel launched its daring attack on front-line Arab states in 1967, Egypt's best troops were stuck in a Yemeni quagmire. As with Lyndon Johnson and Vietnam, Yemen was a war that Gamal Abdel Nasser could not win but would not quit.

Today, Yemen is once more the focus of a war. The remnants of the old order are battling a determined insurgency led by the Houthis. A Shia offshoot, the Houthis cannot be described as clients of Iran, having arrived at their radical stance on America and Israel all on their own. Saudi Arabia's impetuous leader, Prince Muhammad bin Salman, failed to learn the lessons of history, launching a clumsy and cruel invasion of Yemen shortly after coming to power. As Riedel demonstrates, approximately 400,000 Yemenis have died, and the healthcare service has all but collapsed. As is usual in the developing world, most of the victims of this war have been children. Riedel chides successive American presidents, both Democrats and Republicans, for indulging the Saudis. The war seems to have subsided not through Saudi victory – despite Riyadh spending billions – but Chinese mediation. It was China that brokered an agreement between Saudi Arabia and Iran that saw the lowering of temperatures in Yemen.

More accustomed to war than peace, the Houthis have taken sides in the Gaza war. With Iranian support, they have launched attacks on commercial shipping in the Persian Gulf, disrupting maritime traffic in those critical waterways. The United States and United Kingdom have launched retaliatory strikes, but it remains to be seen whether such action will deter the perennially reckless Houthis. As another conflict looms in the Gulf, *America and the Yemens* should prove a valuable resource for both general readers and policymakers alike.

Hezbollahland: Mapping Dahiya and Lebanon's Shia Community
Hanin Ghaddar. Washington DC: The Washington Institute for
Near East Policy, 2022. £46.00/$60.00. 132 pp.

Hizbullah is one of the most lethal terrorist organisations in the Middle East. Its record includes killing 241 American marines in Lebanon and attacking a Jewish centre in Argentina. It is a terror group with a truly global reach. Hizbullah, more so than any other Iranian proxy, is a direct creation of the Islamic Republic, and is its most prized protégé. In the early 1980s, Tehran began to amalgamate various Shia groups into Hizbullah, beginning a relationship that has brought the group billions of dollars in Iranian assistance. In this important monograph, Hanin Ghaddar focuses on the small Shia enclave of Dahiya, a suburb in southern Beirut, to draw larger and sensible conclusions about Hizbullah.

Dahiya might be overwhelmingly Shia, but it features its own class stratifications. Hizbullah's message of Shia inclusion has evidently not stopped it from seeking to enrich its elite, aid its supporters and deny resources to those deemed insufficiently loyal. Brutality and targeted killings have been the hallmarks of its power grab, but it has also participated in electoral politics and gained control of state ministries, whose funds it has misused for its own purposes. At a time when Lebanon's financial order is collapsing, Hizbullah's state-within-a-state is doing more harm than the usual inefficiencies and corruption of Lebanese leaders.

The core question that this monograph addresses is whether Hizbullah is losing support within the Shia community. For a long time, Hizbullah was assumed to be a vanguard organisation that forced Lebanon's Sunni and Christian notables, who had long divided power among themselves, to pay attention to the Shia slums. Hizbullah developed a sophisticated armed militia, but it also created social services, hospitals and schools that attracted Shi'ites with little affection for its anti-America and anti-Israeli crusades. The group all but dispensed with the other Shia political organisation, Amal, and made itself central to Lebanon. And then came Israel's departure in 2000 from its security sector in southern Lebanon, a withdrawal that was largely attributed to Hizbullah's hit-and-run tactics. The organisation seemed to have reached the peak of its influence.

All of this began to change in the wake of some catastrophic mistakes. In 2006, Hizbullah engaged in a war with Israel that devastated Beirut. While Hizbullah was not defeated, its leader, Hassan Nasrallah, made the unusual admission that, had he anticipated the scale of Israeli retaliation, he would not have inflamed the southern border. This was cold comfort for those Lebanese

– many of whom were Shia – whose homes and businesses were destroyed during the Israeli strikes.

Then came the Arab Spring and the revolt against Bashar al-Assad in Syria. Iran was determined to enter the fray and save Assad, and made use of Hizbullah troops to do so. Suddenly, the Shia militia was involved in slaughtering hundreds of thousands of Sunnis. Assad survived, but it is hard to see how that benefited Hizbullah in a multi-confessional Lebanese society. With the advent of Hamas's 7 October 2023 attack against Israel, Hizbullah is once more threatening intervention, with all its attendant consequences for Lebanon.

The price of being Iran's proxy and surrogate in the region has indeed been costly. As this monograph demonstrates, many Shi'ites are beginning to question the price they have paid for Hizbullah's subordination of Lebanese interests to Iran's revolutionary priorities.

Asia-Pacific
Lanxin Xiang

The Light of Asia: A History of Western Fascination with the East
Christopher Harding. London: Allen Lane, 2024. £30.00.
464 pp.

This is an ambitious yet timely project to identify continuities and discontinuities in the interactions between two ancient civilisations in the East – China and India – with so-called Greco-Roman civilisation, broadly known today as the 'West', across several millennia. Christopher Harding seems able to manage the subject with flying colours, and his analysis illuminates features of East–West interaction in the present day.

Harding writes that from the early modern era, Asia attracted Western fascination as a place of 'wealth and wonder', and as a source of 'fresh wisdom for the West'. The 'light of Asia', he says, 'appeared, for a time, to shine especially brightly in China'. Europeans such as Voltaire and Gottfried Wilhelm Leibniz were 'thrilled to discover an ancient and successful society, built and maintained on learning and merit' rather than feudal and clerical privilege (p. 3). Early Portuguese visitors to China, who were 'not especially welcome' (p. 69), found a 'learned place' that was 'peaceable, and well-fed', with 'impressive' architecture and 'sophisticated' arts and crafts (pp. 71–2). There was little cause for Europeans, who were classified as 'outer barbarians' by the Chinese world view, to feel superior (p. 69).

Westerners have been more confident in their encounters with Indian civilisation, which, unlike China's, was known for its poverty and a chaotic cultural identity comprising many religions and languages – a consequence of India having been conquered on numerous occasions by foreign powers, starting with Alexander the Great. China had some experience with foreign conquest too, notably by the Mongols and Manchus, but the alien rulers had quickly become assimilated to Chinese culture and ways of governance. Thus, there was, from the beginning, a major difference in the interactions between the Western world and the two Asian civilisations. Indo-Western relations started in ancient times and involved direct military conquest, while Sino-Western relations involved minimal direct contact until the 1840s (the first Opium War). Interactions with India were more of a one-way street, with Western culture often prevailing, while there was greater resistance to Western influence in China. Both patterns have lasted to our times.

Two fantasies dominate contemporary Western thinking about Asia. One is that India will overtake China, a prospect seen as welcome in the West because

 https://doi.org/10.1080/00396338.2024.2332070

India is 'one of us', the world's 'most populous democracy'. The second is that China will eventually converge with Western systems of governance. Neither vision seems realisable.

Nevertheless, India is still being enthusiastically courted by contemporary Greco-Romans, who have invented the geopolitical concept of 'Indo-Pacific' to highlight its importance. Yet India is not part of the Greco-Roman world. It is resisting the Western-led international order, known today as Pax Americana, in a variety of ways, such as buying Russian energy products in massive quantities.

The United States–South Korea Alliance: Why It May Fail and Why It Must Not
Scott A. Snyder. New York: Columbia University Press, 2023.
£30.00/$35.00. 336 pp.

The United States and South Korea have enjoyed a cooperative alliance relationship for more than 70 years, but Scott Snyder warns that

> it would be a mistake to ignore emerging domestic political vulnerabilities that threaten alliance cooperation resulting from a combination of narrow nationalism and deepening domestic political polarization in both countries that became visible during the Trump and Moon administrations. (pp. ix–x)

According to the author, these trends suggest that the greatest risk to alliance cohesion lies not in 'external threats such as North Korea's nuclear development or China's ambition to recreate a Sinocentric world order', but rather in domestic developments such as 'political polarization and new conceptions of national interest in both the United States and South Korea' (p. x).

Snyder writes that the alliance's vulnerability to 'exclusive forms of self-interested nationalism' was on full display in Donald Trump's '"America-First" extortionist demands' for increased financial contributions by South Korea to maintain the presence of US troops on the Korean Peninsula (p. 4). Trump portrayed South Korea as a rich free-rider that had 'conned' the United States into defending it:

> When top U.S. military commanders stationed in the country showed Trump the revamped and gleaming Camp Humphreys, a U.S. military base … that was expanded with an almost $10 billion investment from South Korea, Trump used it as evidence that South Korea should and could pay even more for the presence of U.S. forces in South Korea rather than as evidence of South Korean commitment to the alliance. (p. 4)

Things may have improved somewhat under the leadership of Joe Biden in the US and Yoon Suk-yeol in South Korea, but the threat remains. Opposition leader Lee Jae-myung, who has displayed an inclination to 'prioritize inter-Korean reconciliation over U.S.–South Korea alliance coordination', lost the 2022 election to Yoon by only 0.7 percentage points (p. 5). His party will be in a strong position to reclaim power in 2027, leaving open the possibility that differences over North Korea policy will re-emerge as an irritant within the alliance relationship. Likewise, a return to Trumpism in the United States, and with it the possible 'rekindling of an unconventional Trump-style "bromance" with [North Korean leader] Kim Jong-un', might encourage 'conservative fears of abandonment that would motivate a South Korea no longer confident in U.S. defense commitments to pursue its own independent nuclear capability' (p. 7).

Snyder offers a good analysis of the ways in which domestic political conditions might undermine the US–South Korean alliance. Unfortunately, his book was published before Kim Jong-un decided to repudiate the goal of reunification with South Korea, thus undercutting one of the leading causes of the South Korean opposition.

Living U.S.–China Relations: From Cold War to Cold War
David M. Lampton. Lanham, MD: Rowman & Littlefield, 2024.
£30.00/$36.00. 440 pp.

In *Living U.S.–China Relations*, author David (Mike) Lampton uses an auto-biographical approach to explain the tumultuous trajectory of US–China relations during his lifetime. Now nearly 80 years old, Lampton belongs to a tight-knit intellectual circle dedicated to furthering the work of the late John Wilson Lewis, a leading China-policy guru at Stanford University, and the late A. Doak Barnett, the child of American missionaries in China who also made a career of studying the country. This group is known for eschewing the traditional Western approach to Sinology, preferring to emphasise 'practical matters' in dealing with China rather than seeking to understand the country more deeply. Some of Lewis's students went on to gain important policy-making positions in Washington, mostly in Democratic administrations. As a group, they have taken pride in promoting good US–China ties and contributing to US policy.

The group's collective understanding of China's history, language, culture and traditional governing philosophy, however, has produced judgements about China that are often wishful in character. Group members may have grasped that their policy legacy is being threatened, but they don't seem to understand why.

Lampton laments that 'developments in the U.S.–China relationship are converging in a fashion that is setting off alarm bells … Friction between America and China is increasing, unlike anything we have seen in a half century' (p. xiii). The fact that this is occurring during a Democratic administration, the natural habitat of Lampton and his group, is raising painful questions about their favoured theories of convergence and positive engagement with China. Lampton acknowledges that the pendulum is swinging 'from Cold War to Cold War', but fails to see how decades of promoting false optimism on both sides of the Pacific have contributed to this outcome.

Indeed, it seems off the mark to refer to growing distrust between the US and China as a new cold war – we should be so lucky! Today's US–China relations more closely resemble the great-power tensions of 1914 than US–Soviet relations during the Cold War, given the lack of any stabilising mechanism for dangerous issues such as Taiwan and the South China Sea. Lampton is correct to say that 'for U.S. foreign policy to be strong and realistic, it must be founded on knowledge, empathy, and accurately assessed capabilities and weaknesses' (p. 313), but in the main his book reads as a swan song for a bygone golden era that will not come back.

Advantage China: Agent of Change in an Era of Global Disruption
Jeremy Garlick. London: Bloomsbury Academic, 2023. £21.99.
232 pp.

Jeremy Garlick argues forcefully that the Chinese economic miracle is widely misunderstood in the West, not just because there is a lack of knowledge about what works in the Chinese system, but also because cultural hubris encourages Westerners to conclude that the Chinese economic miracle is either Western-made, or the product of some mistake or misjudgement. Hence, the West cannot accept that the Chinese system may have inherent advantages over its Western counterpart in many fundamental respects.

Despite containing scathing criticism of the Western approach to China, *Advantage China* is not a left-wing screed, but rather a serious case study of China's Belt and Road Initiative (BRI). In seeking to explain why and how China has an advantage over the West in the Global South, Garlick makes three main arguments. These are, firstly, that the West should draw lessons from China's experience dealing with global-development issues in a way that differs substantially from Western approaches; secondly, that the West's reluctance to recognise the advantages China possesses in its dealings with the Global South is reducing Western competitiveness; and thirdly, that the West's lack of competitiveness in the Global South is drastically enhancing China's influence in many areas of geopolitical concern to the West.

Westerners tend to focus on what they see as the negative aspects of the BRI, citing 'debt traps', the support of autocratic regimes and environmental damage (p. 67). But the question of debt-building, perhaps the criticism most often levelled by the West against the BRI, is not a uniquely Chinese problem. The Western world has been grappling with the debt problem since the mid-twentieth century, with little success. Neither the IMF nor the Paris Club have managed to restructure the debt problems of the Global South, despite decades of trying. The Paris Club in particular is run by representatives of the creditors, its mechanism lacks transparency and the debtor countries have no input into its decision-making.

Another comparative disadvantage of the West lies in its lack of competitiveness in infrastructure-building, either at home or overseas. China offers expertise, technological innovation and cost-effectiveness, and Garlick argues that its strengths in infrastructure construction 'are the key to whatever success the BRI has enjoyed so far' (p. 69). The principle of non-interference in the affairs of other countries gives China another advantage. This principle is vehemently attacked in the West as protecting dictatorial governments, but it is enshrined in the United Nations Charter, which mandates respect for member states' national sovereignty. The Western habit of interventionism, especially the United States' penchant for regime change, represents a violation of the UN Charter. Moreover, the US often destroys regimes with no follow-up plan for reconstruction and development. This approach lacks appeal in the Global South.

The author concludes that, although the West and China both stand to benefit from better cooperation in the search for solutions to development problems in the Global South, 'given the entrenched geopolitical rivalries and lack of mutual understanding this seems highly unlikely' (p. 7).

The Emergence of China's Smart State
Rogier Creemers, Straton Papagianneas and Adam Knight,
eds. Lanham, MD: Rowman & Littlefield, 2023. £85.00/$110.00.
260 pp.

This edited volume offers a comprehensive study of China's cyber strategy and policymaking, a topic that has received scant attention to date. In chapter one ('The Cyberspace Administration of China: A Portrait'), the authors note that China's ambition is to become 'a technological leader with greater international competitiveness and self-sufficiency, universal high-bandwidth connectivity and a powerful digital economy'. At the same time, it maintains the 'most elaborate content censorship system in the world' and is 'imposing ever stricter regulations surrounding data protection and cybersecurity' (p. 10).

The central institution regulating these policies is the Cyberspace Administration of China (CAC). The CAC discharges many responsibilities, such as maintaining the so-called Great Firewall, disseminating propaganda and disinformation as required by government policy, and overseeing cyber security. However, the CAC is not a traditional government agency. Jamie Horsley and Rogier Creemers describe it as an 'opaque, seemingly dual Party–state institution … As such, it is solely accountable to the CCP [Chinese Communist Party] Central Committee, not the State Council, China's central government' (p. 19). The CAC's 'institutional parent' is the Party Central Cybersecurity and Informatisation Commission, which is chaired by the CCP's general secretary, Xi Jinping.

The authors offer several case studies to illustrate the role played by the CAC in building a smart state. One is the notorious Social Credit System (SCS). This system tends to be viewed in the West through the lens of 'authoritarian resilience' and human rights (p. 36), but this kind of analysis can be simplistic and static. As one of the government's flagship 'smart' projects (another being Smart Court Reform), the SCS has 'relied heavily on a decentralised model of decision making and localised piloting' (p. 41). As such, local administrations found themselves interpreting and applying the system in ways that sometimes violated Chinese law. Recognising this, the Chinese government announced changes intended to create an SCS that 'sits within China's legal system, not in parallel to it' (p. 45). Between July 2020 and March 2022, five new legislative updates were published by state bodies, and progress has also been made toward the creation of a Social Credit Law. Cases like these demonstrate the dynamism of Chinese cyber policy and the importance the government places on its goal of developing 'world-class indigenous technologies, top-notch information services, flourishing online culture, solid network infrastructure, and a powerful digital economy' (p. 1).

Letter to the Editor

Balancing the necessary and the possible

Sir,

As an author and someone who deeply appreciates his own limitations, I found the review and analysis of my recent book by James J. Wirtz an honour ('The US Navy and the Western Pacific', *Survival*, vol. 66, no. 1). I especially enjoyed his story about briefing Kazakhstan's National Defense University and the implicit caution not to talk past each other in foreign affairs – a too-regular occurrence in American diplomacy as US viewpoints are pushed without consideration for a foreign audience's needs. One of the objectives of the book was to offer a way to do better using 'naval statecraft'.

James rightly points out that there is too little discussion in the book about educating future naval leaders. It is a topic that in fact merits its own book, though there is a section in chapter nine ('Required Focus on Tradition While Building New Core Competencies') that does address the challenge faced by the US Navy. It must return to basics to ensure its fleet is competently operated while adjusting to the demands of future naval warfare and deciding what platforms to invest in. On this the military has a perfect record – it always guesses wrong.

James suggests the book advocates adhering to a traditional force structure. In fact, the chapters 'New Model Navy' and 'Fleet Design 2035' attempt to lay out a force structure that will allow the United States to win future wars and prevail in the emerging cold war with China and Russia. Knowing the historical record on predicting how future wars will be fought, the best approach, and the one I recommend, is to hedge – that is, to retain conventional warships and concepts of operations while at the same time

Survival | vol. 66 no. 2 | April–May 2024 | pp. 187–188   https://doi.org/10.1080/00396338.2024.2332072

developing next-generation formations, such as the teaming of the crewed and uncrewed fleets of the future. That way, if any given prediction is wrong, the navy will still have the capacity and options to adjust the fleet to unfolding conditions.

James correctly states that any rethinking of the Goldwater–Nichols construct of joint operations will cause turbulence. However, rather than suggesting that the Goldwater–Nichols Act be overturned, my book embraces it and seeks to adapt it to evolving world events. For example, making the US Navy an operational command like Transportation Command or Cyber Command would make it a combat power and naval-presence provider to the geographic commands. The intent is to enable naval operations both on a global scale and in distinct maritime regions such as the Indian Ocean or the South China Sea. This would be controversial, of course, but competing with China in a new cold war will require the US to more fully leverage the advantages of its global naval forces' mobility. Furthermore, to enhance wartime joint operations in the first island chain, the book details new task-force constructs and exercises to practise the needed concept of operations (see chapter seven).

To conclude, I greatly appreciated James's review and mostly agree with his analysis. In the end, the book attempts to balance the art of the possible with the urgent necessities of preserving global peace and prevailing in the new cold war. It is likely too late to do this easily or cheaply.

Brent D. Sadler
Senior Research Fellow, Naval Warfare and Advanced Technology, Heritage Foundation.

Author of *U.S. Naval Power in the 21st Century: A New Strategy for Facing the Chinese and Russian Threat* (Naval Institute Press, 2023)

Will America Fail Ukraine?

Dana H. Allin and Jonathan Stevenson

In January 1941, President Franklin Roosevelt came to this chamber to speak to the nation. He said, 'I address you at a moment unprecedented in the history of the Union.' Hitler was on the march. War was raging in Europe. President Roosevelt's purpose was to wake up the Congress and alert the American people that this was no ordinary moment. Freedom and democracy were under assault in the world. Tonight I come to the same chamber to address the nation. Now it is we who face an unprecedented moment in the history of the Union. And yes, my purpose tonight is to both wake up this Congress, and alert the American people that this is no ordinary moment either. Not since President Lincoln and the Civil War have freedom and democracy been under assault here at home as they are today. What makes our moment rare is that freedom and democracy are under attack, both at home and overseas, at the very same time.[1]

I

This opening of the American president's State of the Union address to Congress on 7 March 2024 sounded a familiar Joe Biden refrain. The Russian forces that invaded Ukraine in February 2022 belonged to the same historical

Dana H. Allin is an IISS Senior Fellow and Editor of *Survival*, and an adjunct professor at the Johns Hopkins School of Advanced International Studies (SAIS–Europe) in Bologna, Italy. **Jonathan Stevenson** is an IISS Senior Fellow and Managing Editor of *Survival*.

Survival | vol. 66 no. 2 | April–May 2024 | pp. 189–196   https://doi.org/10.1080/00396338.2024.2332073

threat and malignancy as the violent acolytes of Donald Trump who stormed the US Capitol in January 2021. Trump, the current front-runner in the 2024 US presidential election, was now celebrating those 6 January storm troopers and promising to pardon them if he wins in November. Meanwhile, Trump's fiercest supporters in Congress were blocking $60 billion in renewed military aid for a Ukrainian army running short of ammunition to fend off the troops of an increasingly confident Vladimir Putin.

Biden gave an energetic speech on that Thursday night and his cheering section on the Democratic side of the aisle interrupted him with raucous, even joyful, vigour in return. Aside from a coterie of MAGA hecklers, Republicans sat sullenly still throughout. (This dynamic works in reverse when a Republican is president.) The tableau was repeated in miniature for the 30 million television viewers who could watch the reactions of Vice President Kamala Harris and Speaker of the House Mike Johnson sitting behind Biden. Harris stood repeatedly to lead the Democratic cheering and applause. Johnson stayed fixed in his chair, with cameras recording heroic facial efforts to reveal neither approval nor overt contempt.

Johnson's face was hiding a lot. In Ukraine itself and among America's NATO allies, there is dumbfounded disbelief that in a United States with still-strong public support for Ukraine, and two Houses of Congress that reflect that support in large, bipartisan, pro-Ukraine majorities, the aid bill may nonetheless remain forever blocked. It might also, to be clear, become unblocked before this essay is published. In either case, however, the circumstances constitute a crisis of American global power and, indeed, as Biden has asserted, of American democracy. They require some explanation.

Trump is not yet president again, but he dominates his party in the way identified by William Saletan at the very outset of the 2016 Republican primary season, when the idea of Trump actually moving into the White House still seemed far-fetched. In an article in *Slate* titled 'Donald Trump Is the GOP's Warlord' and subtitled 'The Republican Party Is Officially a Failed State', Saletan argued that

> since President [Barack] Obama's election, the GOP [Republican Party] has
> abandoned its role as a national governing party. It has seized Congress not

by pursuing an alternative agenda but by campaigning and staging votes against anything Obama says or does. The party's so-called leaders have become followers, chasing the pet issues of right-wing radio audiences. Now the mob to whom these elders have surrendered – angry white voters who are determined to 'take back their country' from immigrants and liberals – is ready to install its own presidential nominee. The Trump–Cruz takeover is the culmination of the Grand Old Party's moral collapse.[2]

A year ago, when American support for Ukraine appeared strong and enduring, it also looked implausible that Trump could return from electoral defeat; from his unconstitutional attempt to overturn that result; and from the initial revulsion of congressional Republicans over the violent siege of the Capitol that he summoned. The comeback looked less and less likely when prosecutors in various jurisdictions brought 98 criminal indictments against the former president, related, in part, to that attempt and the ensuing violence; when he was held civilly liable for sexual abuse and defamation, and ordered to pay $83m in damages; and when he was hit with a civil-fraud judgment totalling more than $450m. Yet he has not just rebounded. He is the de facto presidential nominee of his party and leading Biden in the polls.

Meanwhile, Speaker Johnson, who inherited a thin Republican House majority that is getting thinner, can be toppled from his post if he courts the ire of just a few MAGA members, in the same way his predecessor Kevin McCarthy was ousted six months ago. The MAGA ringleader, Marjorie Taylor Greene, says they will in fact pull the plug on Johnson if he brings the Ukraine-aid bill to the floor for a vote. There were in theory other possibilities. A 'discharge petition' signed by a majority of House members would bypass the speaker, but any Republican who signed it would have a MAGA target on his or her back. Democrats might offer the votes to keep Johnson in the speakership, but if Johnson accepted the favour it would put a practically indelible bullseye on *his* back. There is no strong evidence, in any event, that Johnson himself wants the bill to pass.[3]

Our colleague Nigel Gould-Davies writes in this issue of a 'balance of resources and a balance of resolve' with respect to Ukraine. The former favours the West, but it has started to look as though the latter favours Putin. As Gould-Davies's essay indicates, however, national resolve is not the same as the kind of individual willpower that is required to stay on a diet. Rather, national resolve is a composite of political realities.[4] Political leadership has a role, of course, but it also has limits. For Republican leadership on Ukraine, the limiting condition even now is Trump. A full ten months before he might return to the White House, he has decisive say over whether House Republicans will approve the $60bn for Ukraine. That prospect appears abhorrent to him because approval would be both good for Ukraine and good for Biden.

II

In mid-January of this year, one of us joined a meeting with a US congressional delegation visiting London. Republican members of the delegation argued that a) the Ukraine debate was really a debate over security on the US southern border, and aid would pass if coupled with sufficiently tough border measures; b) the Trump administration in any event provided more serious support to Ukraine than the Obama administration did; and c) Trump's supposed hostility to NATO was a myth created to obscure the sensibleness of his demand that NATO members meet their defence-spending targets.

A couple of weeks later Trump definitively killed a bipartisan Senate effort to tighten border security, calling it a 'great gift to the Democrats, and a Death Wish for The Republican Party'.[5] About five weeks after that, he received Hungarian Prime Minister Viktor Orbán, the most autocratic and pro-Putin leader in both NATO and the European Union, for a kind of faux state visit at Mar-a-Lago, where Orbán fawned over Trump and vice versa. Among other genuflections, Orbán proclaimed that returning Trump to the presidency would offer the 'only serious chance' of ending the Russia–Ukraine war.[6] 'He will not give a penny in the Ukraine–Russia war. That is why the war will end', Orbán reported with great confidence.[7]

It is a good idea to keep the actual record in mind. Following Russia's invasion of Ukraine in February 2022, Trump extolled Putin's 'savvy' and 'genius'.[8] More fundamentally, his conduct as president vis-à-vis

Ukraine before the war geopolitically compromised the country. Trump and several of his more outlandish advisers believed they could make a case that Joe Biden had improperly curried favour with Ukraine's previous government to advance his son Hunter's business ventures and that Kyiv had conspired with the Democratic National Committee to frame Russia for interfering in the 2016 presidential election, evidence for which could be found on an imaginary server owned by CrowdStrike and physically located in Ukraine. When Ukrainian President Volodymyr Zelenskyy demurred in response to Trump's pressure for his help in substantiating these hallucinatory claims in an infamous 25 July 2019 phone conversation, Trump withheld $400m in congressionally authorised foreign assistance. It was released only when Trump's machinations became public in September 2019.

Trump's attempt to blackmail Zelenskyy, for which he was impeached but not convicted, effectively signalled to Putin that American support for and interests in Ukraine were subject to barter. In addition, the call illuminated Trump's indifference to Putin's revanchism. More broadly, it unequivocally demonstrated Trump's preference for illiberal autocrats as American partners insofar as they could steamroller democratic governance in the service of his personal political interests. It reflected Trump's dismantling of the National Security Council-managed inter-agency process for formulating and executing US foreign policy.[9] Finally, it showcased his disdain for constitutionally sanctioned standards of governance. One of us noted in 2020 that 'Trump used Ukraine's precarious position in the face of ongoing Russian aggression as leverage', which was 'precisely the kind of corrupt transaction with a foreign power that the eighteenth-century framers of the United States Constitution were worried about when they drafted the impeachment clause'.[10]

Trump and such accomplices as former New York mayor Rudy Giuliani became conduits for injecting *American* corruption into Ukraine, in what then-national security advisor John Bolton metaphorically called a 'drug deal'.[11] While US assistance to Ukraine subsequently increased, the episode had revealed a grossly transactional administration willing to comprehensively debase US governance and treasured post-war strategic norms. One consequence was damage to the image of the United States, which, according to Ukrainian philosopher Volodymyr Yermolenko, had been seen as a 'perfect democracy functioning very well', with effective checks and balances, but now looked to be 'crumbling' at Trump's hands.[12] Another consequence was the weakening of US deterrence in Europe. As Bolton put it in an interview, the 'unnatural environment' that the Trump administration had created in US–Ukraine relations made it 'that much easier for Putin' to invade Ukraine.[13]

Early this year, as his presidential-election campaign gathered steam, Trump confirmed his disparagement of the long-standing transatlantic security bargain, reiterating that he would 'not protect' NATO members whose financial contribution to the Alliance he deemed insufficient, and in fact would encourage Russia to do 'whatever the hell it wanted' to them.[14] It goes almost without saying that if Trump were to facilitate the end of the war in his second incarnation as the American president, as Orbán suggested he could, it would be on terms favourable to Russia. Beyond selling out Ukraine, such a result would also undermine the United States' strategic brand – a reputational asset that is crucial to the respect and fealty of its allies and partners. If America's democracy is on the ballot in the 2024 presidential election, so, it would seem, is its global power.

III

With Trump ahead in the polls, however, the political–analytical debate reasonably revolves around the question of whether the small number of swing voters in a mere six contested states (Arizona, Georgia, Michigan, Nevada, Pennsylvania and Wisconsin) really care enough about lofty issues of fidelity to democratic norms and US alliances to cast their votes on that basis. The question may seem damning of those voters, yet it is hard to argue that the American electorate has had to answer such questions perhaps since the American Civil War, and in any event since the end of the Second World War. The reason is that the grand-strategic choices on offer, both internationally and domestically, were structured by two parties that shared some basic assumptions. Even George McGovern's 1972 stridently idealistic 'Come Home, America' campaign was about the wrenching US departure from Vietnam, not a wholesale abandonment of allies everywhere.

Biden's campaign strategists appear to believe that they can win by connecting the somewhat abstract questions of constitutionalism and foreign policy to more concrete notions of basic rights under threat and the spectre of national and international disorder. The most palpable right is the right to abortion, which the US Supreme Court removed with its 24 June 2022 *Dobbs v. Jackson Women's Health Organization* decision overturning *Roe v. Wade*, decided half a century earlier. This has helped Democrats in every election since *Dobbs* was announced, but it is not clear whether it will rescue them in the next presidential one. As for disorder, Biden's approval ratings fell precipitously with the chaotic US withdrawal from Afghanistan and have never really recovered. The Democratic coalition, large and inherently fractious, is riven by anguish and anger over Israel's Gaza war. And voters are worried about Biden's age. Trump, only a few years younger and prone to incoherent rants, nonetheless projects more energy. He might plausibly present a rough isolationism as the road back to peace and a return to 'normalcy'.[15]

In that case, the challenge that our colleague Benjamin Rhode poses in his essay 'Europe Without America', also in these pages, may arise in earnest in a matter of months.[16] Biden may very well be re-elected; our hunch, for what it's worth, is that he will be. But the Ukraine impasse shows how that may not be enough to conclusively salvage US strategic leadership or American democracy. America has a two-party system, and the stability of both foreign policy and democratic norms requires some basic consensus between the parties. This consensus cannot exist as long as Trump leads the Republicans, and it is unclear how they will assemble themselves in the event of his defeat or even victory. The future of Republican foreign policy after Trump is as inscrutable as Speaker Johnson's face.

Notes

[1]   White House, 'Remarks of President Joe Biden – State of the Union Address as Prepared for Delivery', 7 March 2024, https://www.whitehouse.gov/briefing-room/speeches-remarks/2024/03/07/remarks-of-president-joe-biden-state-of-the-union-address-as-prepared-for-delivery-2/.

2   William Saletan, 'Donald Trump Is the GOP's Warlord', *Slate*, 28 January 2016, https://slate.com/news-and-politics/2016/01/the-gop-is-a-failed-state-donald-trump-is-its-warlord.html.

3   See, for example, Kayla Guo, 'How Congress Could Bypass Republican Opposition to Funding Ukraine', *New York Times*, 13 February 2024, https://www.nytimes.com/2024/02/13/us/politics/congress-discharge-petition-ukraine.html.

4   See Nigel Gould-Davies, 'Ukraine: The Balance of Resources and the Balance of Resolve', *Survival*, vol. 66, no. 2, April–May 2024, pp. 55–62.

5   Quoted in Brett Samuels, 'Trump Calls Border Bill "a Death Wish" for Republican Party: "Don't be STUPID!!!"', *Hill*, 5 February 2024, https://thehill.com/homenews/campaign/4448556-trump-calls-border-bill-a-death-wish-for-republican-party-dont-be-stupid/.

6   Quoted in Nicholas Riccardi and Justin Spike, 'Trump Meets with Hungary's Leader, Viktor Orbán, Continuing His Embrace of Autocrats', Associated Press, 8 March 2024, https://apnews.com/article/trump-orban-hungary-conservatives-autocrats-biden-97d6998f747d3543f2f1df069b0f9165.

7   Quoted in Jaroslav Lukiv, 'Trump Will Not Give a Penny to Ukraine – Hungary PM Orban', BBC, 11 March 2024, https://www.bbc.com/news/world-europe-68533351.

8   Joseph Gedeon, 'Trump Calls Putin "Genius" and "Savvy" for Ukraine Invasion', *Politico*, 23 February 2022, https://www.politico.com/news/2022/02/23/trump-putin-ukraine-invasion-00010923.

9   See Jonathan Stevenson, 'How Trump Sabotaged Ukraine', *New York Review*, 11 March 2022, https://www.nybooks.com/online/2022/03/11/how-trump-sabotaged-ukraine/.

10 Dana H. Allin, 'Impeachment, Trump and US Foreign Policy', *Survival*, vol. 62, no. 1, February–March 2020, p. 221.

11 John Bolton, *The Room Where It Happened: A White House Memoir* (New York: Simon & Schuster, 2020), p. 465.

12 Quoted in Michelle Goldberg, '"The Beacon Has Gone Out": What Trump and Giuliani Have Wrought', *New York Times*, 12 October 2019, https://www.nytimes.com/2019/10/12/opinion/sunday/ukraine-trump.html.

13 Cameron Joseph, 'John Bolton: Trump Made It "That Much Easier" for Putin to Invade Ukraine', Vice News, 1 March 2022, https://www.vice.com/en/article/3abjgn/john-bolton-interview-russia-ukraine.

14 Michael Gold, 'Trump Says He Gave NATO Allies Warning: Pay In or He'd Urge Russian Aggression', *New York Times*, 10 February 2024, https://www.nytimes.com/2024/02/10/us/politics/trump-nato-russia.html.

15 'Normalcy' for normality was popularised by president Warren G. Harding on the eve of an earlier isolationist idyl.

16 See Benjamin Rhode, 'Europe Without America', *Survival*, vol. 66, no. 2, April–May 2024, pp. 7–18.

Printed in the United States
by Baker & Taylor Publisher Services